MW00791074

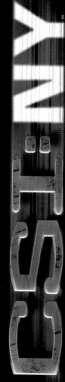

CSI:NY™

BLOODY MURDER

IDW Publishing is:

Robbie Robbins, President
Chris Ryall, Publisher/Editor-in-Chief
Ted Adams, Vice President
Kris Oprisko, Vice President
Neil Uyetake, Art Director
Dan Taylor, Editor
Aaron Myers, Distribution Manager
Tom B. Long, Designer
Chance Boren, Editorial Assistant
Matthew Ruzicka, CPA, Controller
Alex Garner, Creative Director
Yumiko Miyano, Business Development
Rick Privman, Business Development

ISBN: 1-933239-80-8
09 08 07 06 05 1 2 3 4 5

www.idwpublishing.com

CSI:NY Created by Anthony E. Zuiker, Ann Donahue, Carol Mendelsohn Licensed to IDW by CBS Consumer Products
Special thanks to Maryann Martin and Ken Ross at CBS Consumer Products for their invaluable assistance.

CSI:NY

BLOODY MURDER

Written by : **Max Allan Collins**

Artwork by : **J.K. Woodward**

Flashback Artwork by : **Steven Perkins**

Forensics Research/Co-Plot by : **Matthew V. Clemens**

Designed by : **Neil Uyetake**

Lettered by : **Robbie Robbins &
Tom B. Long**

Edited by : **Kris Oprisko**

Cover Photo by : **Timothy White**

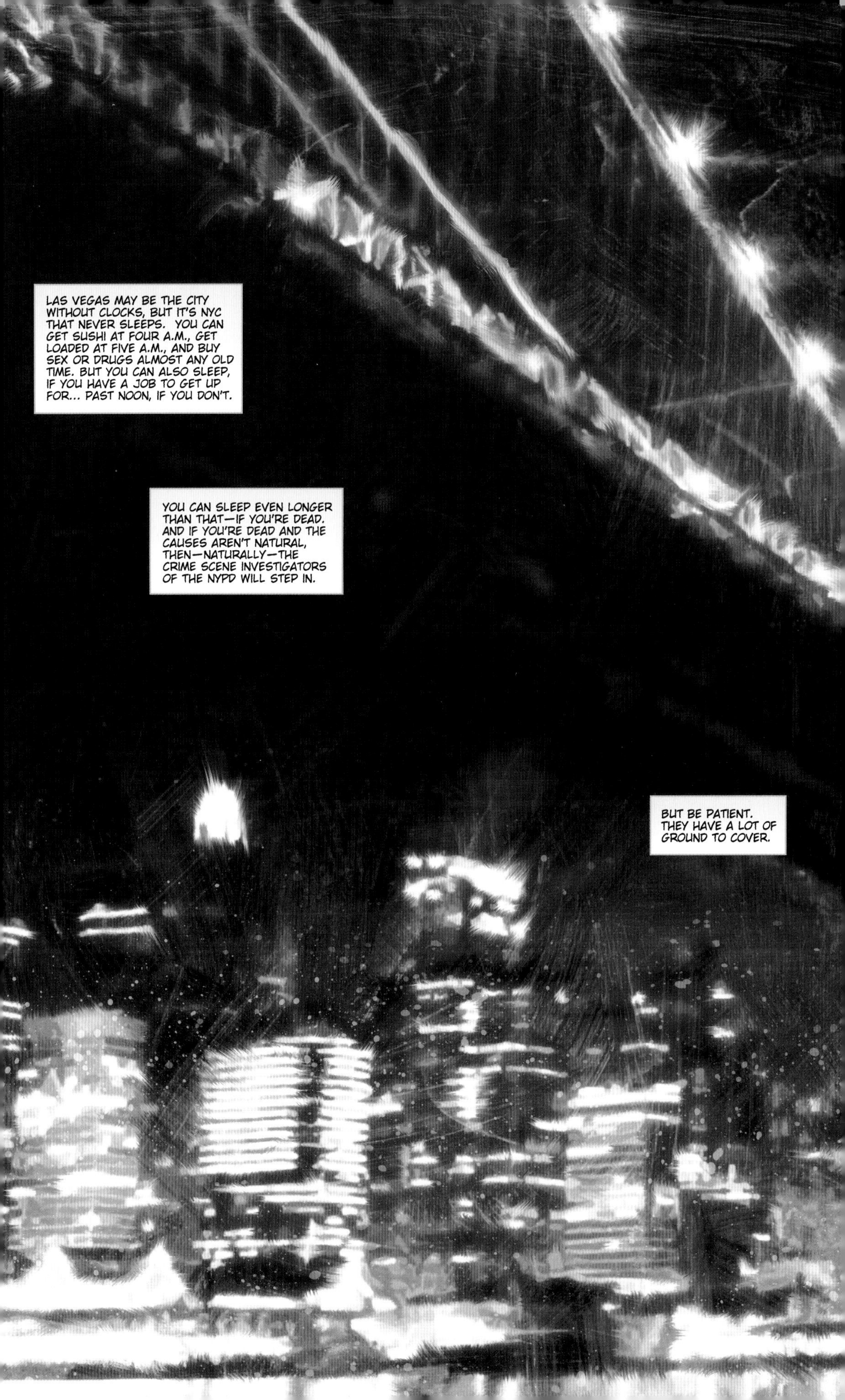
LAS VEGAS MAY BE THE CITY WITHOUT CLOCKS, BUT IT'S NYC THAT NEVER SLEEPS. YOU CAN GET SUSHI AT FOUR A.M., GET LOADED AT FIVE A.M., AND BUY SEX OR DRUGS ALMOST ANY OLD TIME. BUT YOU CAN ALSO SLEEP, IF YOU HAVE A JOB TO GET UP FOR... PAST NOON, IF YOU DON'T.
YOU CAN SLEEP EVEN LONGER THAN THAT—IF YOU'RE DEAD. AND IF YOU'RE DEAD AND THE CAUSES AREN'T NATURAL, THEN—NATURALLY—THE CRIME SCENE INVESTIGATORS OF THE NYPD WILL STEP IN.
BUT BE PATIENT. THEY HAVE A LOT OF GROUND TO COVER.

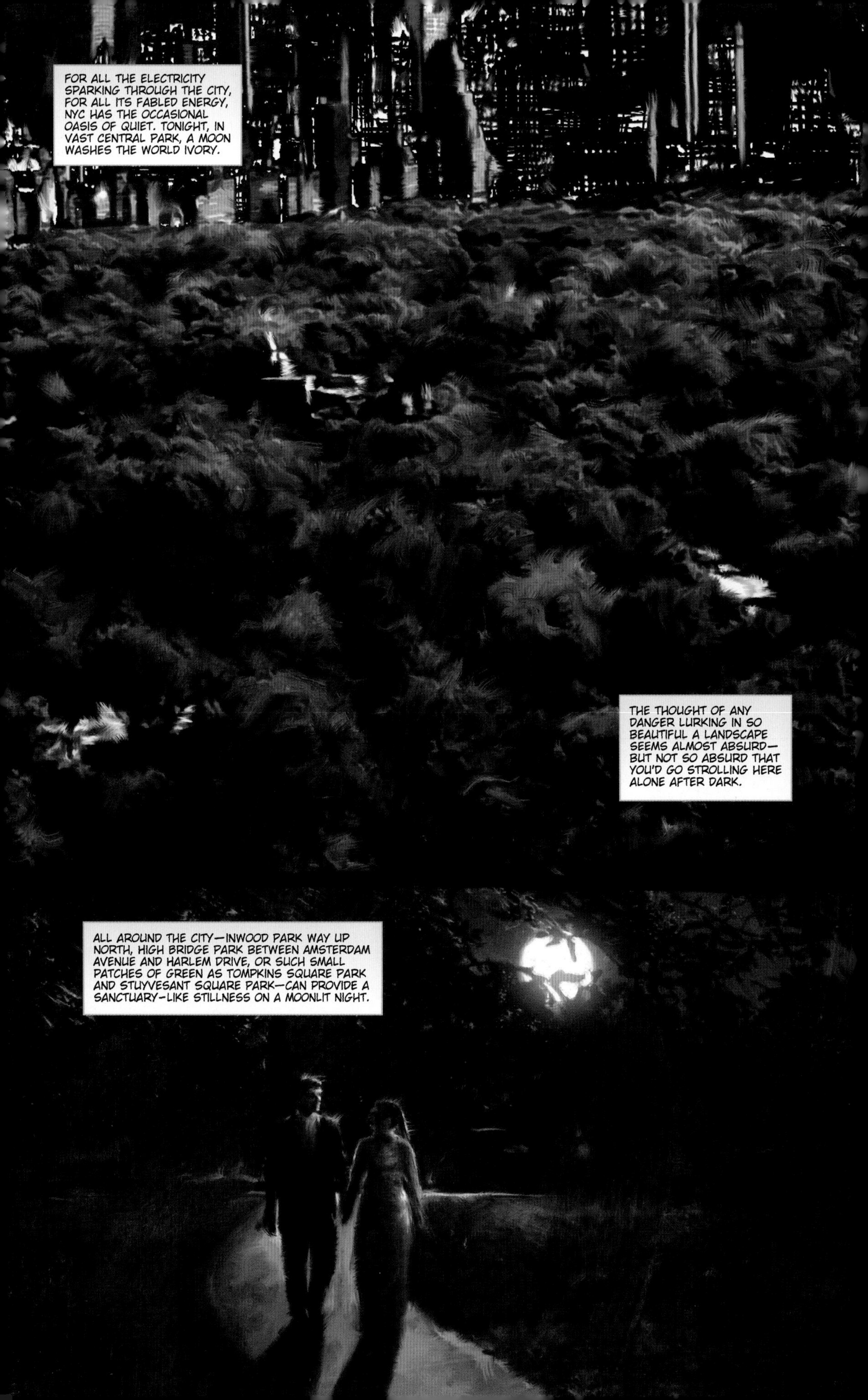
FOR ALL THE ELECTRICITY SPARKING THROUGH THE CITY, FOR ALL ITS FABLED ENERGY, NYC HAS THE OCCASIONAL OASIS OF QUIET. TONIGHT, IN VAST CENTRAL PARK, A MOON WASHES THE WORLD IVORY.
THE THOUGHT OF ANY DANGER LURKING IN SO BEAUTIFUL A LANDSCAPE SEEMS ALMOST ABSURD— BUT NOT SO ABSURD THAT YOU'D GO STROLLING HERE ALONE AFTER DARK.
ALL AROUND THE CITY—INWOOD PARK WAY UP NORTH, HIGH BRIDGE PARK BETWEEN AMSTERDAM AVENUE AND HARLEM DRIVE, OR SUCH SMALL PATCHES OF GREEN AS TOMPKINS SQUARE PARK AND STUYVESANT SQUARE PARK—CAN PROVIDE A SANCTUARY-LIKE STILLNESS ON A MOONLIT NIGHT.

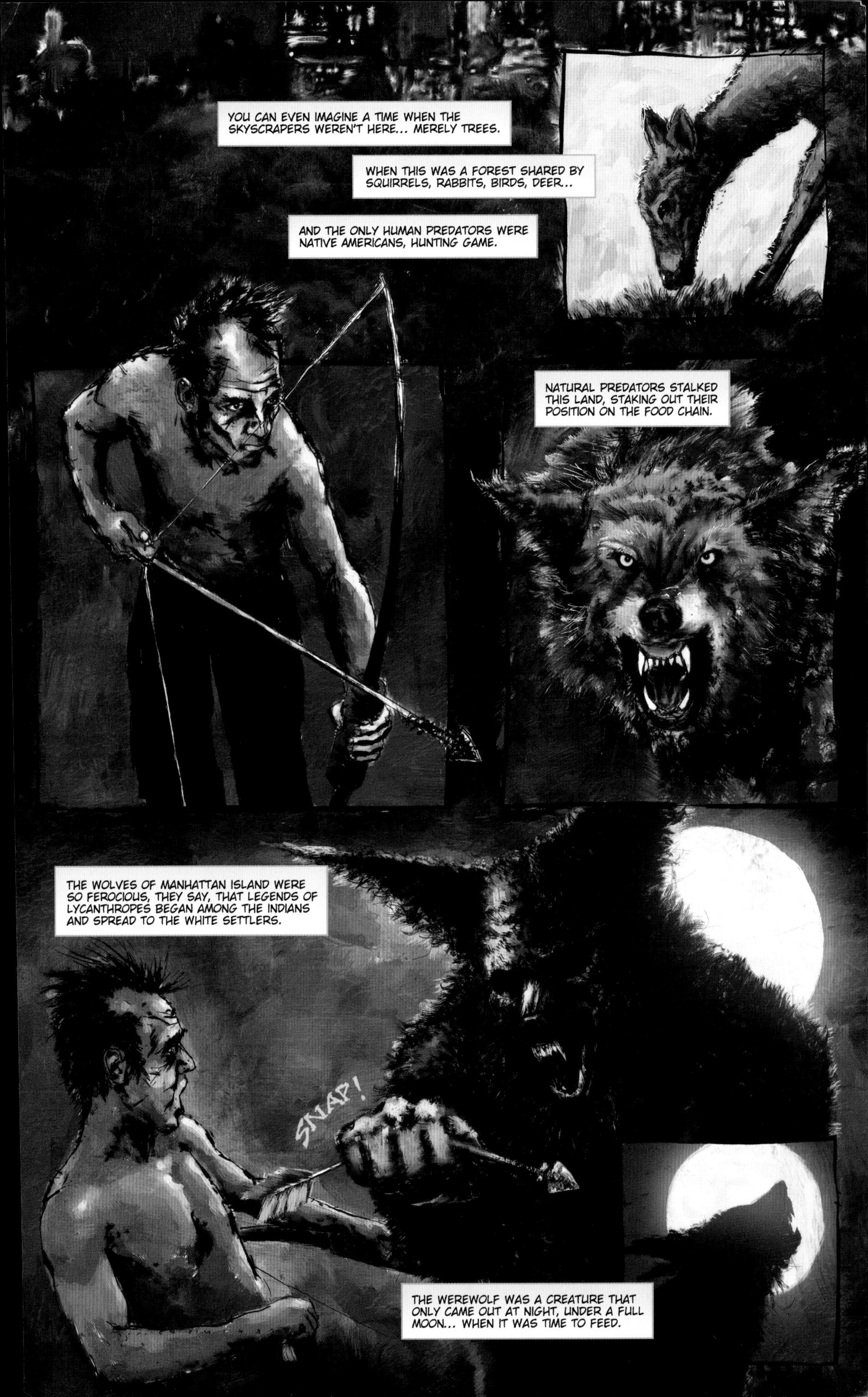
YOU CAN EVEN IMAGINE A TIME WHEN THE SKYSCRAPERS WEREN'T HERE... MERELY TREES.
WHEN THIS WAS A FOREST SHARED BY SQUIRRELS, RABBITS, BIRDS, DEER...
AND THE ONLY HUMAN PREDATORS WERE NATIVE AMERICANS, HUNTING GAME.
NATURAL PREDATORS STALKED THIS LAND, STAKING OUT THEIR POSITION ON THE FOOD CHAIN.
THE WOLVES OF MANHATTAN ISLAND WERE SO FEROCIOUS, THEY SAY, THAT LEGENDS OF LYCANTHROPES BEGAN AMONG THE INDIANS AND SPREAD TO THE WHITE SETTLERS.
SNAP!
THE WEREWOLF WAS A CREATURE THAT ONLY CAME OUT AT NIGHT, UNDER A FULL MOON... WHEN IT WAS TIME TO FEED.

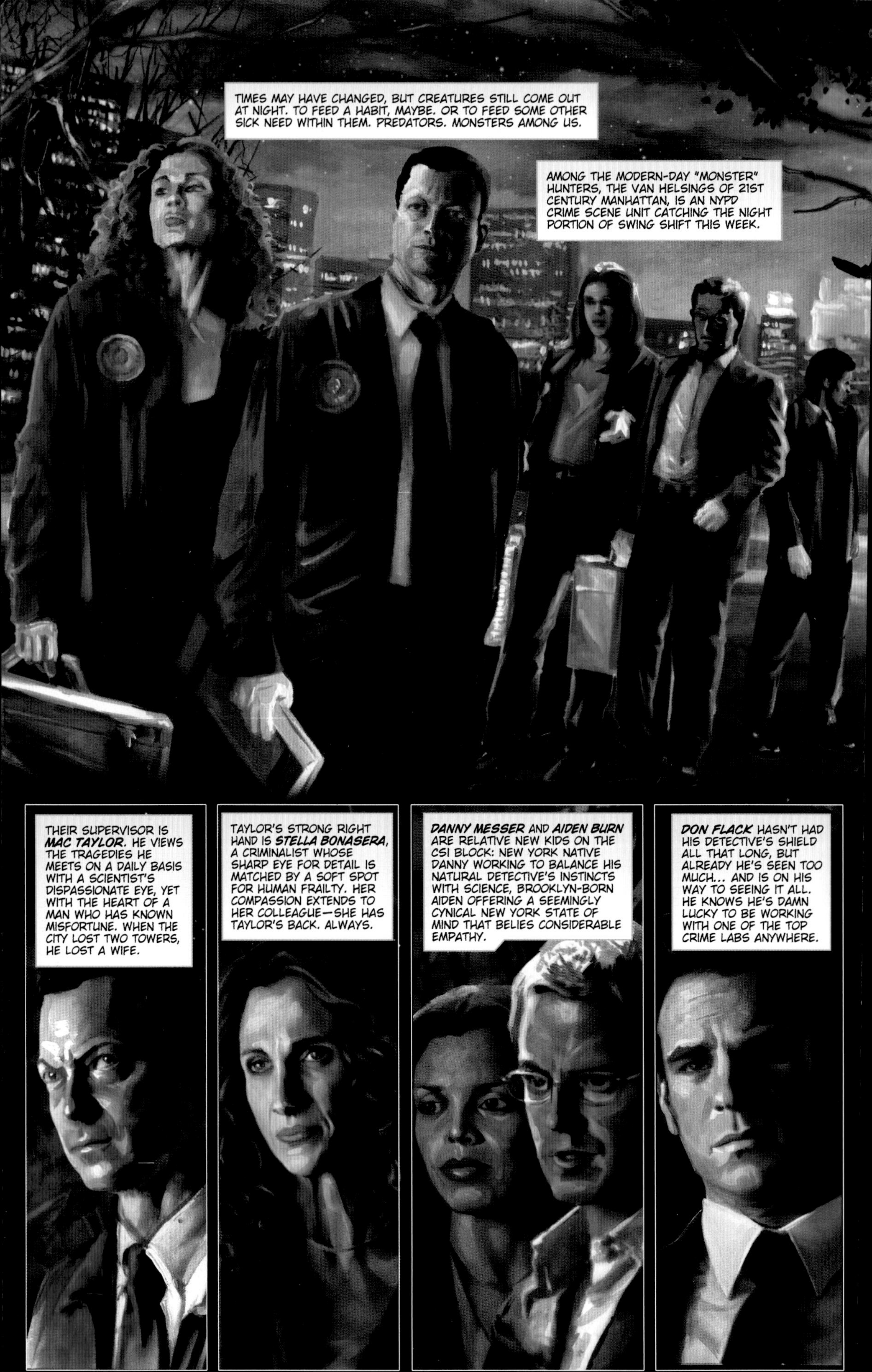
TIMES MAY HAVE CHANGED, BUT CREATURES STILL COME OUT AT NIGHT. TO FEED A HABIT, MAYBE. OR TO FEED SOME OTHER SICK NEED WITHIN THEM. PREDATORS. MONSTERS AMONG US.
AMONG THE MODERN-DAY "MONSTER" HUNTERS, THE VAN HELSINGS OF 21ST CENTURY MANHATTAN, IS AN NYPD CRIME SCENE UNIT CATCHING THE NIGHT PORTION OF SWING SHIFT THIS WEEK.
THEIR SUPERVISOR IS MAC TAYLOR. HE VIEWS THE TRAGEDIES HE MEETS ON A DAILY BASIS WITH A SCIENTIST'S DISPASSIONATE EYE, YET WITH THE HEART OF A MAN WHO HAS KNOWN MISFORTUNE. WHEN THE CITY LOST TWO TOWERS, HE LOST A WIFE.
TAYLOR'S STRONG RIGHT HAND IS STELLA BONASERA, A CRIMINALIST WHOSE SHARP EYE FOR DETAIL IS MATCHED BY A SOFT SPOT FOR HUMAN FRAILTY. HER COMPASSION EXTENDS TO HER COLLEAGUE—SHE HAS TAYLOR'S BACK. ALWAYS.
DANNY MESSER AND AIDEN BURN ARE RELATIVE NEW KIDS ON THE CSI BLOCK: NEW YORK NATIVE DANNY WORKING TO BALANCE HIS NATURAL DETECTIVE'S INSTINCTS WITH SCIENCE, BROOKLYN-BORN AIDEN OFFERING A SEEMINGLY CYNICAL NEW YORK STATE OF MIND THAT BELIES CONSIDERABLE EMPATHY.
DON FLACK HASN'T HAD HIS DETECTIVE'S SHIELD ALL THAT LONG, BUT ALREADY HE'S SEEN TOO MUCH... AND IS ON HIS WAY TO SEEING IT ALL. HE KNOWS HE'S DAMN LUCKY TO BE WORKING WITH ONE OF THE TOP CRIME LABS ANYWHERE.

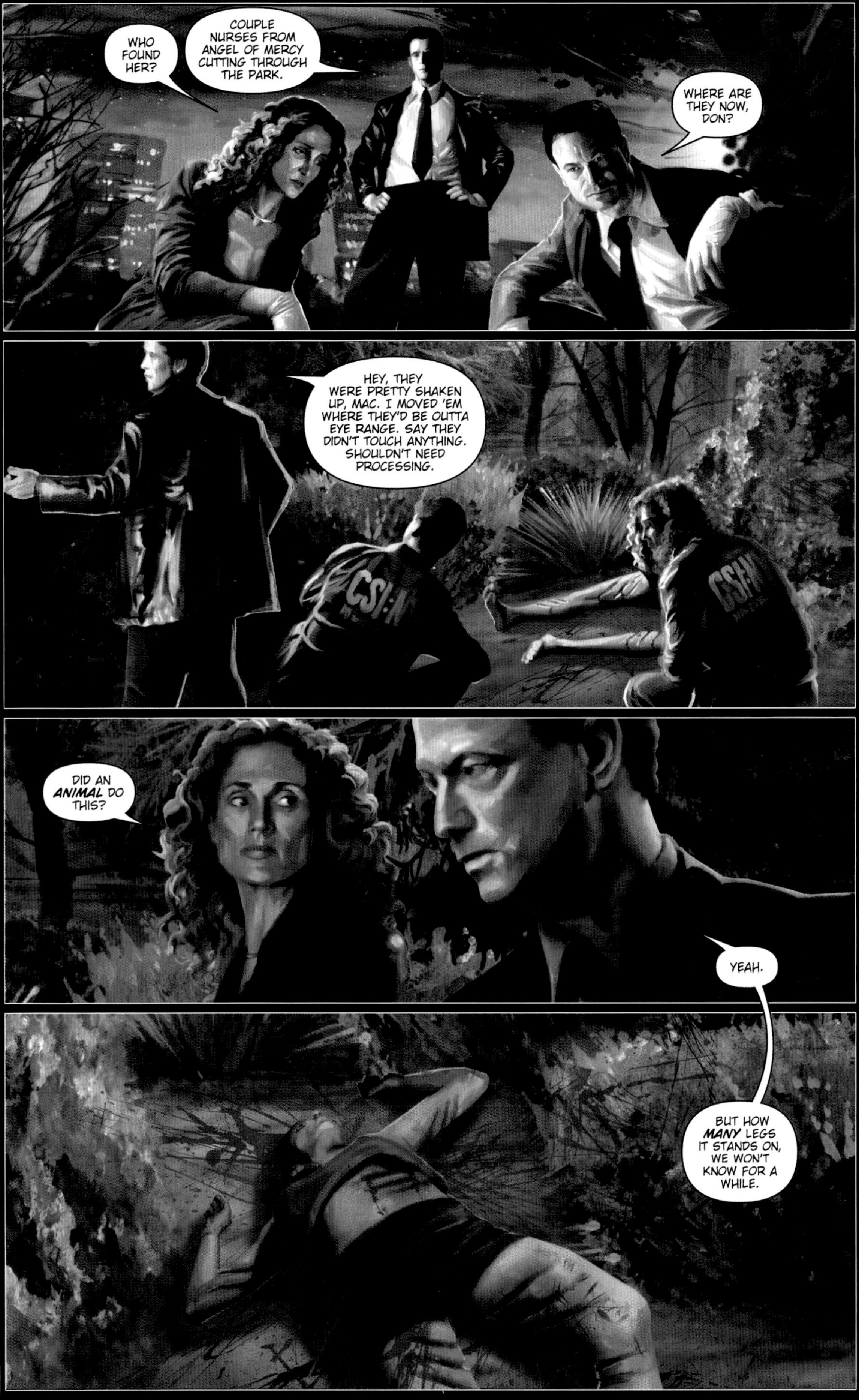
WHO FOUND HER?
COUPLE NURSES FROM ANGEL OF MERCY CUTTING THROUGH THE PARK.
WHERE ARE THEY NOW, DON?
HEY, THEY WERE PRETTY SHAKEN UP, MAC. I MOVED 'EM WHERE THEY'D BE OUTTA EYE RANGE. SAY THEY DIDN'T TOUCH ANYTHING. SHOULDN'T NEED PROCESSING.
CSI:NY
CSI:NY
DID AN ANIMAL DO THIS?
YEAH.
BUT HOW MANY LEGS IT STANDS ON, WE WON'T KNOW FOR A WHILE.

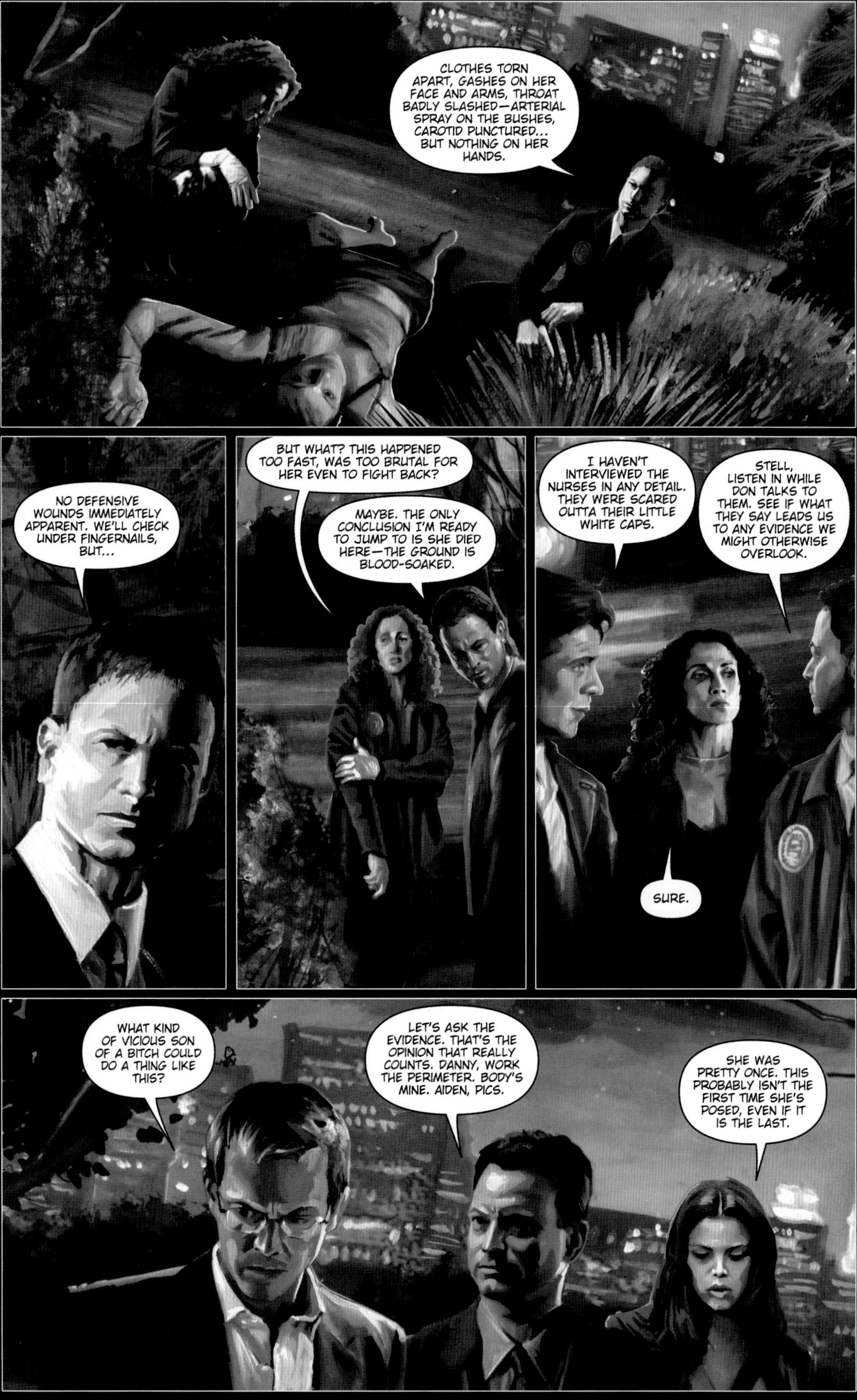
CLOTHES TORN APART, GASHES ON HER FACE AND ARMS, THROAT BADLY SLASHED—ARTERIAL SPRAY ON THE BUSHES, CAROTID PUNCTURED... BUT NOTHING ON HER HANDS.
NO DEFENSIVE WOUNDS IMMEDIATELY APPARENT. WE'LL CHECK UNDER FINGERNAILS, BUT...
BUT WHAT? THIS HAPPENED TOO FAST, WAS TOO BRUTAL FOR HER EVEN TO FIGHT BACK?
MAYBE. THE ONLY CONCLUSION I'M READY TO JUMP TO IS SHE DIED HERE—THE GROUND IS BLOOD-SOAKED.
I HAVEN'T INTERVIEWED THE NURSES IN ANY DETAIL. THEY WERE SCARED OUTTA THEIR LITTLE WHITE CAPS.
STELL, LISTEN IN WHILE DON TALKS TO THEM. SEE IF WHAT THEY SAY LEADS US TO ANY EVIDENCE WE MIGHT OTHERWISE OVERLOOK.
SURE.
WHAT KIND OF VICIOUS SON OF A BITCH COULD DO A THING LIKE THIS?
LET'S ASK THE EVIDENCE. THAT'S THE OPINION THAT REALLY COUNTS. DANNY, WORK THE PERIMETER. BODY'S MINE. AIDEN, PICS.
SHE WAS PRETTY ONCE. THIS PROBABLY ISN'T THE FIRST TIME SHE'S POSED, EVEN IF IT IS THE LAST.

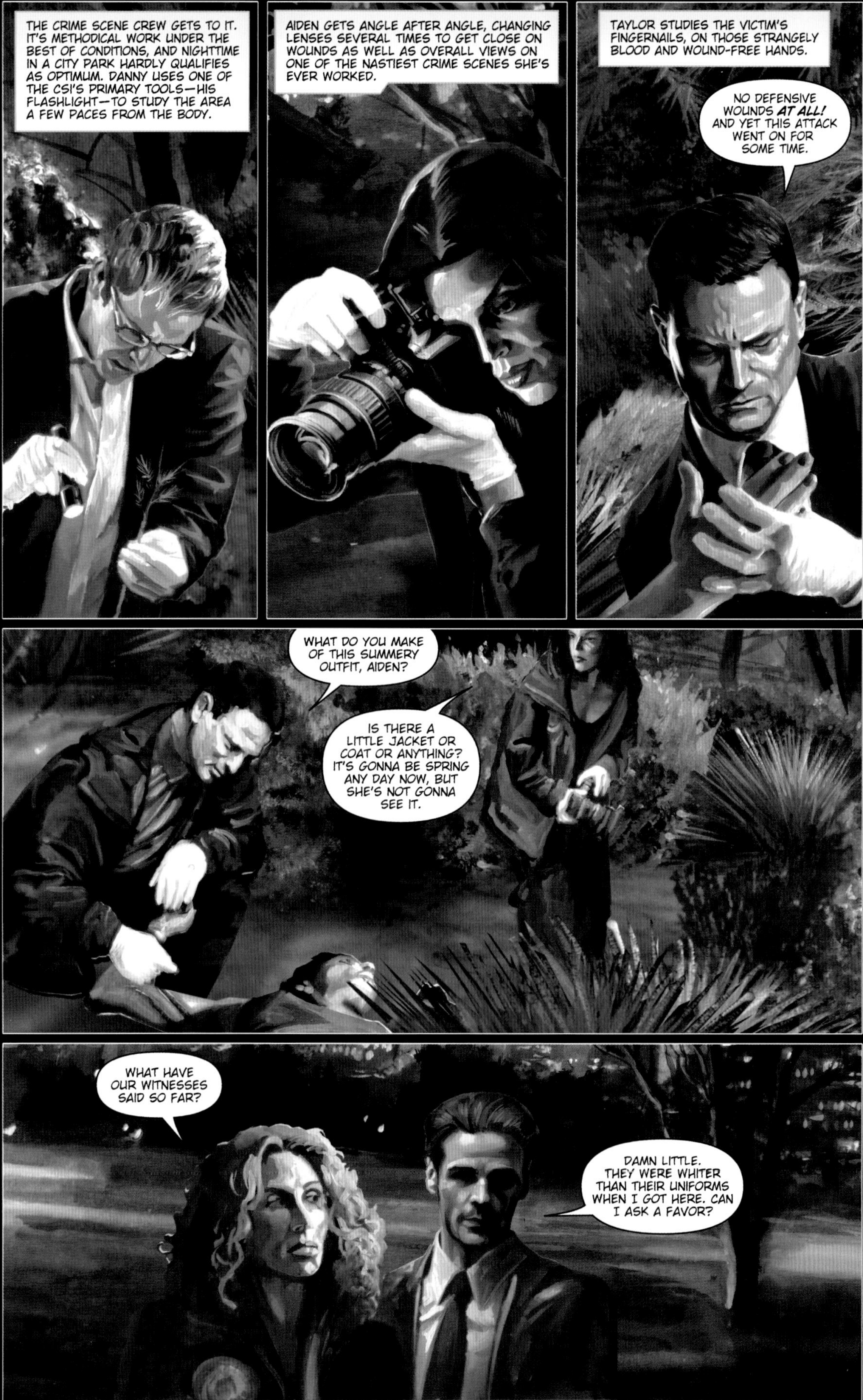
THE CRIME SCENE CREW GETS TO IT. IT'S METHODICAL WORK UNDER THE BEST OF CONDITIONS, AND NIGHTTIME IN A CITY PARK HARDLY QUALIFIES AS OPTIMUM. DANNY USES ONE OF THE CSI'S PRIMARY TOOLS—HIS FLASHLIGHT—TO STUDY THE AREA A FEW PACES FROM THE BODY.
AIDEN GETS ANGLE AFTER ANGLE, CHANGING LENSES SEVERAL TIMES TO GET CLOSE ON WOUNDS AS WELL AS OVERALL VIEWS ON ONE OF THE NASTIEST CRIME SCENES SHE'S EVER WORKED.
TAYLOR STUDIES THE VICTIM'S FINGERNAILS, ON THOSE STRANGELY BLOOD AND WOUND-FREE HANDS.
NO DEFENSIVE WOUNDS ***AT ALL!*** AND YET THIS ATTACK WENT ON FOR SOME TIME.
WHAT DO YOU MAKE OF THIS SUMMERY OUTFIT, AIDEN?
IS THERE A LITTLE JACKET OR COAT OR ANYTHING? IT'S GONNA BE SPRING ANY DAY NOW, BUT SHE'S NOT GONNA SEE IT.
WHAT HAVE OUR WITNESSES SAID SO FAR?
DAMN LITTLE. THEY WERE WHITER THAN THEIR UNIFORMS WHEN I GOT HERE. CAN I ASK A FAVOR?

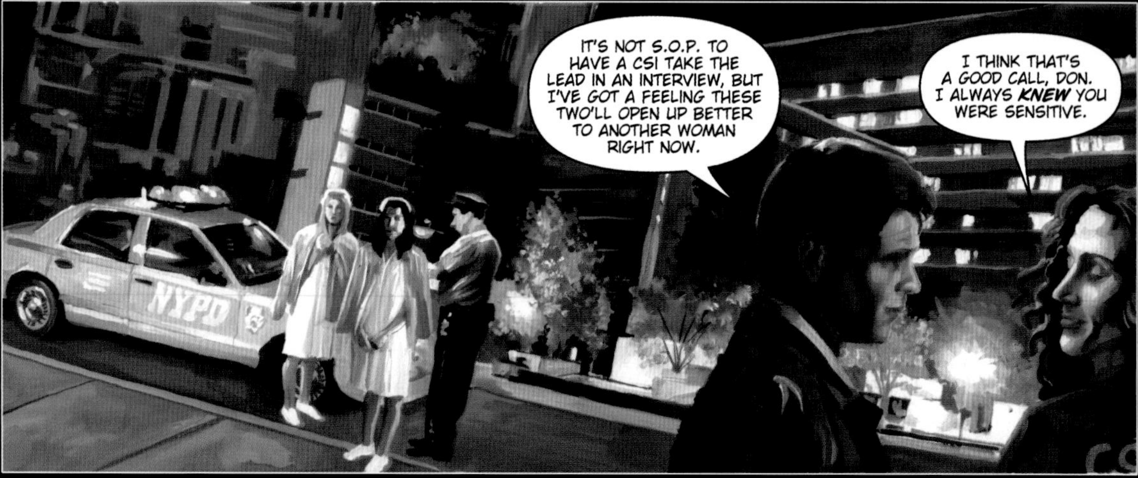
IT'S NOT S.O.P. TO HAVE A CSI TAKE THE LEAD IN AN INTERVIEW, BUT I'VE GOT A FEELING THESE TWO'LL OPEN UP BETTER TO ANOTHER WOMAN RIGHT NOW.
I THINK THAT'S A GOOD CALL, DON. I ALWAYS *KNEW* YOU WERE SENSITIVE.
NYPD

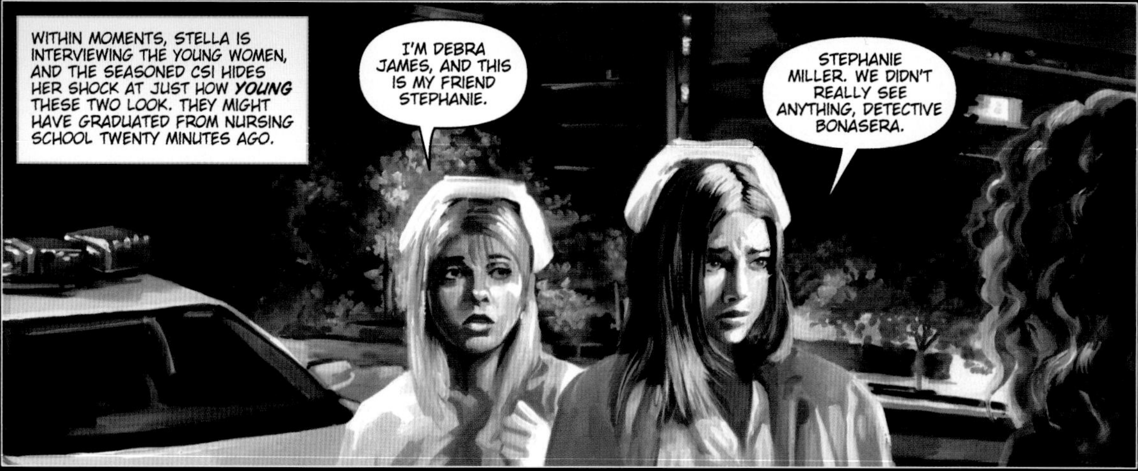
WITHIN MOMENTS, STELLA IS INTERVIEWING THE YOUNG WOMEN, AND THE SEASONED CSI HIDES HER SHOCK AT JUST HOW *YOUNG* THESE TWO LOOK. THEY MIGHT HAVE GRADUATED FROM NURSING SCHOOL TWENTY MINUTES AGO.
I'M DEBRA JAMES, AND THIS IS MY FRIEND STEPHANIE.
STEPHANIE MILLER. WE DIDN'T REALLY SEE ANYTHING, DETECTIVE BONASERA.

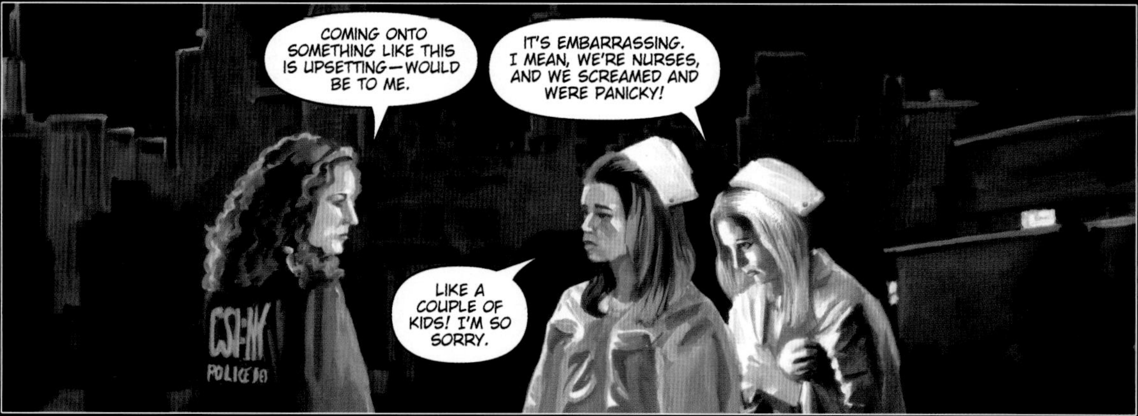
COMING ONTO SOMETHING LIKE THIS IS UPSETTING—WOULD BE TO ME.
IT'S EMBARRASSING. I MEAN, WE'RE NURSES, AND WE SCREAMED AND WERE PANICKY!
LIKE A COUPLE OF KIDS! I'M SO SORRY.
CSI:NY
POLICE DEPT

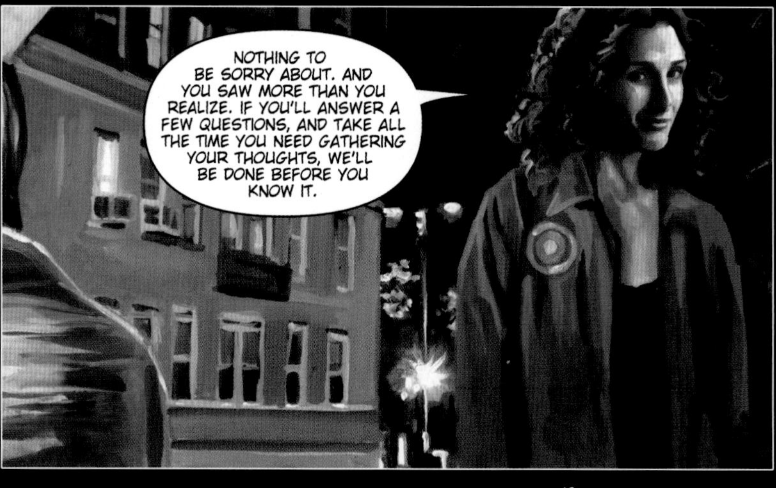
NOTHING TO BE SORRY ABOUT. AND YOU SAW MORE THAN YOU REALIZE. IF YOU'LL ANSWER A FEW QUESTIONS, AND TAKE ALL THE TIME YOU NEED GATHERING YOUR THOUGHTS, WE'LL BE DONE BEFORE YOU KNOW IT.

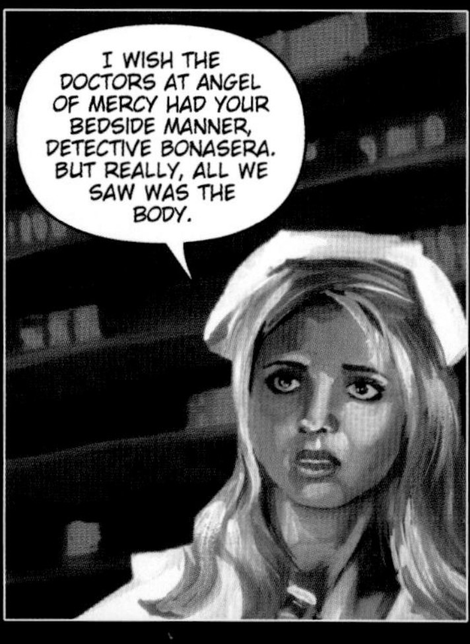
I WISH THE DOCTORS AT ANGEL OF MERCY HAD YOUR BEDSIDE MANNER, DETECTIVE BONASERA. BUT REALLY, ALL WE SAW WAS THE BODY.

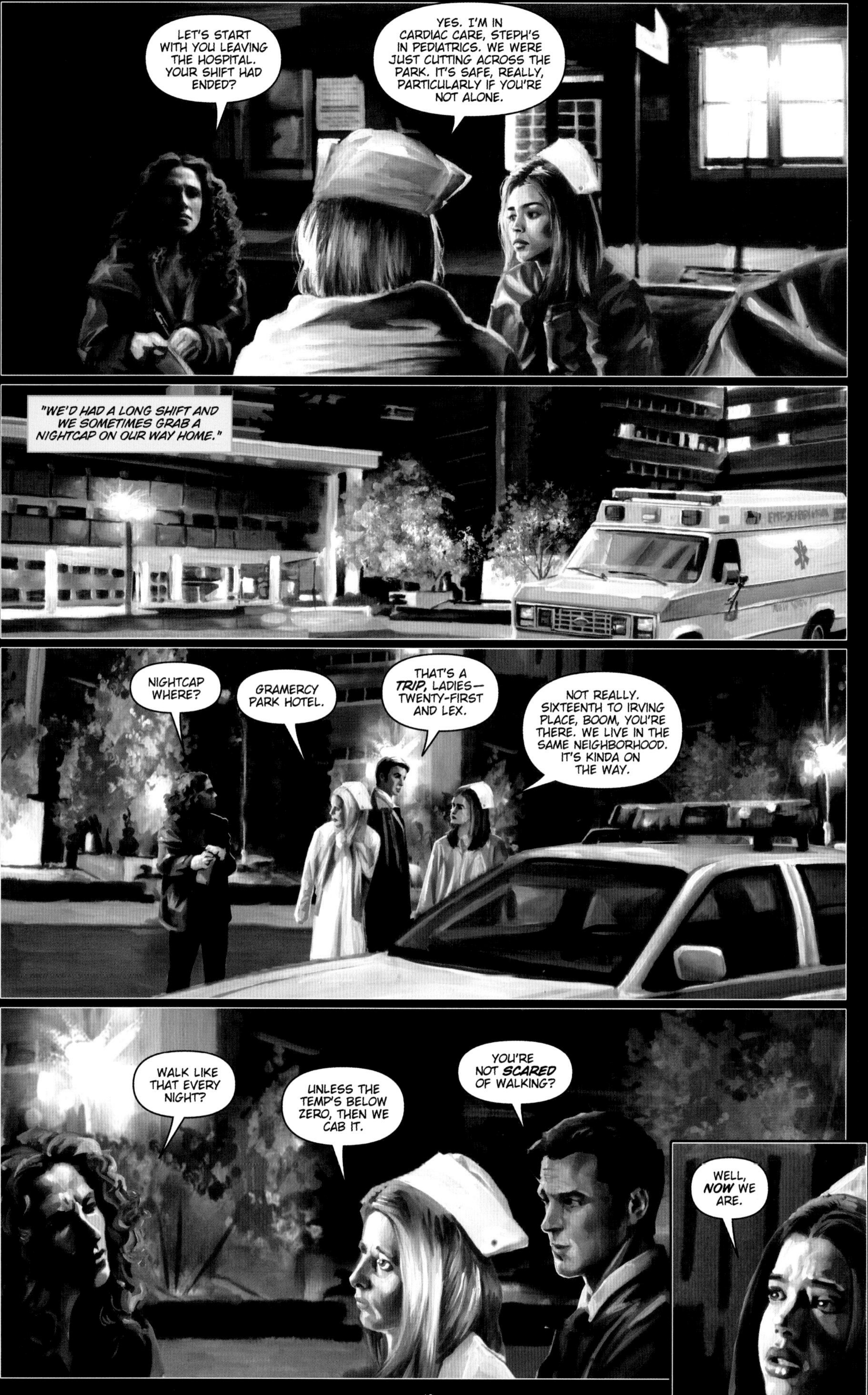

LET'S START WITH YOU LEAVING THE HOSPITAL. YOUR SHIFT HAD ENDED?
YES. I'M IN CARDIAC CARE, STEPH'S IN PEDIATRICS. WE WERE JUST CUTTING ACROSS THE PARK. IT'S SAFE, REALLY, PARTICULARLY IF YOU'RE NOT ALONE.
"WE'D HAD A LONG SHIFT AND WE SOMETIMES GRAB A NIGHTCAP ON OUR WAY HOME."
NIGHTCAP WHERE?
GRAMERCY PARK HOTEL.
THAT'S A *TRIP,* LADIES— TWENTY-FIRST AND LEX.
NOT REALLY. SIXTEENTH TO IRVING PLACE, BOOM, YOU'RE THERE. WE LIVE IN THE SAME NEIGHBORHOOD. IT'S KINDA ON THE WAY.
WALK LIKE THAT EVERY NIGHT?
UNLESS THE TEMP'S BELOW ZERO, THEN WE CAB IT.
YOU'RE NOT *SCARED* OF WALKING?
WELL, *NOW* WE ARE.

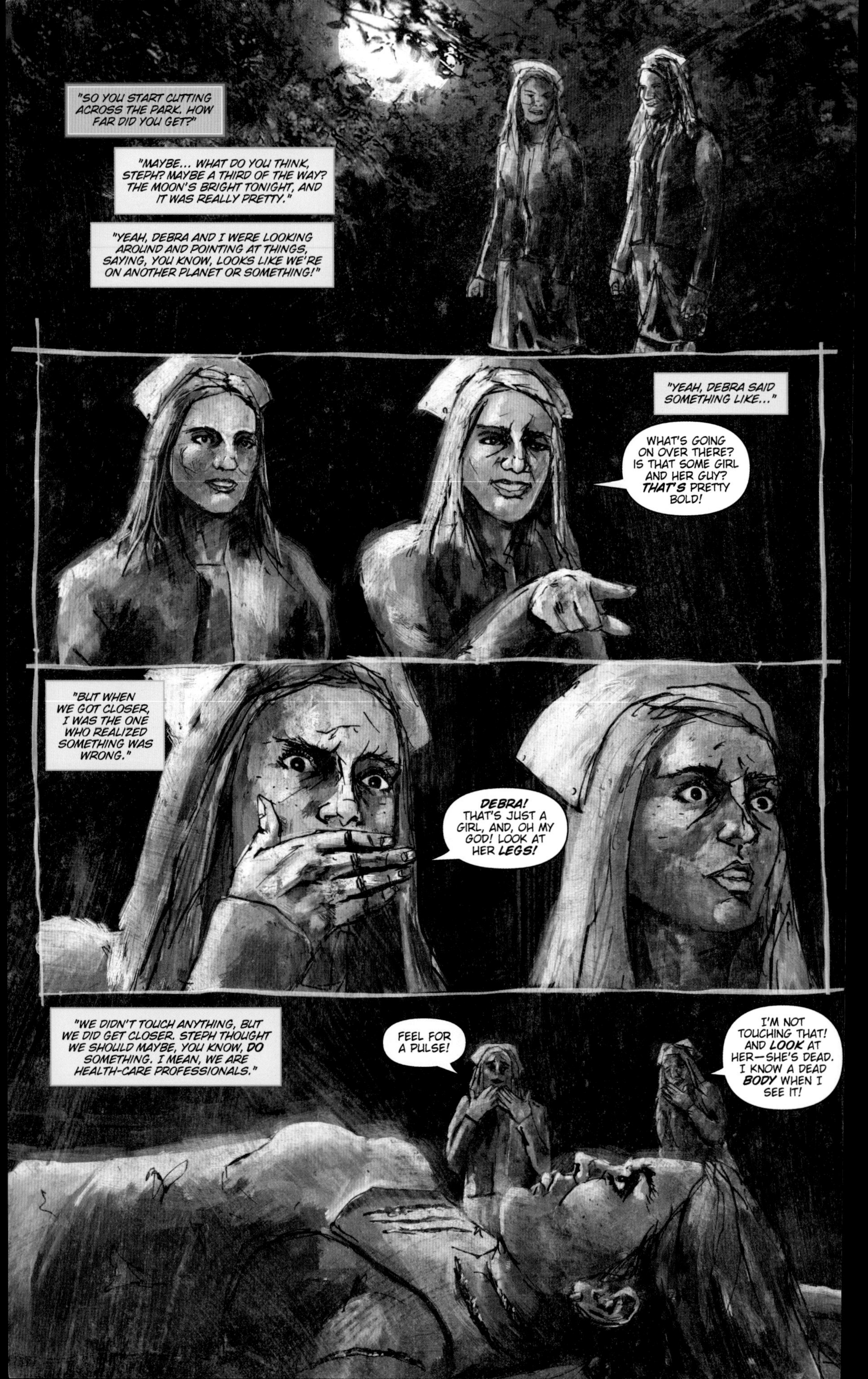
"SO YOU START CUTTING ACROSS THE PARK. HOW FAR DID YOU GET?"
"MAYBE... WHAT DO YOU THINK, STEPH? MAYBE A THIRD OF THE WAY? THE MOON'S BRIGHT TONIGHT, AND IT WAS REALLY PRETTY."
"YEAH, DEBRA AND I WERE LOOKING AROUND AND POINTING AT THINGS, SAYING, YOU KNOW, LOOKS LIKE WE'RE ON ANOTHER PLANET OR SOMETHING!"
"YEAH, DEBRA SAID SOMETHING LIKE..."
WHAT'S GOING ON OVER THERE? IS THAT SOME GIRL AND HER GUY? THAT'S PRETTY BOLD!
"BUT WHEN WE GOT CLOSER, I WAS THE ONE WHO REALIZED SOMETHING WAS WRONG."
DEBRA! THAT'S JUST A GIRL, AND, OH MY GOD! LOOK AT HER LEGS!
"WE DIDN'T TOUCH ANYTHING, BUT WE DID GET CLOSER. STEPH THOUGHT WE SHOULD MAYBE, YOU KNOW, DO SOMETHING. I MEAN, WE ARE HEALTH-CARE PROFESSIONALS."
FEEL FOR A PULSE!
I'M NOT TOUCHING THAT! AND LOOK AT HER—SHE'S DEAD. I KNOW A DEAD BODY WHEN I SEE IT!

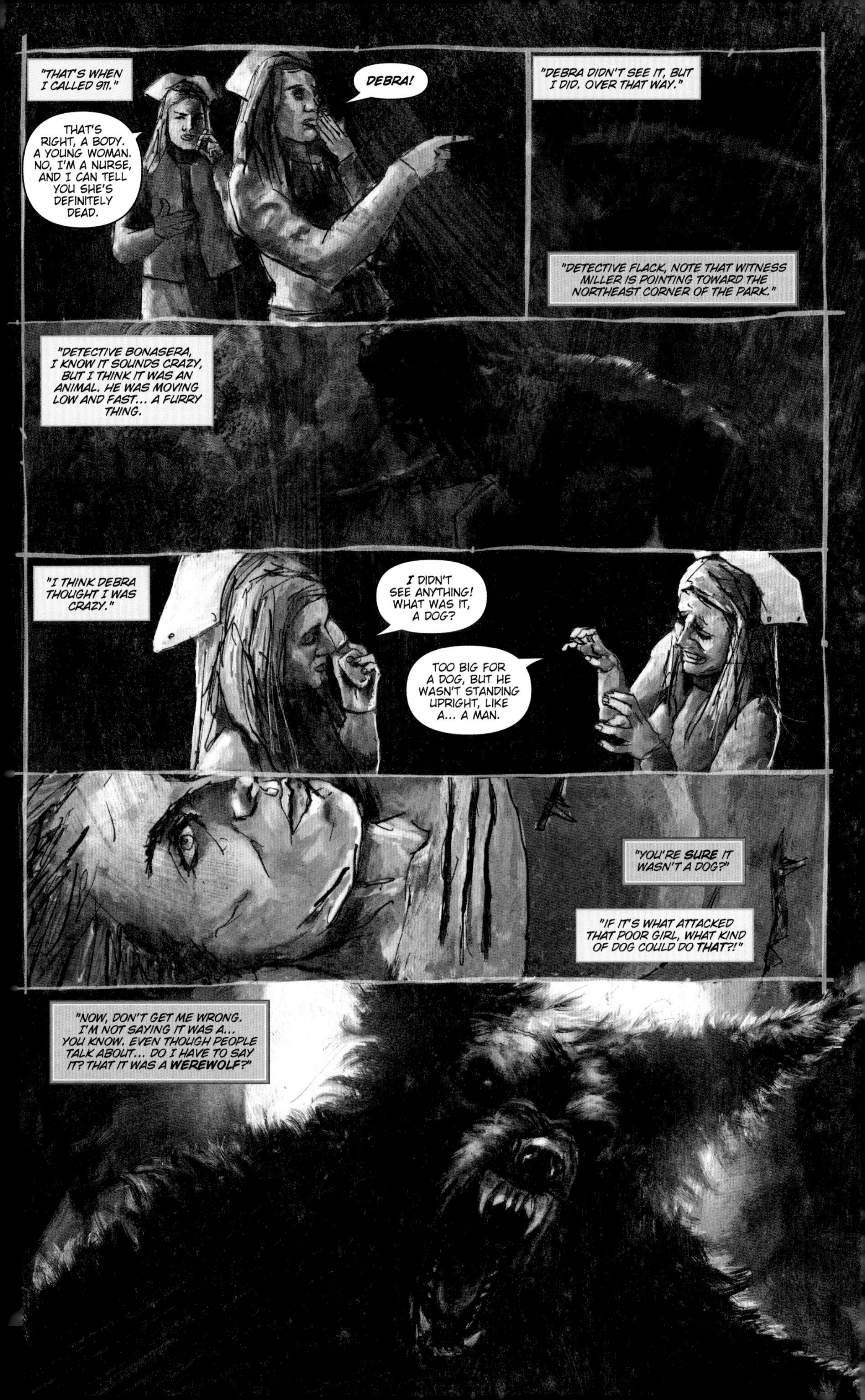
"THAT'S WHEN I CALLED 911."
DEBRA!
THAT'S RIGHT, A BODY. A YOUNG WOMAN. NO, I'M A NURSE, AND I CAN TELL YOU SHE'S DEFINITELY DEAD.
"DEBRA DIDN'T SEE IT, BUT I DID. OVER THAT WAY."
"DETECTIVE FLACK, NOTE THAT WITNESS MILLER IS POINTING TOWARD THE NORTHEAST CORNER OF THE PARK."
"DETECTIVE BONASERA, I KNOW IT SOUNDS CRAZY, BUT I THINK IT WAS AN ANIMAL. HE WAS MOVING LOW AND FAST... A FURRY THING.
"I THINK DEBRA THOUGHT I WAS CRAZY."
I DIDN'T SEE ANYTHING! WHAT WAS IT, A DOG?
TOO BIG FOR A DOG, BUT HE WASN'T STANDING UPRIGHT, LIKE A... A MAN.
"YOU'RE SURE IT WASN'T A DOG?"
"IF IT'S WHAT ATTACKED THAT POOR GIRL, WHAT KIND OF DOG COULD DO THAT?!"
"NOW, DON'T GET ME WRONG. I'M NOT SAYING IT WAS A... YOU KNOW. EVEN THOUGH PEOPLE TALK ABOUT... DO I HAVE TO SAY IT? THAT IT WAS A WEREWOLF?"

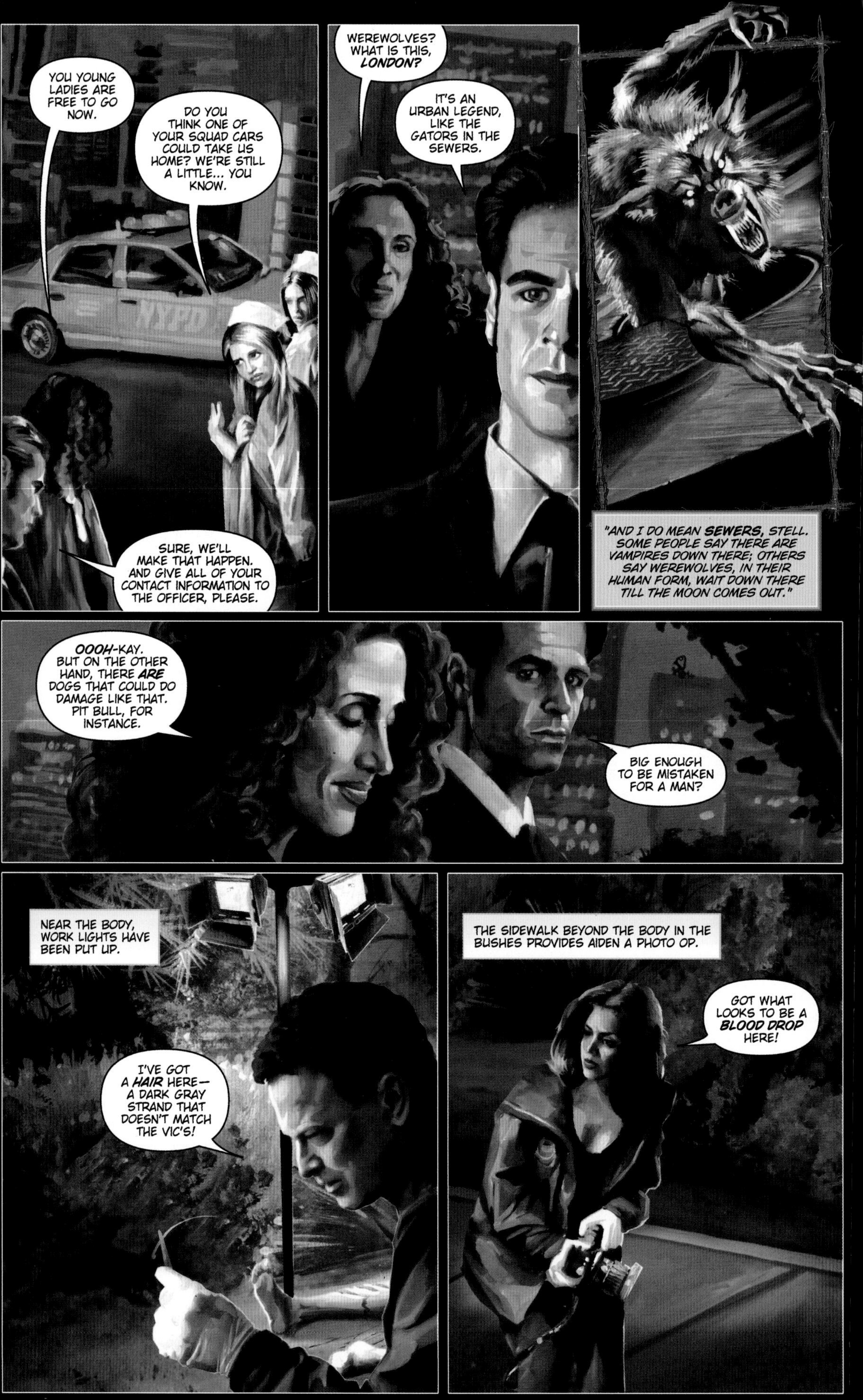

YOU YOUNG LADIES ARE FREE TO GO NOW.
DO YOU THINK ONE OF YOUR SQUAD CARS COULD TAKE US HOME? WE'RE STILL A LITTLE... YOU KNOW.
SURE, WE'LL MAKE THAT HAPPEN. AND GIVE ALL OF YOUR CONTACT INFORMATION TO THE OFFICER, PLEASE.
NYPD
WEREWOLVES? WHAT IS THIS, *LONDON?*
IT'S AN URBAN LEGEND, LIKE THE GATORS IN THE SEWERS.
*"AND I DO MEAN **SEWERS,** STELL. SOME PEOPLE SAY THERE ARE VAMPIRES DOWN THERE; OTHERS SAY WEREWOLVES, IN THEIR HUMAN FORM, WAIT DOWN THERE TILL THE MOON COMES OUT."*
OOOH-KAY. BUT ON THE OTHER HAND, THERE ***ARE*** DOGS THAT COULD DO DAMAGE LIKE THAT. PIT BULL, FOR INSTANCE.
BIG ENOUGH TO BE MISTAKEN FOR A MAN?
NEAR THE BODY, WORK LIGHTS HAVE BEEN PUT UP.
I'VE GOT A ***HAIR*** HERE— A DARK GRAY STRAND THAT DOESN'T MATCH THE VIC'S!
THE SIDEWALK BEYOND THE BODY IN THE BUSHES PROVIDES AIDEN A PHOTO OP.
GOT WHAT LOOKS TO BE A ***BLOOD DROP*** HERE!

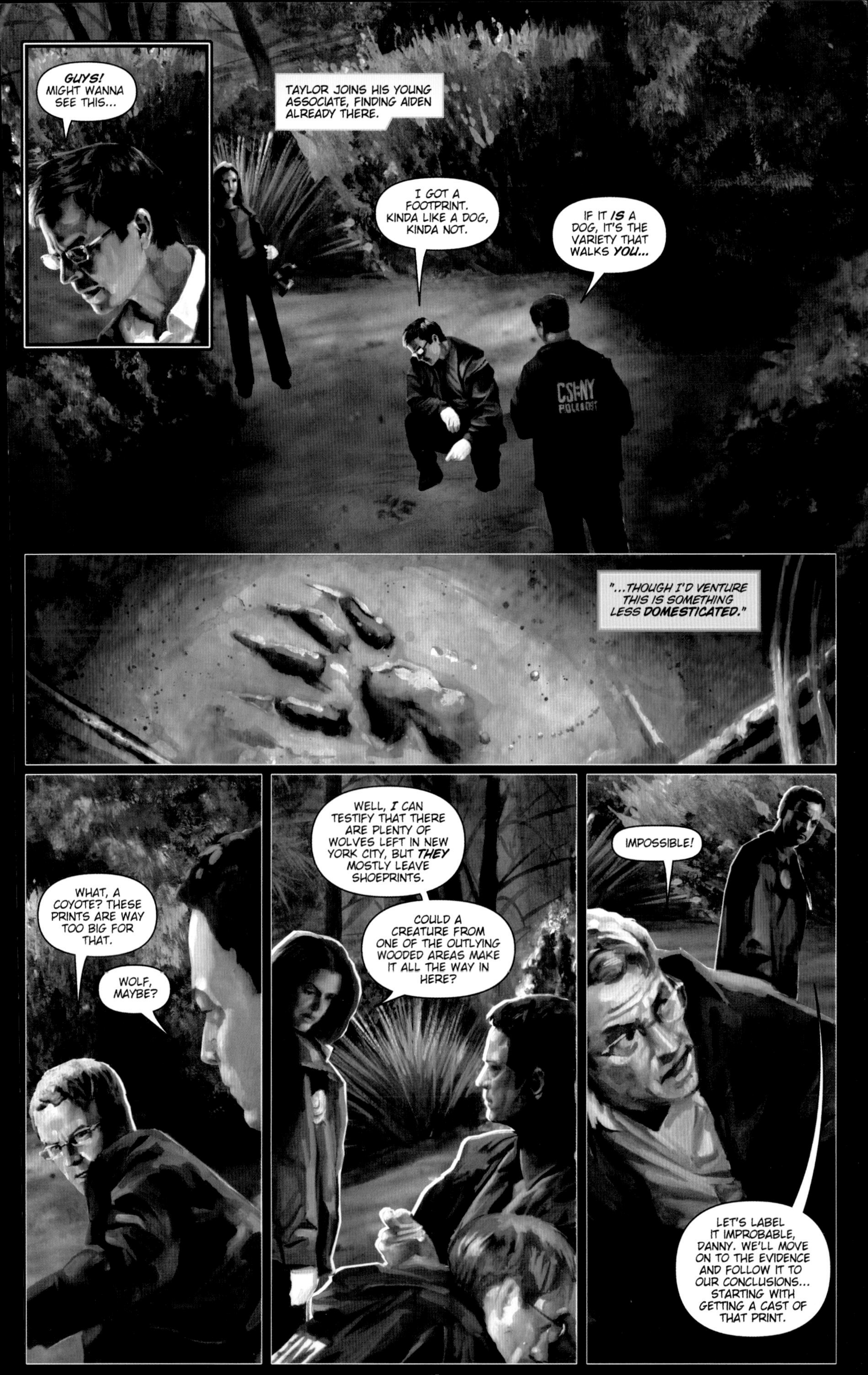
GUYS! MIGHT WANNA SEE THIS...
TAYLOR JOINS HIS YOUNG ASSOCIATE, FINDING AIDEN ALREADY THERE.
I GOT A FOOTPRINT. KINDA LIKE A DOG, KINDA NOT.
IF IT IS A DOG, IT'S THE VARIETY THAT WALKS YOU...
CSI:NY
"...THOUGH I'D VENTURE THIS IS SOMETHING LESS DOMESTICATED."
WHAT, A COYOTE? THESE PRINTS ARE WAY TOO BIG FOR THAT.
WOLF, MAYBE?
WELL, I CAN TESTIFY THAT THERE ARE PLENTY OF WOLVES LEFT IN NEW YORK CITY, BUT THEY MOSTLY LEAVE SHOEPRINTS.
COULD A CREATURE FROM ONE OF THE OUTLYING WOODED AREAS MAKE IT ALL THE WAY IN HERE?
IMPOSSIBLE!
LET'S LABEL IT IMPROBABLE, DANNY. WE'LL MOVE ON TO THE EVIDENCE AND FOLLOW IT TO OUR CONCLUSIONS... STARTING WITH GETTING A CAST OF THAT PRINT.

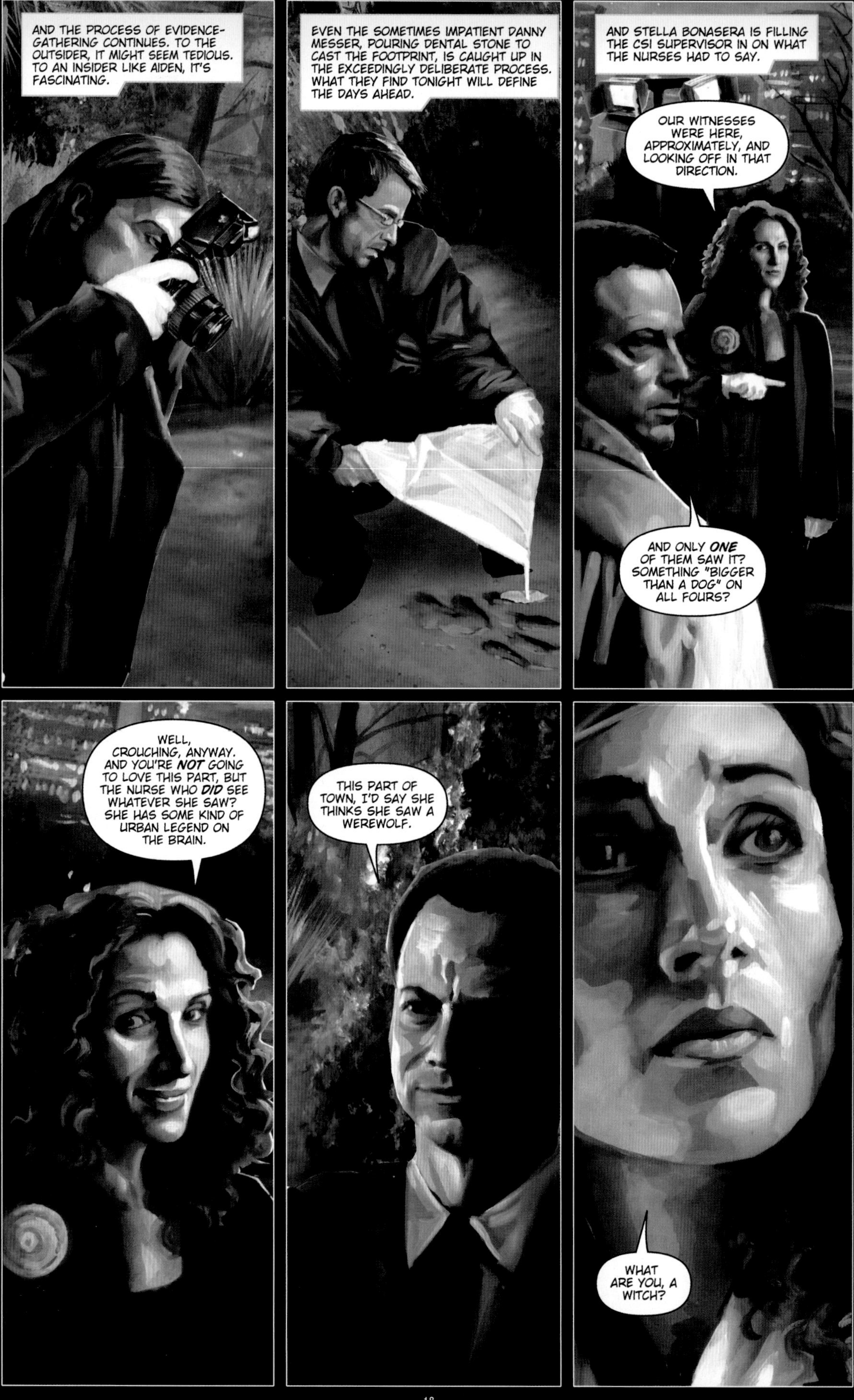
AND THE PROCESS OF EVIDENCE-GATHERING CONTINUES. TO THE OUTSIDER, IT MIGHT SEEM TEDIOUS. TO AN INSIDER LIKE AIDEN, IT'S FASCINATING.
EVEN THE SOMETIMES IMPATIENT DANNY MESSER, POURING DENTAL STONE TO CAST THE FOOTPRINT, IS CAUGHT UP IN THE EXCEEDINGLY DELIBERATE PROCESS. WHAT THEY FIND TONIGHT WILL DEFINE THE DAYS AHEAD.
AND STELLA BONASERA IS FILLING THE CSI SUPERVISOR IN ON WHAT THE NURSES HAD TO SAY.
OUR WITNESSES WERE HERE, APPROXIMATELY, AND LOOKING OFF IN THAT DIRECTION.
AND ONLY ***ONE*** OF THEM SAW IT? SOMETHING "BIGGER THAN A DOG" ON ALL FOURS?
WELL, CROUCHING, ANYWAY. AND YOU'RE ***NOT*** GOING TO LOVE THIS PART, BUT THE NURSE WHO ***DID*** SEE WHATEVER SHE SAW? SHE HAS SOME KIND OF URBAN LEGEND ON THE BRAIN.
THIS PART OF TOWN, I'D SAY SHE THINKS SHE SAW A WEREWOLF.
WHAT ARE YOU, A WITCH?

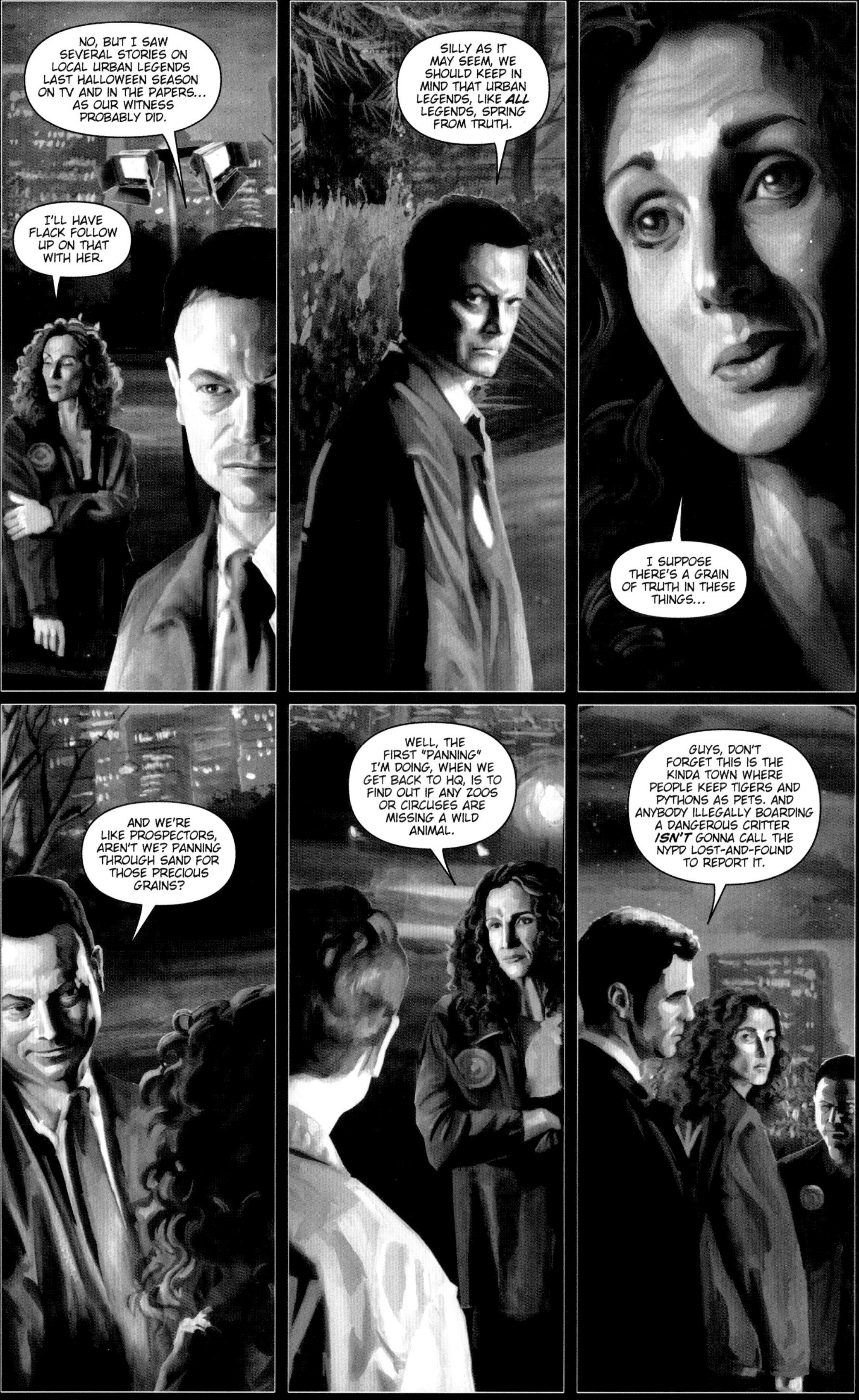
NO, BUT I SAW SEVERAL STORIES ON LOCAL URBAN LEGENDS LAST HALLOWEEN SEASON ON TV AND IN THE PAPERS... AS OUR WITNESS PROBABLY DID.
I'LL HAVE FLACK FOLLOW UP ON THAT WITH HER.
SILLY AS IT MAY SEEM, WE SHOULD KEEP IN MIND THAT URBAN LEGENDS, LIKE ***ALL*** LEGENDS, SPRING FROM TRUTH.
I SUPPOSE THERE'S A GRAIN OF TRUTH IN THESE THINGS...
AND WE'RE LIKE PROSPECTORS, AREN'T WE? PANNING THROUGH SAND FOR THOSE PRECIOUS GRAINS?
WELL, THE FIRST "PANNING" I'M DOING, WHEN WE GET BACK TO HQ, IS TO FIND OUT IF ANY ZOOS OR CIRCUSES ARE MISSING A WILD ANIMAL.
GUYS, DON'T FORGET THIS IS THE KINDA TOWN WHERE PEOPLE KEEP TIGERS AND PYTHONS AS PETS. AND ANYBODY ILLEGALLY BOARDING A DANGEROUS CRITTER ***ISN'T*** GONNA CALL THE NYPD LOST-AND-FOUND TO REPORT IT.

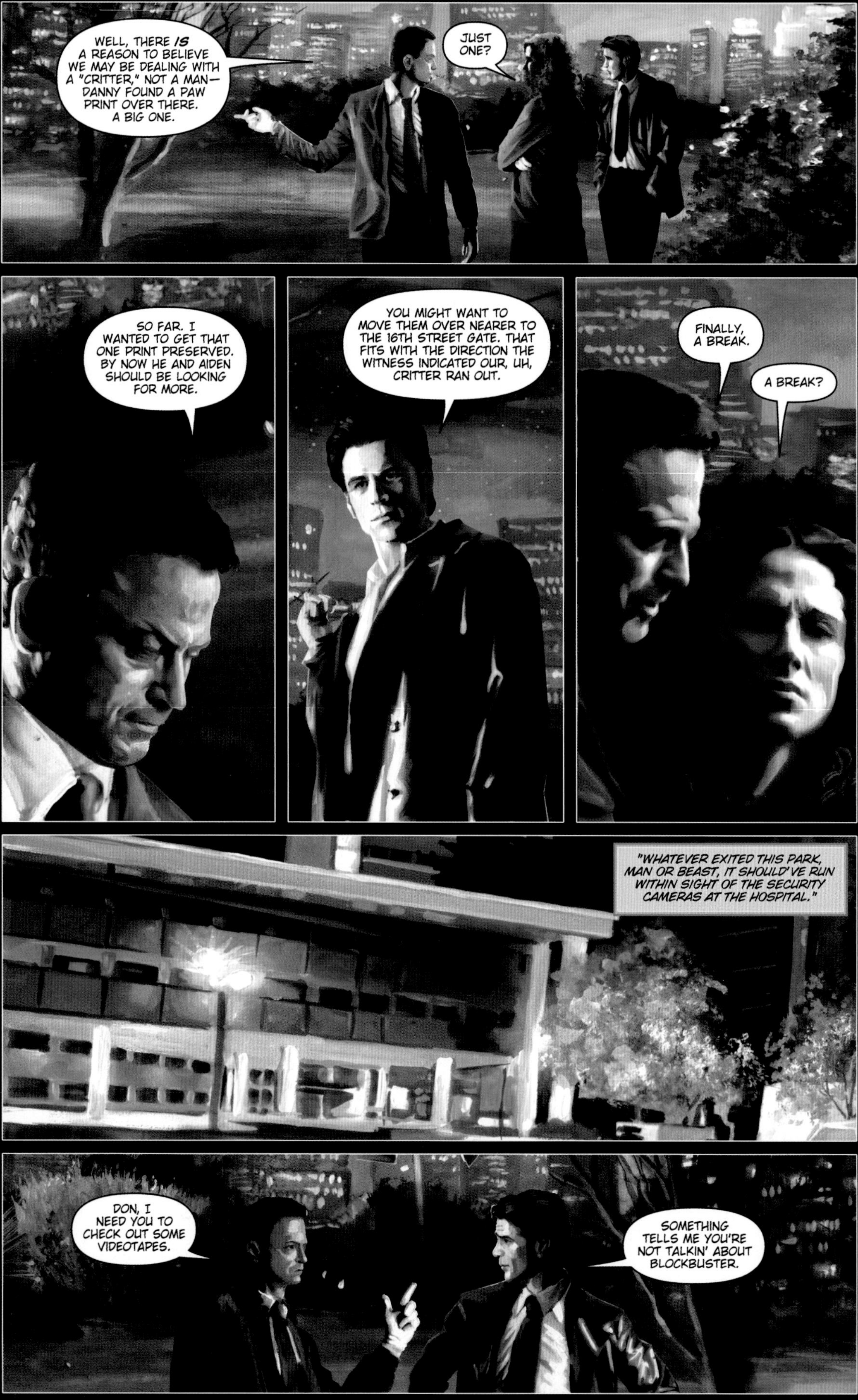

WELL, THERE *IS* A REASON TO BELIEVE WE MAY BE DEALING WITH A "CRITTER," NOT A MAN— DANNY FOUND A PAW PRINT OVER THERE. A BIG ONE.
JUST ONE?
SO FAR. I WANTED TO GET THAT ONE PRINT PRESERVED. BY NOW HE AND AIDEN SHOULD BE LOOKING FOR MORE.
YOU MIGHT WANT TO MOVE THEM OVER NEARER TO THE 16TH STREET GATE. THAT FITS WITH THE DIRECTION THE WITNESS INDICATED OUR, UH, CRITTER RAN OUT.
FINALLY, A BREAK.
A BREAK?
"WHATEVER EXITED THIS PARK, MAN OR BEAST, IT SHOULD'VE RUN WITHIN SIGHT OF THE SECURITY CAMERAS AT THE HOSPITAL."
DON, I NEED YOU TO CHECK OUT SOME VIDEOTAPES.
SOMETHING TELLS ME YOU'RE NOT TALKIN' ABOUT BLOCKBUSTER.

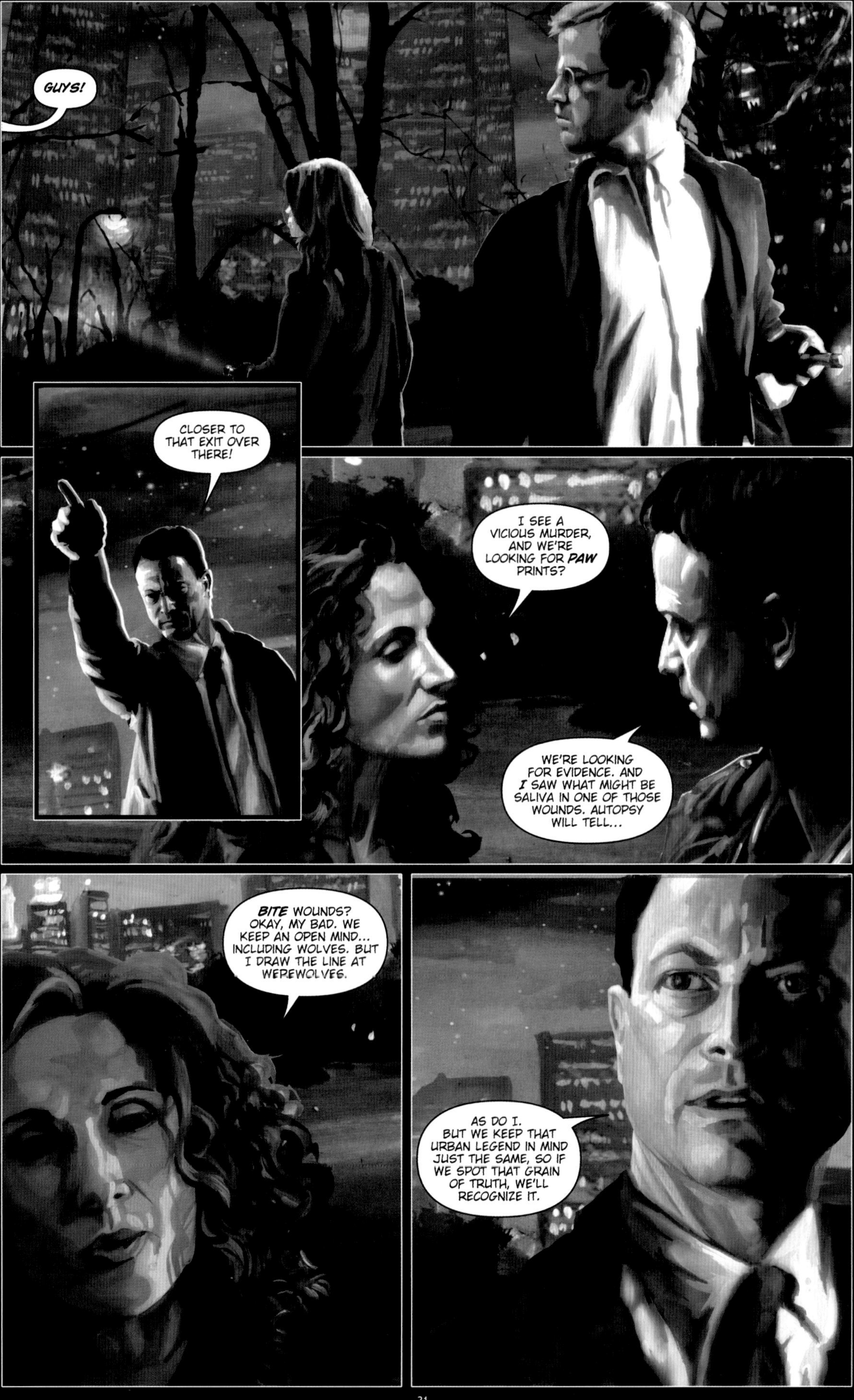
GUYS!
CLOSER TO THAT EXIT OVER THERE!
I SEE A VICIOUS MURDER, AND WE'RE LOOKING FOR PAW PRINTS?
WE'RE LOOKING FOR EVIDENCE. AND I SAW WHAT MIGHT BE SALIVA IN ONE OF THOSE WOUNDS. AUTOPSY WILL TELL...
BITE WOUNDS? OKAY, MY BAD. WE KEEP AN OPEN MIND... INCLUDING WOLVES. BUT I DRAW THE LINE AT WEREWOLVES.
AS DO I. BUT WE KEEP THAT URBAN LEGEND IN MIND JUST THE SAME, SO IF WE SPOT THAT GRAIN OF TRUTH, WE'LL RECOGNIZE IT.

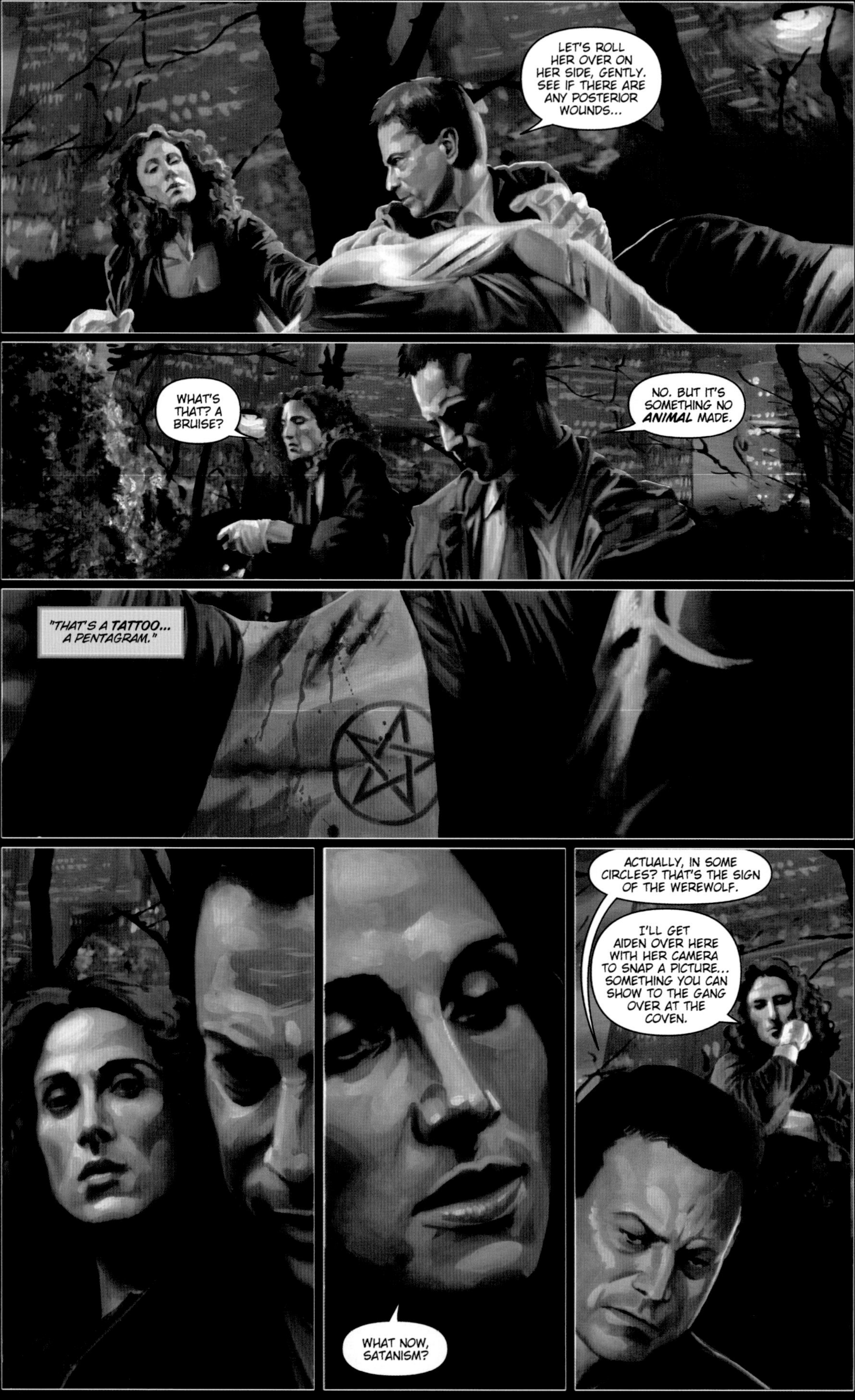
LET'S ROLL HER OVER ON HER SIDE, GENTLY. SEE IF THERE ARE ANY POSTERIOR WOUNDS...
WHAT'S THAT? A BRUISE?
NO. BUT IT'S SOMETHING NO ANIMAL MADE.
"THAT'S A TATTOO... A PENTAGRAM."
WHAT NOW, SATANISM?
ACTUALLY, IN SOME CIRCLES? THAT'S THE SIGN OF THE WEREWOLF.
I'LL GET AIDEN OVER HERE WITH HER CAMERA TO SNAP A PICTURE... SOMETHING YOU CAN SHOW TO THE GANG OVER AT THE COVEN.

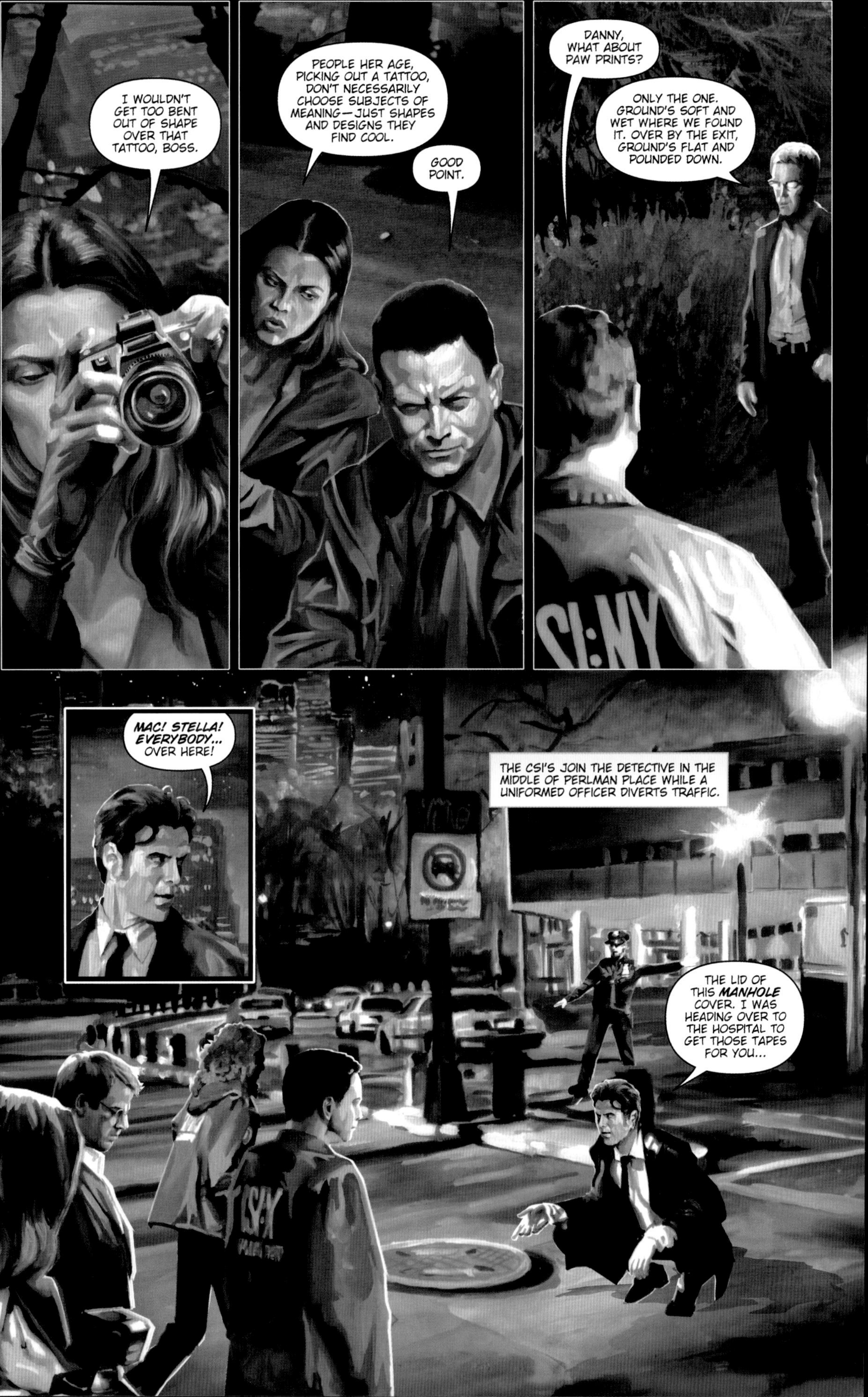
I WOULDN'T GET TOO BENT OUT OF SHAPE OVER THAT TATTOO, BOSS.
PEOPLE HER AGE, PICKING OUT A TATTOO, DON'T NECESSARILY CHOOSE SUBJECTS OF MEANING—JUST SHAPES AND DESIGNS THEY FIND COOL.
GOOD POINT.
DANNY, WHAT ABOUT PAW PRINTS?
ONLY THE ONE. GROUND'S SOFT AND WET WHERE WE FOUND IT. OVER BY THE EXIT, GROUND'S FLAT AND POUNDED DOWN.
CSI:NY
MAC! STELLA! EVERYBODY... OVER HERE!
THE CSI'S JOIN THE DETECTIVE IN THE MIDDLE OF PERLMAN PLACE WHILE A UNIFORMED OFFICER DIVERTS TRAFFIC.
THE LID OF THIS MANHOLE COVER. I WAS HEADING OVER TO THE HOSPITAL TO GET THOSE TAPES FOR YOU...

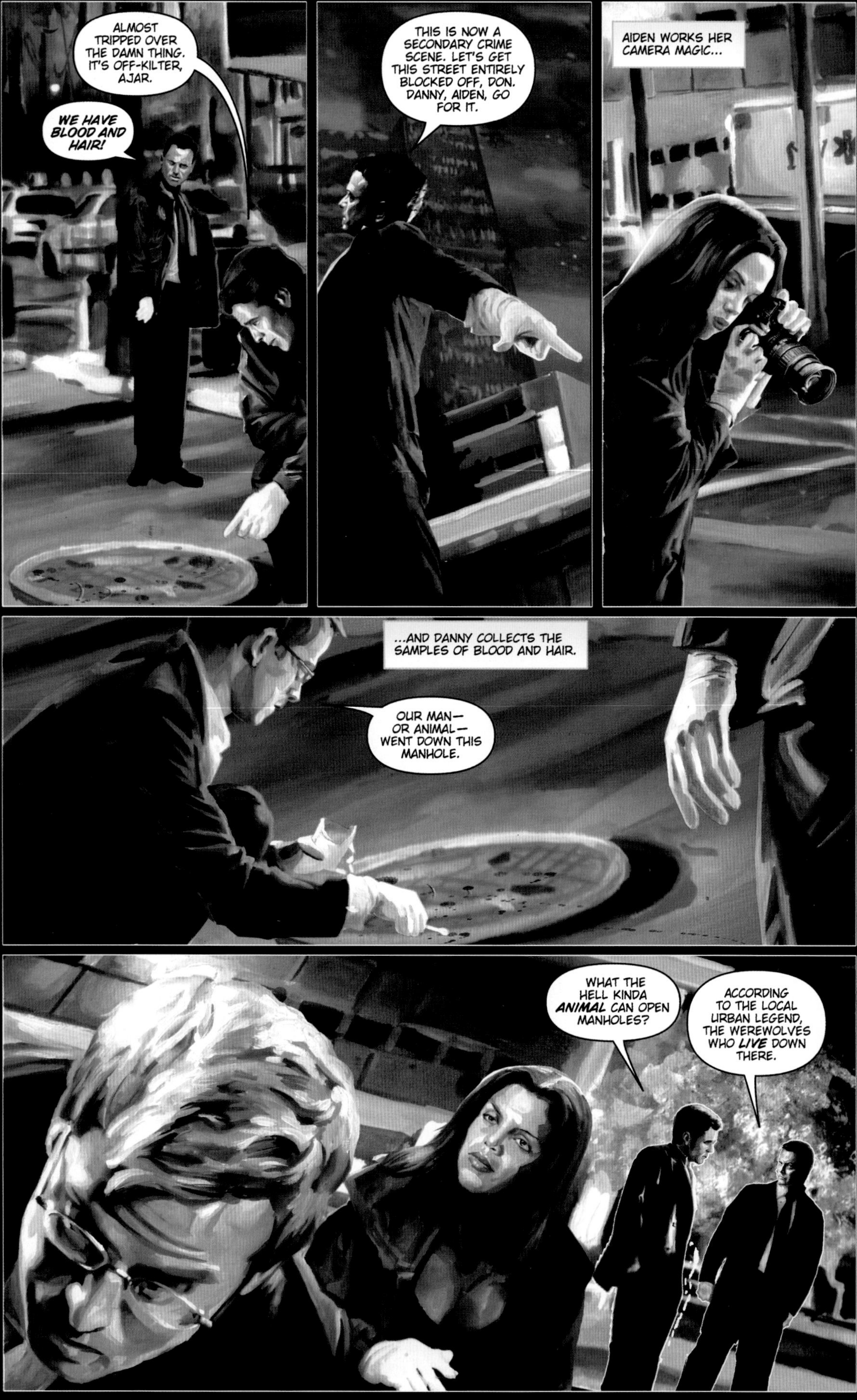
ALMOST TRIPPED OVER THE DAMN THING. IT'S OFF-KILTER, AJAR.
WE HAVE BLOOD AND HAIR!
THIS IS NOW A SECONDARY CRIME SCENE. LET'S GET THIS STREET ENTIRELY BLOCKED OFF, DON. DANNY, AIDEN, GO FOR IT.
AIDEN WORKS HER CAMERA MAGIC...
...AND DANNY COLLECTS THE SAMPLES OF BLOOD AND HAIR.
OUR MAN— OR ANIMAL— WENT DOWN THIS MANHOLE.
WHAT THE HELL KINDA *ANIMAL* CAN OPEN MANHOLES?
ACCORDING TO THE LOCAL URBAN LEGEND, THE WEREWOLVES WHO *LIVE* DOWN THERE.

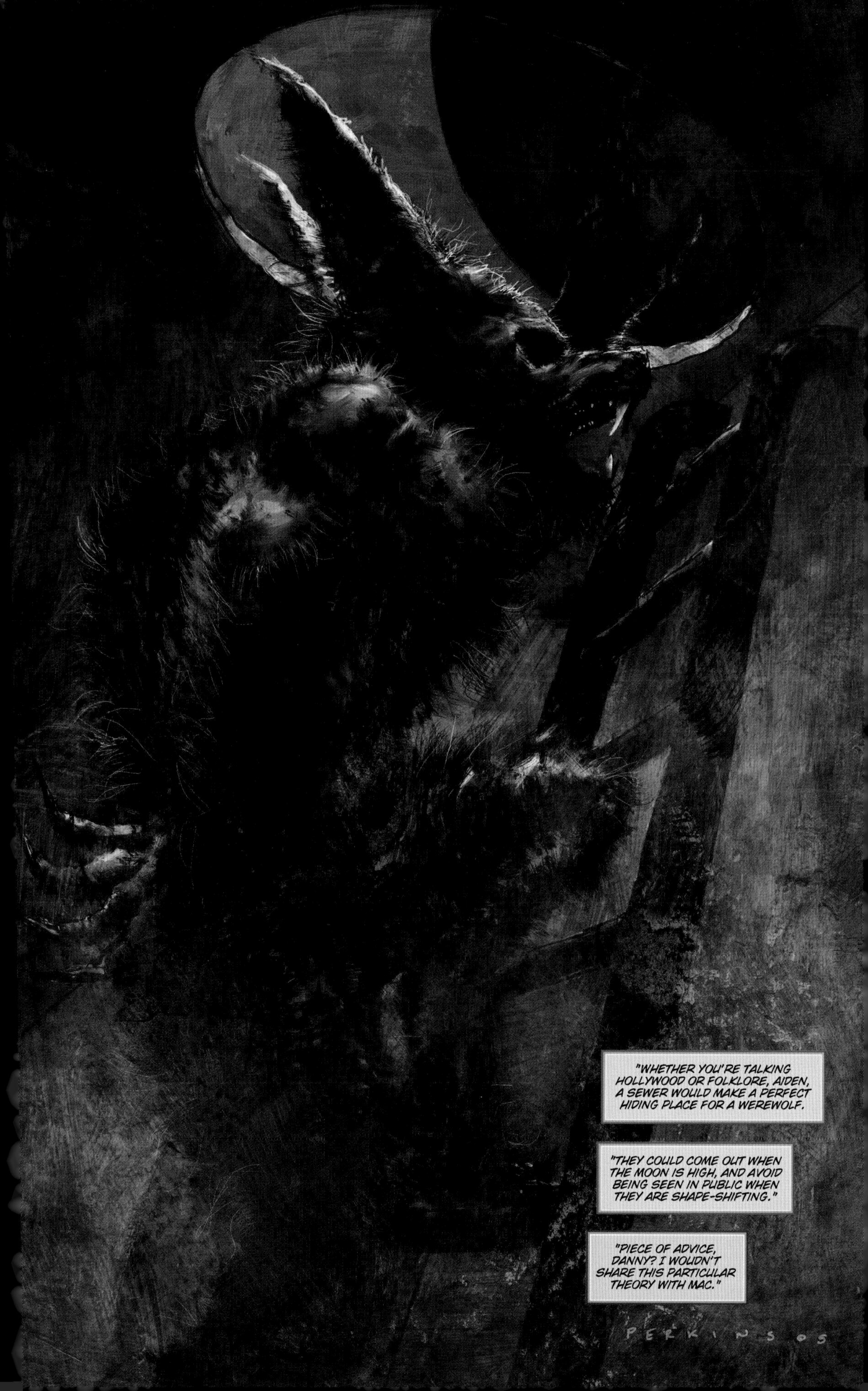
"WHETHER YOU'RE TALKING HOLLYWOOD OR FOLKLORE, AIDEN, A SEWER WOULD MAKE A PERFECT HIDING PLACE FOR A WEREWOLF.
"THEY COULD COME OUT WHEN THE MOON IS HIGH, AND AVOID BEING SEEN IN PUBLIC WHEN THEY ARE SHAPE-SHIFTING."
"PIECE OF ADVICE, DANNY? I WOUDN'T SHARE THIS PARTICULAR THEORY WITH MAC."
PERKINS 05

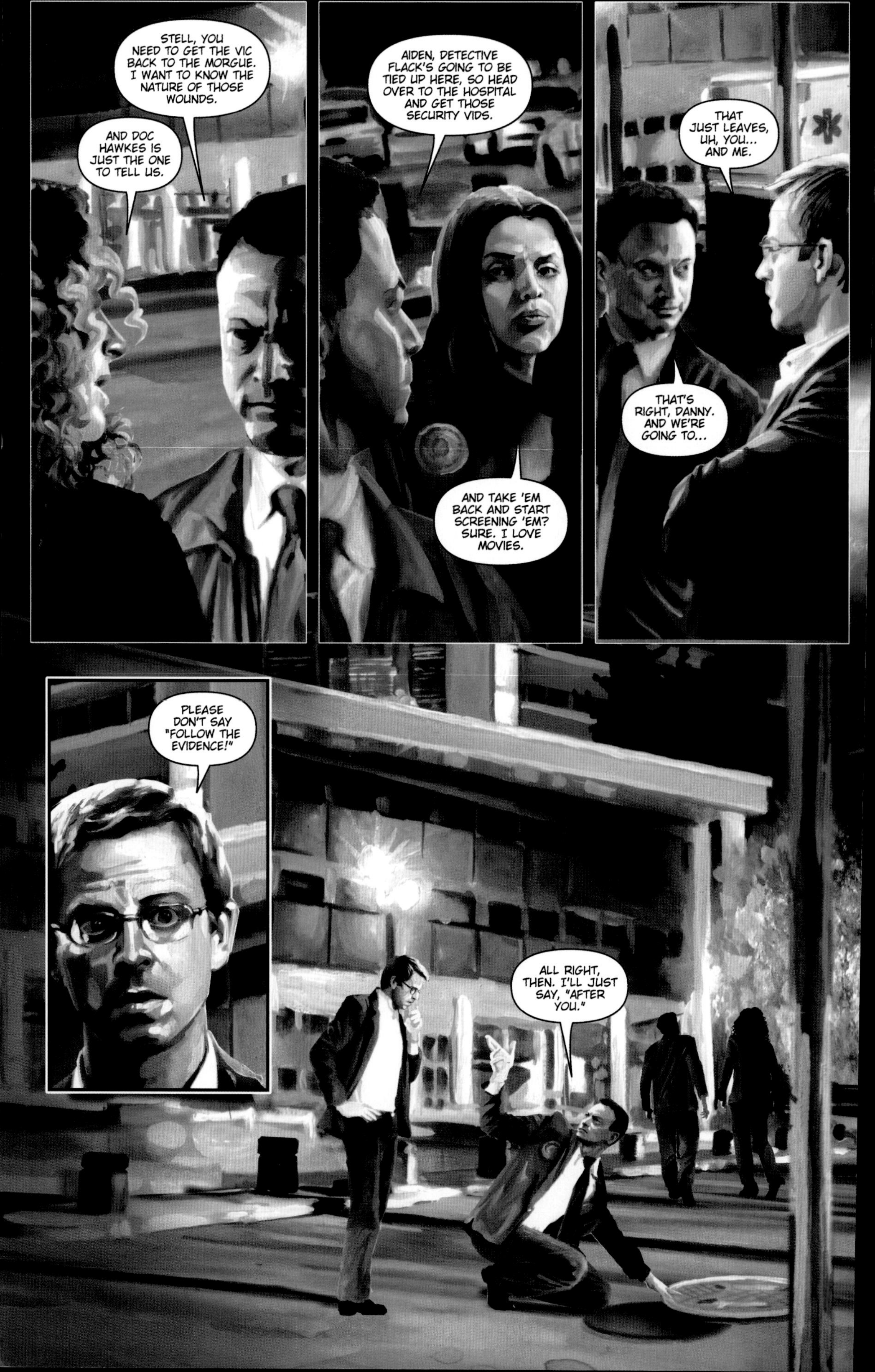
STELL, YOU NEED TO GET THE VIC BACK TO THE MORGUE. I WANT TO KNOW THE NATURE OF THOSE WOUNDS.
AND DOC HAWKES IS JUST THE ONE TO TELL US.
AIDEN, DETECTIVE FLACK'S GOING TO BE TIED UP HERE, SO HEAD OVER TO THE HOSPITAL AND GET THOSE SECURITY VIDS.
AND TAKE 'EM BACK AND START SCREENING 'EM? SURE. I LOVE MOVIES.
THAT JUST LEAVES, UH, YOU... AND ME.
THAT'S RIGHT, DANNY. AND WE'RE GOING TO...
PLEASE DON'T SAY "FOLLOW THE EVIDENCE!"
ALL RIGHT, THEN. I'LL JUST SAY, "AFTER YOU."

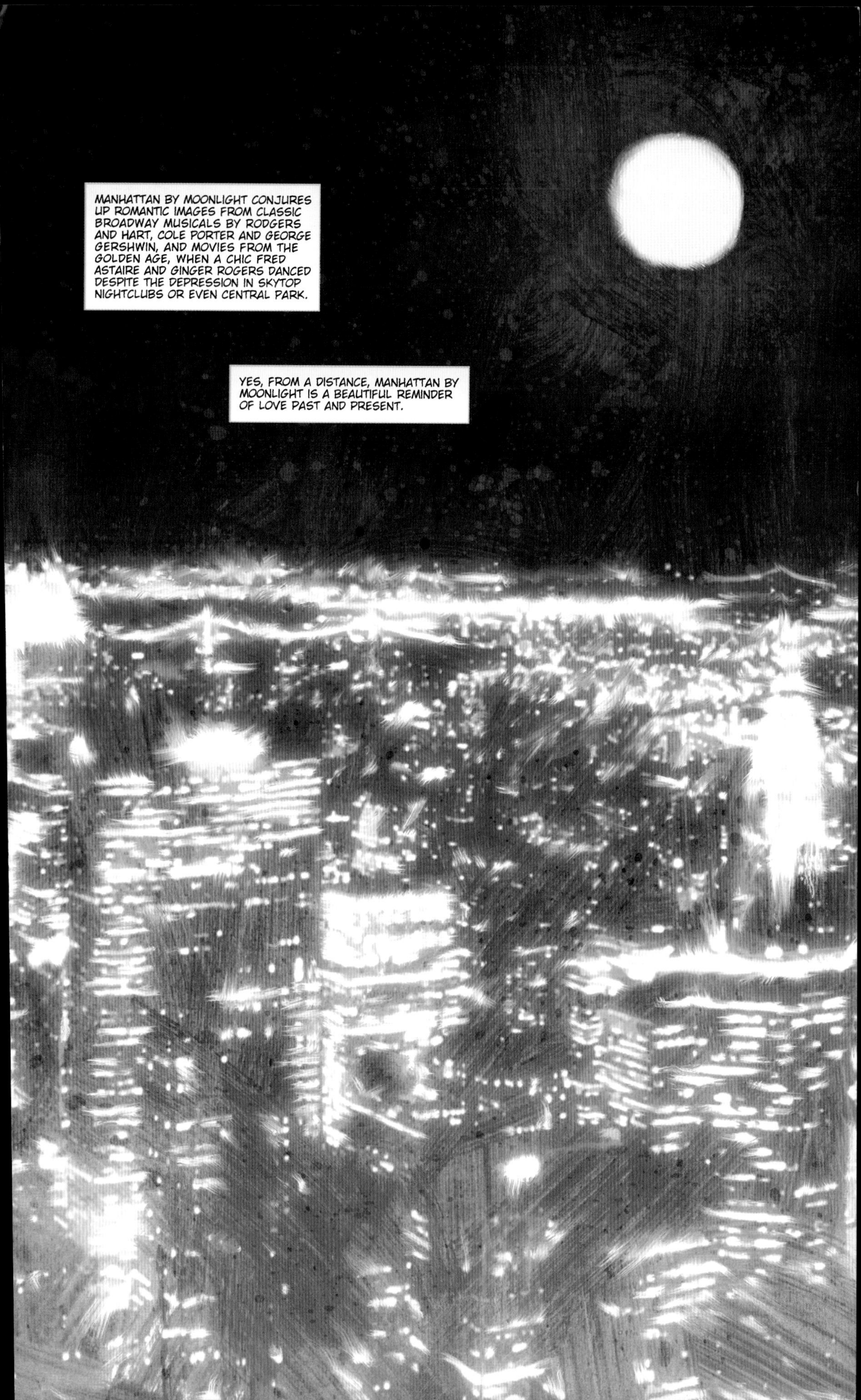
MANHATTAN BY MOONLIGHT CONJURES UP ROMANTIC IMAGES FROM CLASSIC BROADWAY MUSICALS BY RODGERS AND HART, COLE PORTER AND GEORGE GERSHWIN, AND MOVIES FROM THE GOLDEN AGE, WHEN A CHIC FRED ASTAIRE AND GINGER ROGERS DANCED DESPITE THE DEPRESSION IN SKYTOP NIGHTCLUBS OR EVEN CENTRAL PARK.
YES, FROM A DISTANCE, MANHATTAN BY MOONLIGHT IS A BEAUTIFUL REMINDER OF LOVE PAST AND PRESENT.

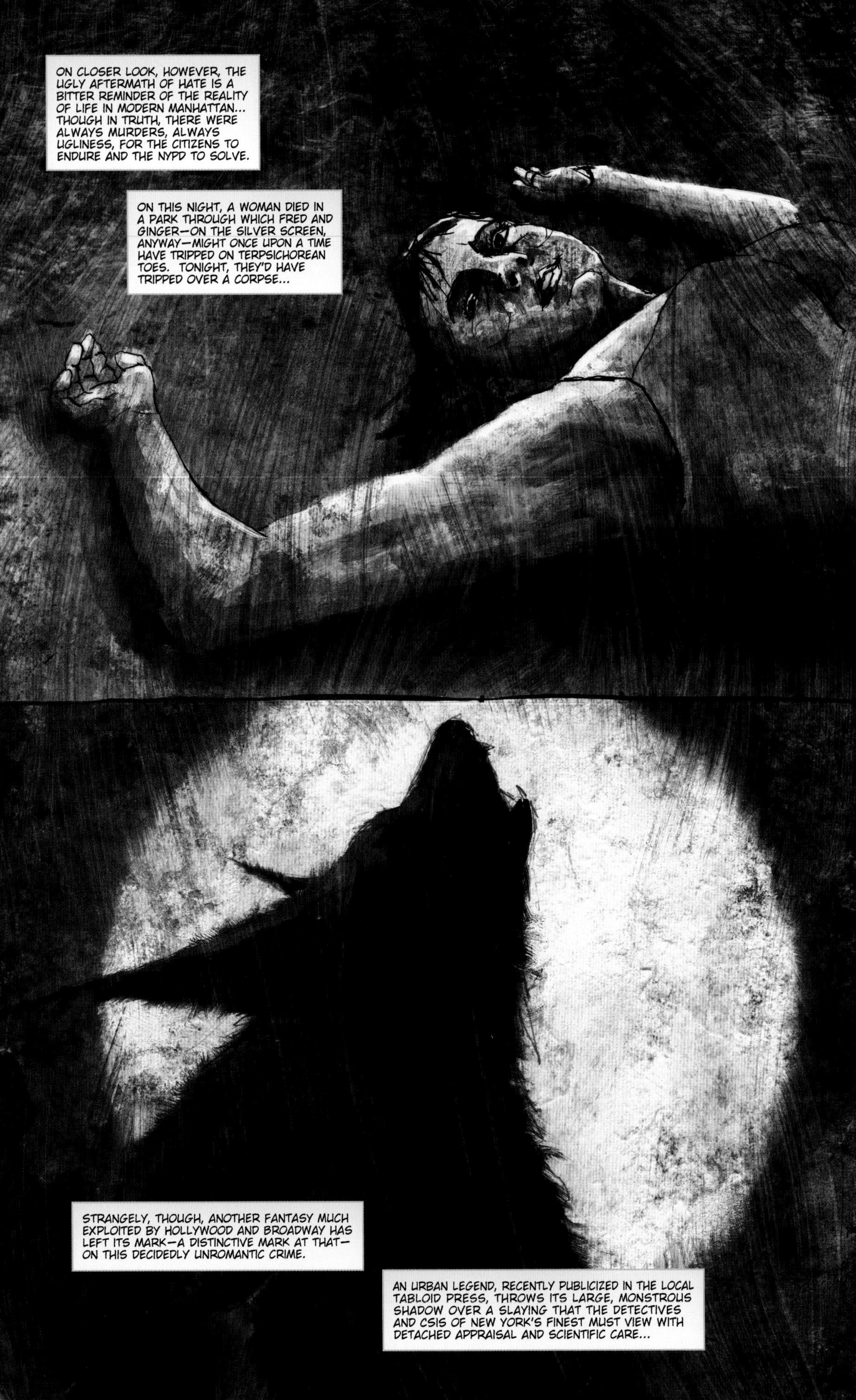
ON CLOSER LOOK, HOWEVER, THE UGLY AFTERMATH OF HATE IS A BITTER REMINDER OF THE REALITY OF LIFE IN MODERN MANHATTAN... THOUGH IN TRUTH, THERE WERE ALWAYS MURDERS, ALWAYS UGLINESS, FOR THE CITIZENS TO ENDURE AND THE NYPD TO SOLVE.
ON THIS NIGHT, A WOMAN DIED IN A PARK THROUGH WHICH FRED AND GINGER—ON THE SILVER SCREEN, ANYWAY—MIGHT ONCE UPON A TIME HAVE TRIPPED ON TERPSICHOREAN TOES. TONIGHT, THEY'D HAVE TRIPPED OVER A CORPSE...
STRANGELY, THOUGH, ANOTHER FANTASY MUCH EXPLOITED BY HOLLYWOOD AND BROADWAY HAS LEFT ITS MARK—A DISTINCTIVE MARK AT THAT—ON THIS DECIDEDLY UNROMANTIC CRIME.
AN URBAN LEGEND, RECENTLY PUBLICIZED IN THE LOCAL TABLOID PRESS, THROWS ITS LARGE, MONSTROUS SHADOW OVER A SLAYING THAT THE DETECTIVES AND CSIS OF NEW YORK'S FINEST MUST VIEW WITH DETACHED APPRAISAL AND SCIENTIFIC CARE...

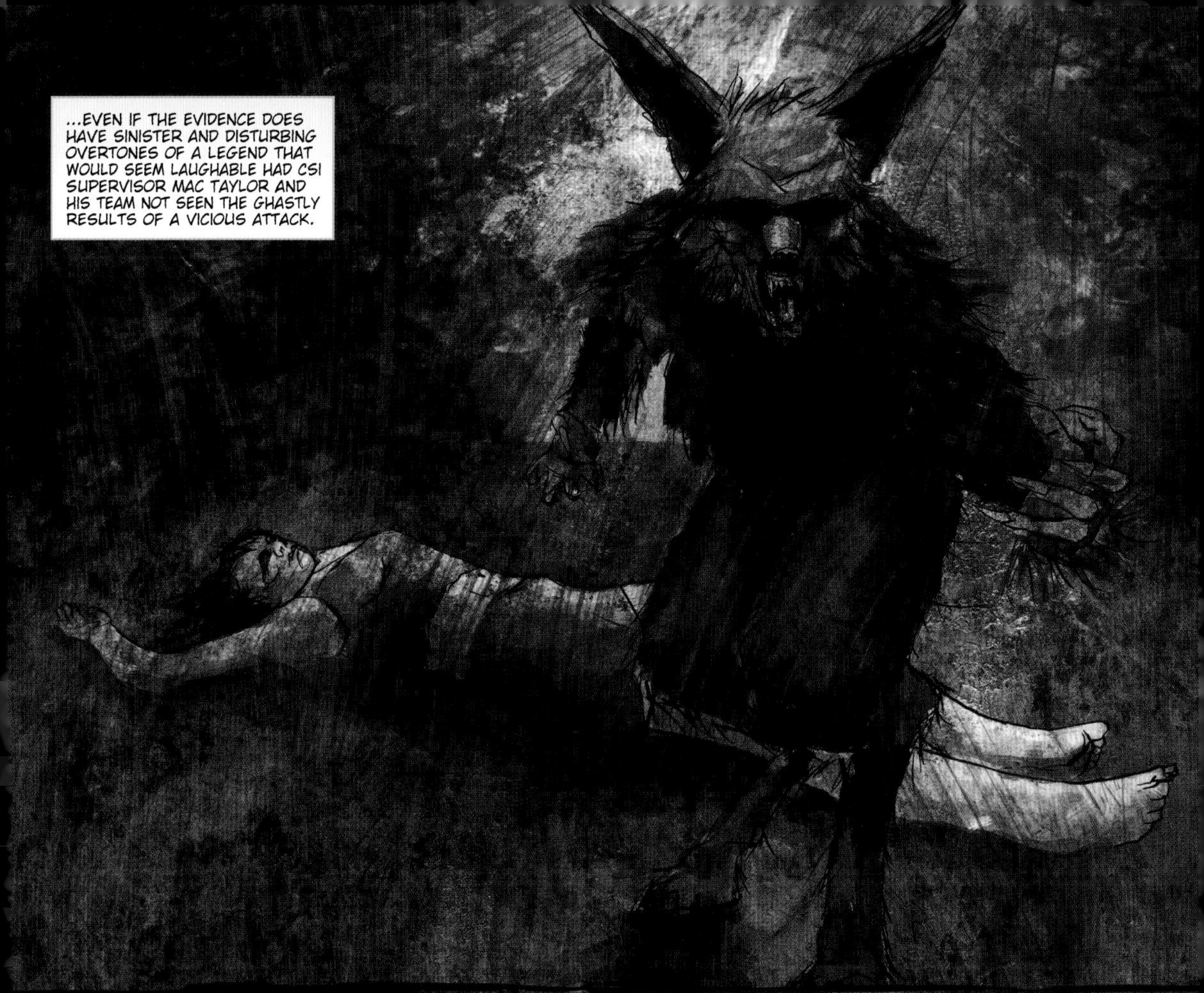
...EVEN IF THE EVIDENCE DOES HAVE SINISTER AND DISTURBING OVERTONES OF A LEGEND THAT WOULD SEEM LAUGHABLE HAD CSI SUPERVISOR MAC TAYLOR AND HIS TEAM NOT SEEN THE GHASTLY RESULTS OF A VICIOUS ATTACK.

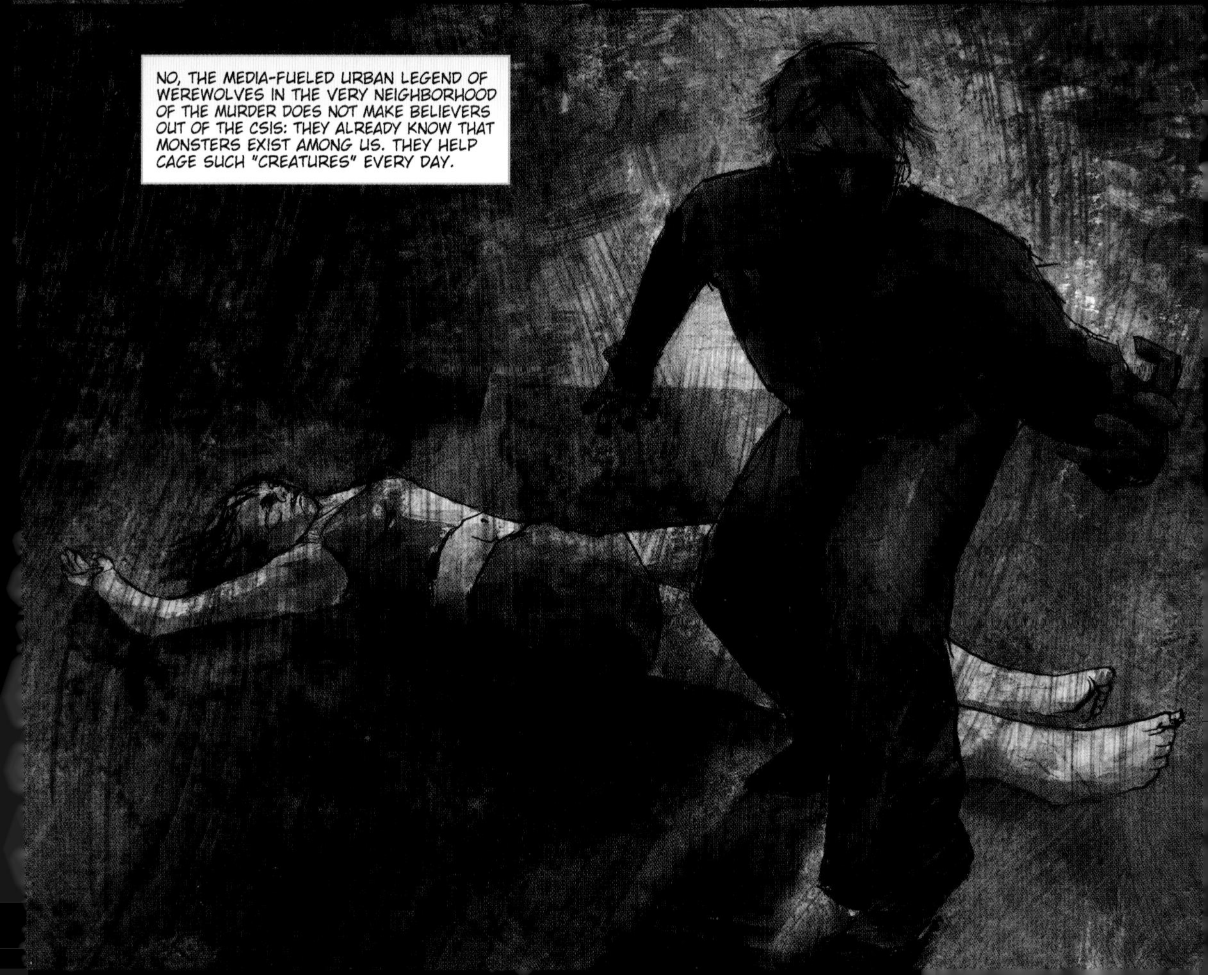
NO, THE MEDIA-FUELED URBAN LEGEND OF WEREWOLVES IN THE VERY NEIGHBORHOOD OF THE MURDER DOES NOT MAKE BELIEVERS OUT OF THE CSIS: THEY ALREADY KNOW THAT MONSTERS EXIST AMONG US. THEY HELP CAGE SUCH "CREATURES" EVERY DAY.

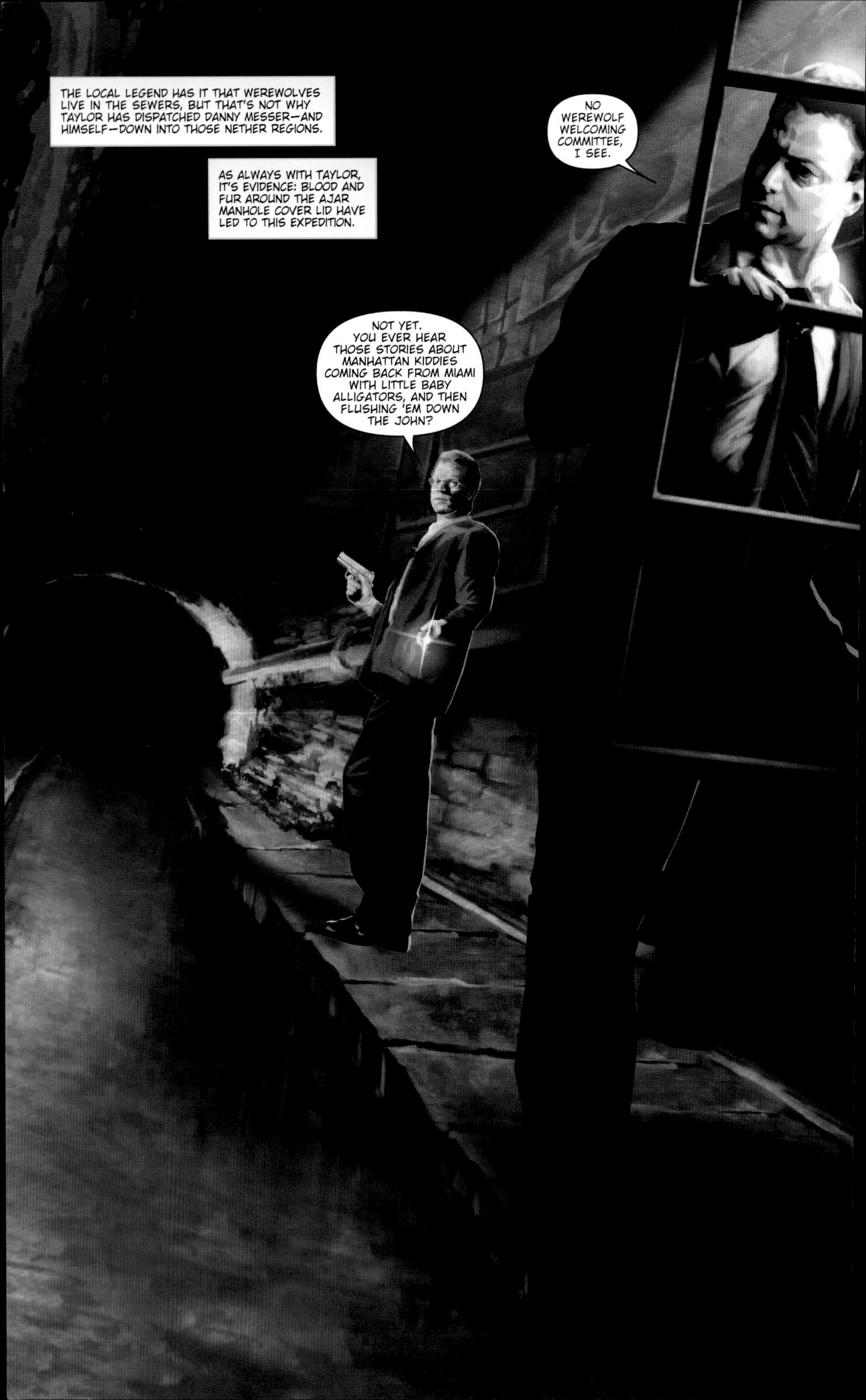
THE LOCAL LEGEND HAS IT THAT WEREWOLVES LIVE IN THE SEWERS, BUT THAT'S NOT WHY TAYLOR HAS DISPATCHED DANNY MESSER—AND HIMSELF—DOWN INTO THOSE NETHER REGIONS.
AS ALWAYS WITH TAYLOR, IT'S EVIDENCE: BLOOD AND FUR AROUND THE AJAR MANHOLE COVER LID HAVE LED TO THIS EXPEDITION.
NO WEREWOLF WELCOMING COMMITTEE, I SEE.
NOT YET. YOU EVER HEAR THOSE STORIES ABOUT MANHATTAN KIDDIES COMING BACK FROM MIAMI WITH LITTLE BABY ALLIGATORS, AND THEN FLUSHING 'EM DOWN THE JOHN?

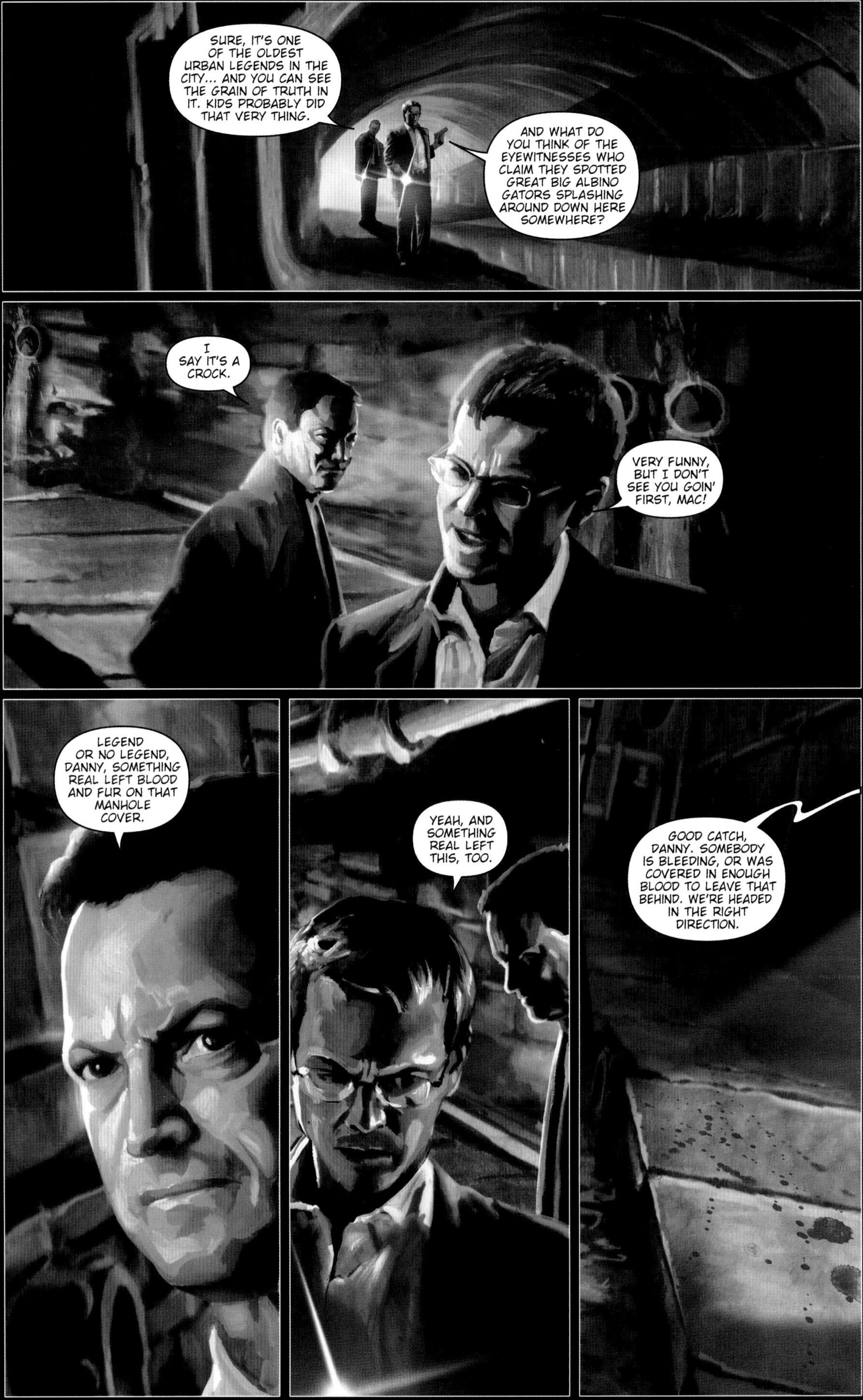
SURE, IT'S ONE OF THE OLDEST URBAN LEGENDS IN THE CITY... AND YOU CAN SEE THE GRAIN OF TRUTH IN IT. KIDS PROBABLY DID THAT VERY THING.
AND WHAT DO YOU THINK OF THE EYEWITNESSES WHO CLAIM THEY SPOTTED GREAT BIG ALBINO GATORS SPLASHING AROUND DOWN HERE SOMEWHERE?
I SAY IT'S A CROCK.
VERY FUNNY, BUT I DON'T SEE YOU GOIN' FIRST, MAC!
LEGEND OR NO LEGEND, DANNY, SOMETHING REAL LEFT BLOOD AND FUR ON THAT MANHOLE COVER.
YEAH, AND SOMETHING REAL LEFT THIS, TOO.
GOOD CATCH, DANNY. SOMEBODY IS BLEEDING, OR WAS COVERED IN ENOUGH BLOOD TO LEAVE THAT BEHIND. WE'RE HEADED IN THE RIGHT DIRECTION.

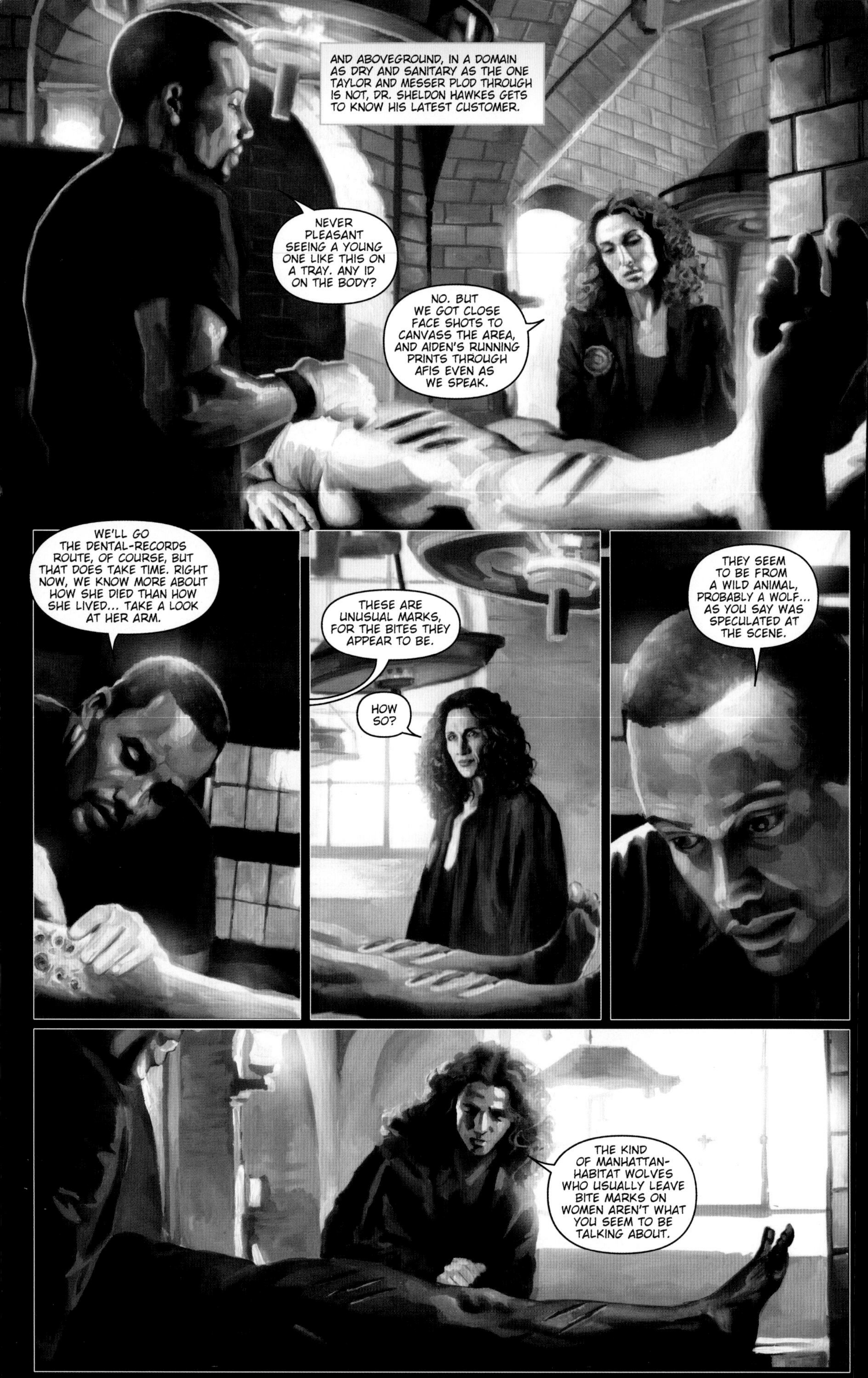

AND ABOVEGROUND, IN A DOMAIN AS DRY AND SANITARY AS THE ONE TAYLOR AND MESSER PLOD THROUGH IS NOT, DR. SHELDON HAWKES GETS TO KNOW HIS LATEST CUSTOMER.
NEVER PLEASANT SEEING A YOUNG ONE LIKE THIS ON A TRAY. ANY ID ON THE BODY?
NO. BUT WE GOT CLOSE FACE SHOTS TO CANVASS THE AREA, AND AIDEN'S RUNNING PRINTS THROUGH AFIS EVEN AS WE SPEAK.
WE'LL GO THE DENTAL-RECORDS ROUTE, OF COURSE, BUT THAT DOES TAKE TIME. RIGHT NOW, WE KNOW MORE ABOUT HOW SHE DIED THAN HOW SHE LIVED... TAKE A LOOK AT HER ARM.
THESE ARE UNUSUAL MARKS, FOR THE BITES THEY APPEAR TO BE.
HOW SO?
THEY SEEM TO BE FROM A WILD ANIMAL, PROBABLY A WOLF... AS YOU SAY WAS SPECULATED AT THE SCENE.
THE KIND OF MANHATTAN-HABITAT WOLVES WHO USUALLY LEAVE BITE MARKS ON WOMEN AREN'T WHAT YOU SEEM TO BE TALKING ABOUT.

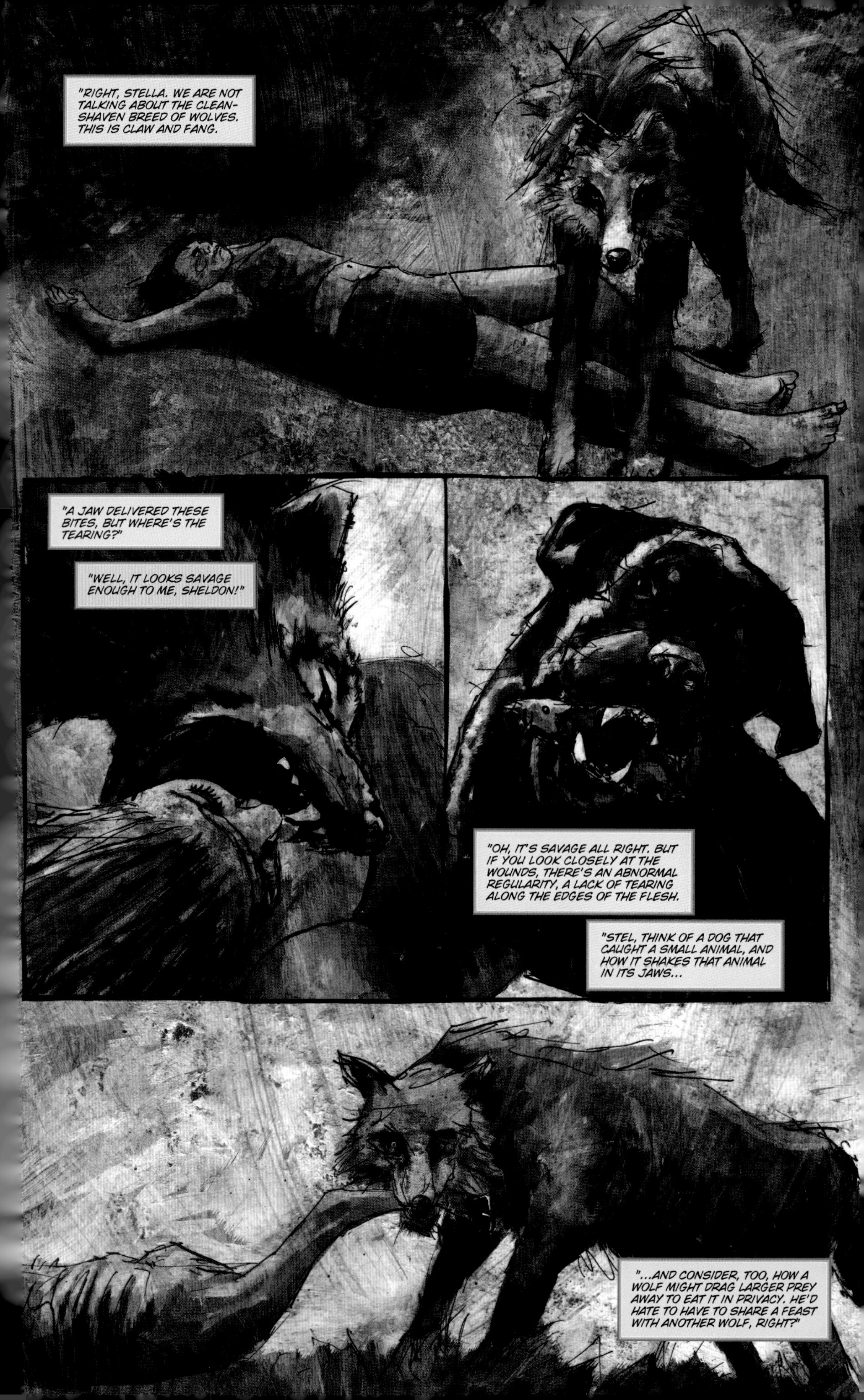
"RIGHT, STELLA. WE ARE NOT TALKING ABOUT THE CLEAN-SHAVEN BREED OF WOLVES. THIS IS CLAW AND FANG.
"A JAW DELIVERED THESE BITES, BUT WHERE'S THE TEARING?"
"WELL, IT LOOKS SAVAGE ENOUGH TO ME, SHELDON!"
"OH, IT'S SAVAGE ALL RIGHT. BUT IF YOU LOOK CLOSELY AT THE WOUNDS, THERE'S AN ABNORMAL REGULARITY, A LACK OF TEARING ALONG THE EDGES OF THE FLESH.
"STEL, THINK OF A DOG THAT CAUGHT A SMALL ANIMAL, AND HOW IT SHAKES THAT ANIMAL IN ITS JAWS...
"...AND CONSIDER, TOO, HOW A WOLF MIGHT DRAG LARGER PREY AWAY TO EAT IT IN PRIVACY. HE'D HATE TO HAVE TO SHARE A FEAST WITH ANOTHER WOLF, RIGHT?"

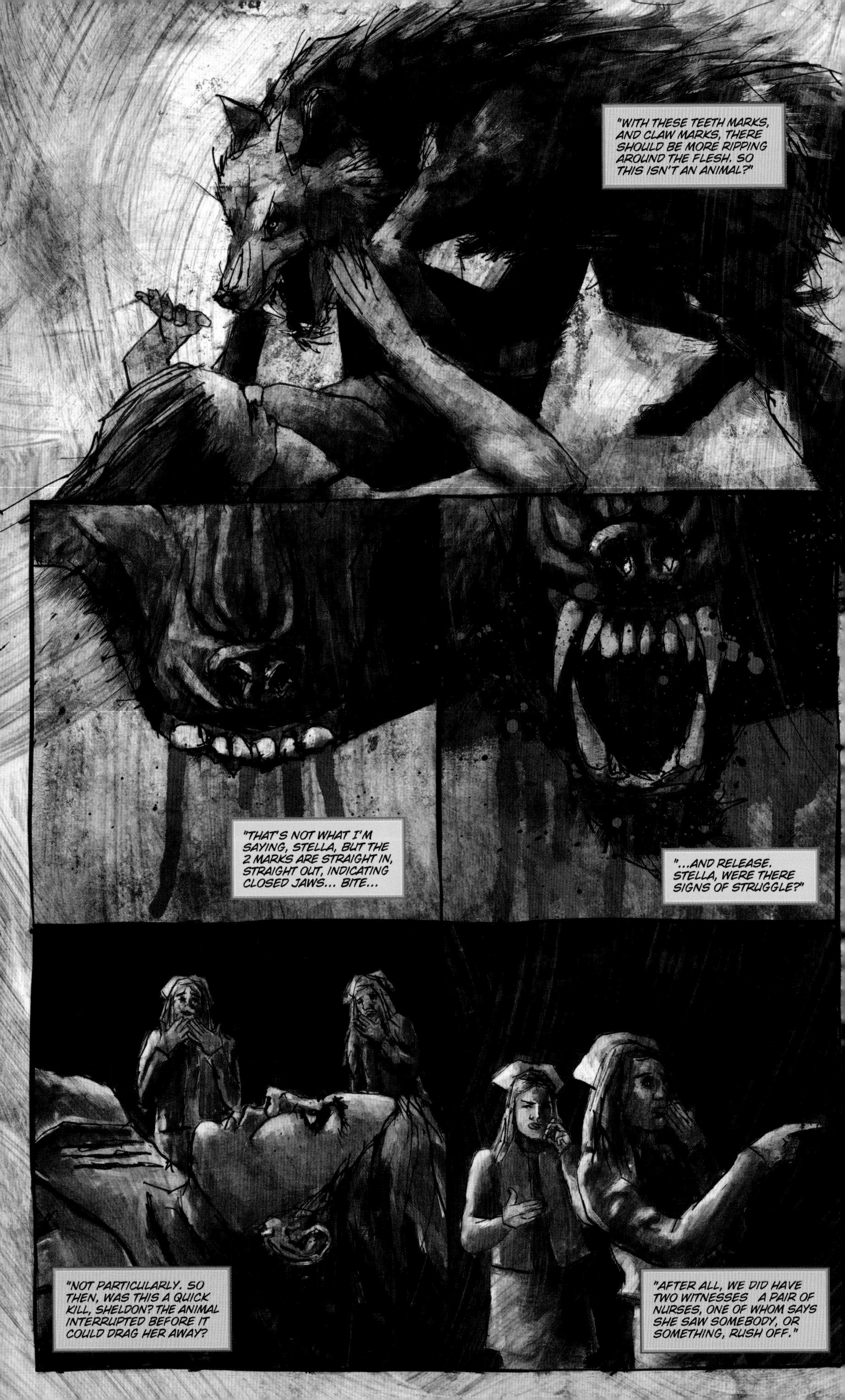
"WITH THESE TEETH MARKS, AND CLAW MARKS, THERE SHOULD BE MORE RIPPING AROUND THE FLESH. SO THIS ISN'T AN ANIMAL?"
"THAT'S NOT WHAT I'M SAYING, STELLA, BUT THE 2 MARKS ARE STRAIGHT IN, STRAIGHT OUT, INDICATING CLOSED JAWS... BITE...
"...AND RELEASE. STELLA, WERE THERE SIGNS OF STRUGGLE?"
"NOT PARTICULARLY. SO THEN, WAS THIS A QUICK KILL, SHELDON? THE ANIMAL INTERRUPTED BEFORE IT COULD DRAG HER AWAY?
"AFTER ALL, WE DID HAVE TWO WITNESSES A PAIR OF NURSES, ONE OF WHOM SAYS SHE SAW SOMEBODY, OR SOMETHING, RUSH OFF."

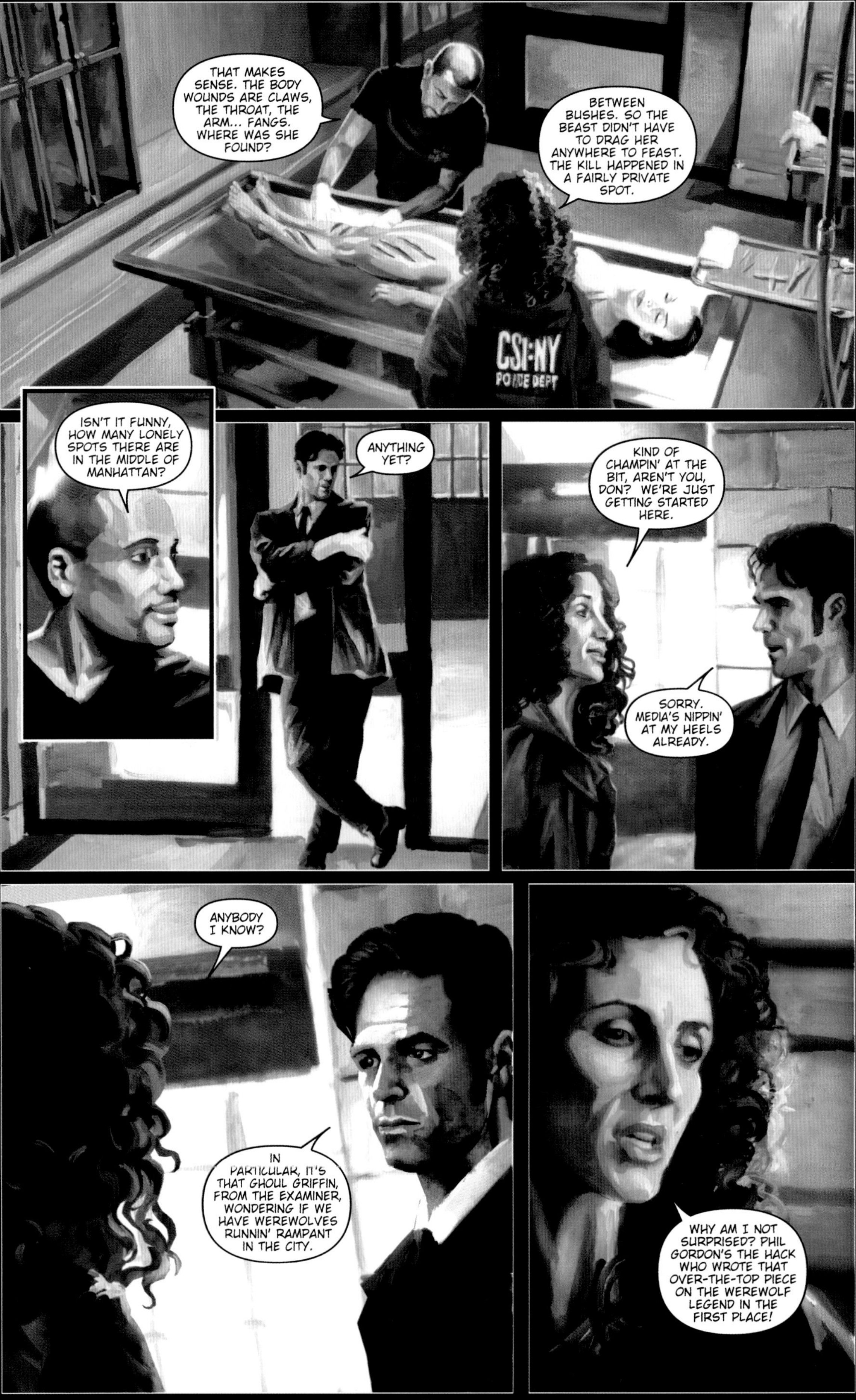
THAT MAKES SENSE. THE BODY WOUNDS ARE CLAWS, THE THROAT, THE ARM... FANGS. WHERE WAS SHE FOUND?
BETWEEN BUSHES. SO THE BEAST DIDN'T HAVE TO DRAG HER ANYWHERE TO FEAST. THE KILL HAPPENED IN A FAIRLY PRIVATE SPOT.
CSI:NY
ISN'T IT FUNNY, HOW MANY LONELY SPOTS THERE ARE IN THE MIDDLE OF MANHATTAN?
ANYTHING YET?
KIND OF CHAMPIN' AT THE BIT, AREN'T YOU, DON? WE'RE JUST GETTING STARTED HERE.
SORRY. MEDIA'S NIPPIN' AT MY HEELS ALREADY.
ANYBODY I KNOW?
IN PARTICULAR, IT'S THAT GHOUL GRIFFIN, FROM THE EXAMINER, WONDERING IF WE HAVE WEREWOLVES RUNNIN' RAMPANT IN THE CITY.
WHY AM I NOT SURPRISED? PHIL GORDON'S THE HACK WHO WROTE THAT OVER-THE-TOP PIECE ON THE WEREWOLF LEGEND IN THE FIRST PLACE!

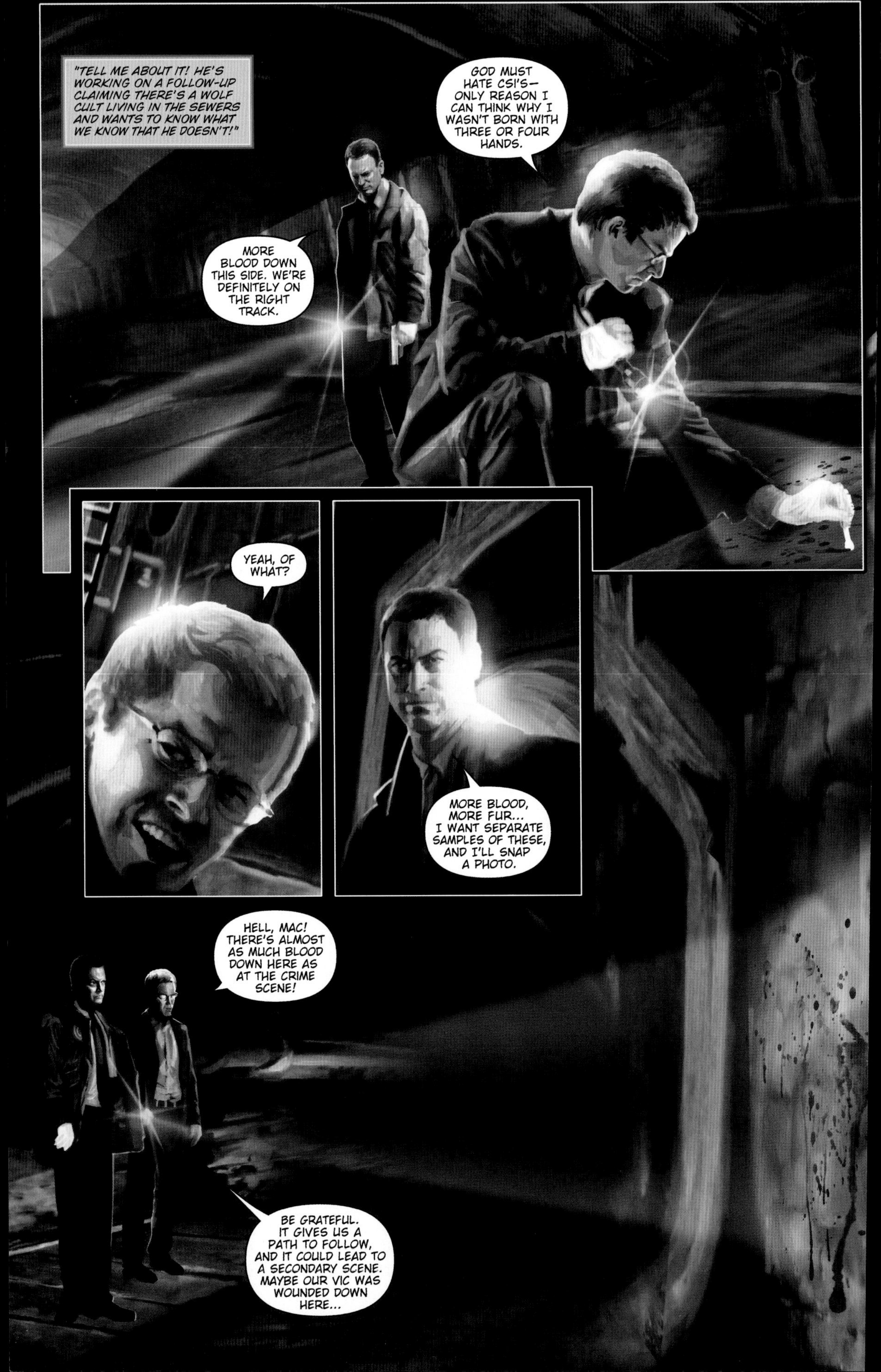
"TELL ME ABOUT IT! HE'S WORKING ON A FOLLOW-UP CLAIMING THERE'S A WOLF CULT LIVING IN THE SEWERS AND WANTS TO KNOW WHAT WE KNOW THAT HE DOESN'T!"
GOD MUST HATE CSI'S— ONLY REASON I CAN THINK WHY I WASN'T BORN WITH THREE OR FOUR HANDS.
MORE BLOOD DOWN THIS SIDE. WE'RE DEFINITELY ON THE RIGHT TRACK.
YEAH, OF WHAT?
MORE BLOOD, MORE FUR... I WANT SEPARATE SAMPLES OF THESE, AND I'LL SNAP A PHOTO.
HELL, MAC! THERE'S ALMOST AS MUCH BLOOD DOWN HERE AS AT THE CRIME SCENE!
BE GRATEFUL. IT GIVES US A PATH TO FOLLOW, AND IT COULD LEAD TO A SECONDARY SCENE. MAYBE OUR VIC WAS WOUNDED DOWN HERE...

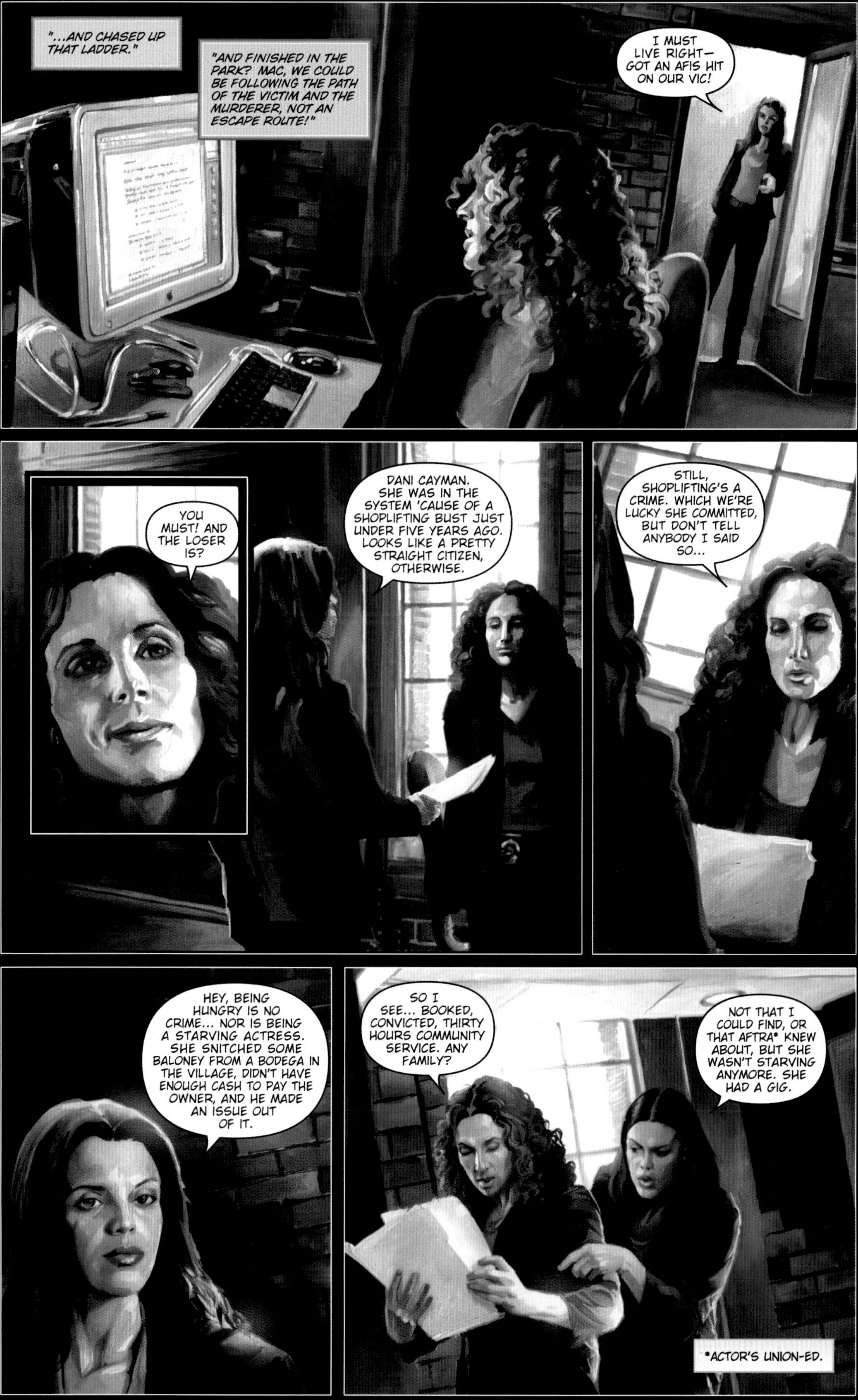
"...AND CHASED UP THAT LADDER."
"AND FINISHED IN THE PARK? MAC, WE COULD BE FOLLOWING THE PATH OF THE VICTIM AND THE MURDERER, NOT AN ESCAPE ROUTE!"
I MUST LIVE RIGHT— GOT AN AFIS HIT ON OUR VIC!
YOU MUST! AND THE LOSER IS?
DANI CAYMAN. SHE WAS IN THE SYSTEM 'CAUSE OF A SHOPLIFTING BUST JUST UNDER FIVE YEARS AGO. LOOKS LIKE A PRETTY STRAIGHT CITIZEN, OTHERWISE.
STILL, SHOPLIFTING'S A CRIME. WHICH WE'RE LUCKY SHE COMMITTED, BUT DON'T TELL ANYBODY I SAID SO...
HEY, BEING HUNGRY IS NO CRIME... NOR IS BEING A STARVING ACTRESS. SHE SNITCHED SOME BALONEY FROM A BODEGA IN THE VILLAGE, DIDN'T HAVE ENOUGH CASH TO PAY THE OWNER, AND HE MADE AN ISSUE OUT OF IT.
SO I SEE... BOOKED, CONVICTED, THIRTY HOURS COMMUNITY SERVICE. ANY FAMILY?
NOT THAT I COULD FIND, OR THAT AFTRA* KNEW ABOUT, BUT SHE WASN'T STARVING ANYMORE. SHE HAD A GIG.
*ACTOR'S UNION-ED.

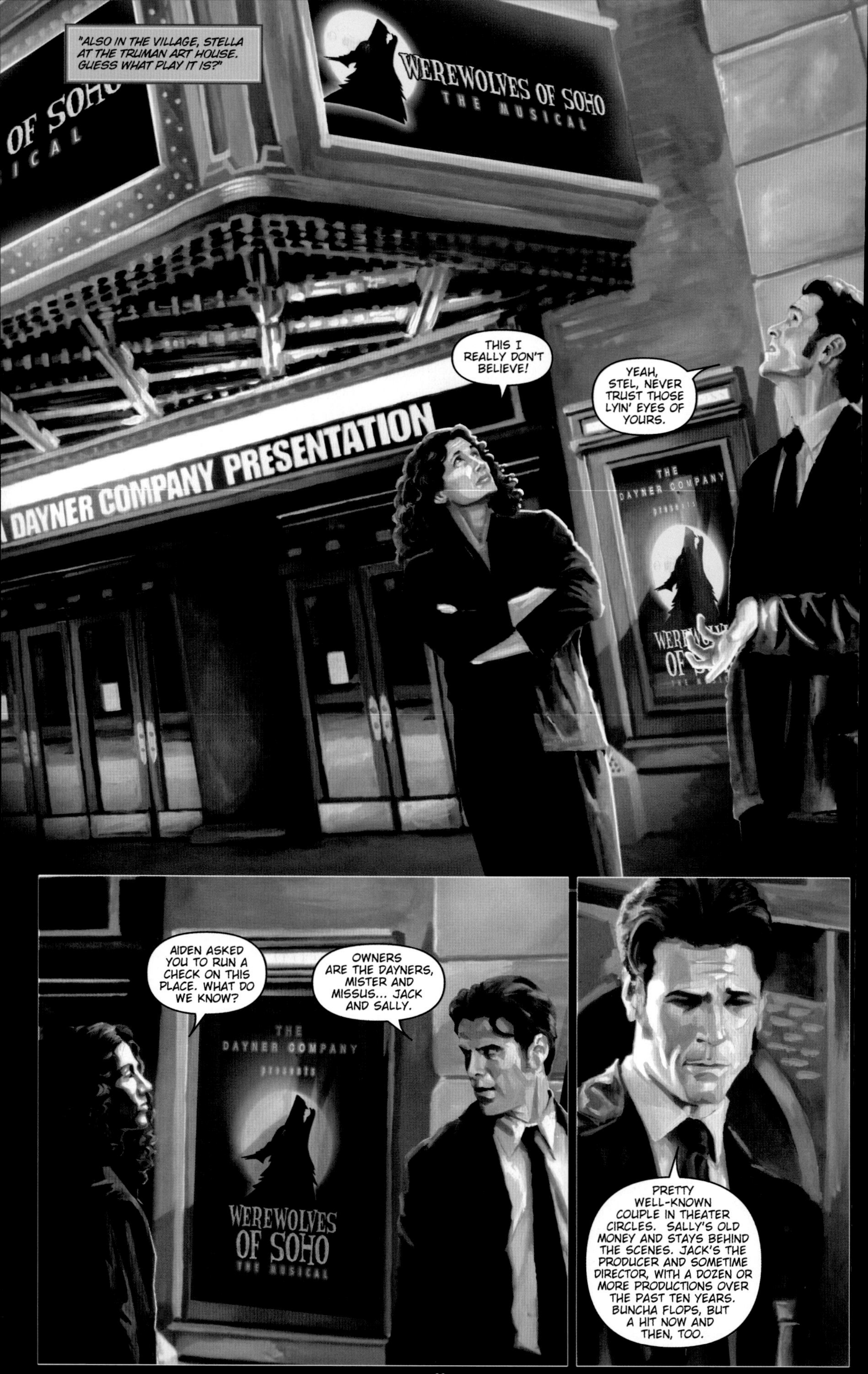
"ALSO IN THE VILLAGE, STELLA AT THE TRUMAN ART HOUSE. GUESS WHAT PLAY IT IS?"
WEREWOLVES OF SOHO
THE MUSICAL
DAYNER COMPANY PRESENTATION
THIS I REALLY DON'T BELIEVE!
YEAH, STEL, NEVER TRUST THOSE LYIN' EYES OF YOURS.
THE DAYNER COMPANY
AIDEN ASKED YOU TO RUN A CHECK ON THIS PLACE. WHAT DO WE KNOW?
OWNERS ARE THE DAYNERS, MISTER AND MISSUS... JACK AND SALLY.
THE DAYNER COMPANY
presents
WEREWOLVES OF SOHO
THE MUSICAL
PRETTY WELL-KNOWN COUPLE IN THEATER CIRCLES. SALLY'S OLD MONEY AND STAYS BEHIND THE SCENES. JACK'S THE PRODUCER AND SOMETIME DIRECTOR, WITH A DOZEN OR MORE PRODUCTIONS OVER THE PAST TEN YEARS. BUNCHA FLOPS, BUT A HIT NOW AND THEN, TOO.

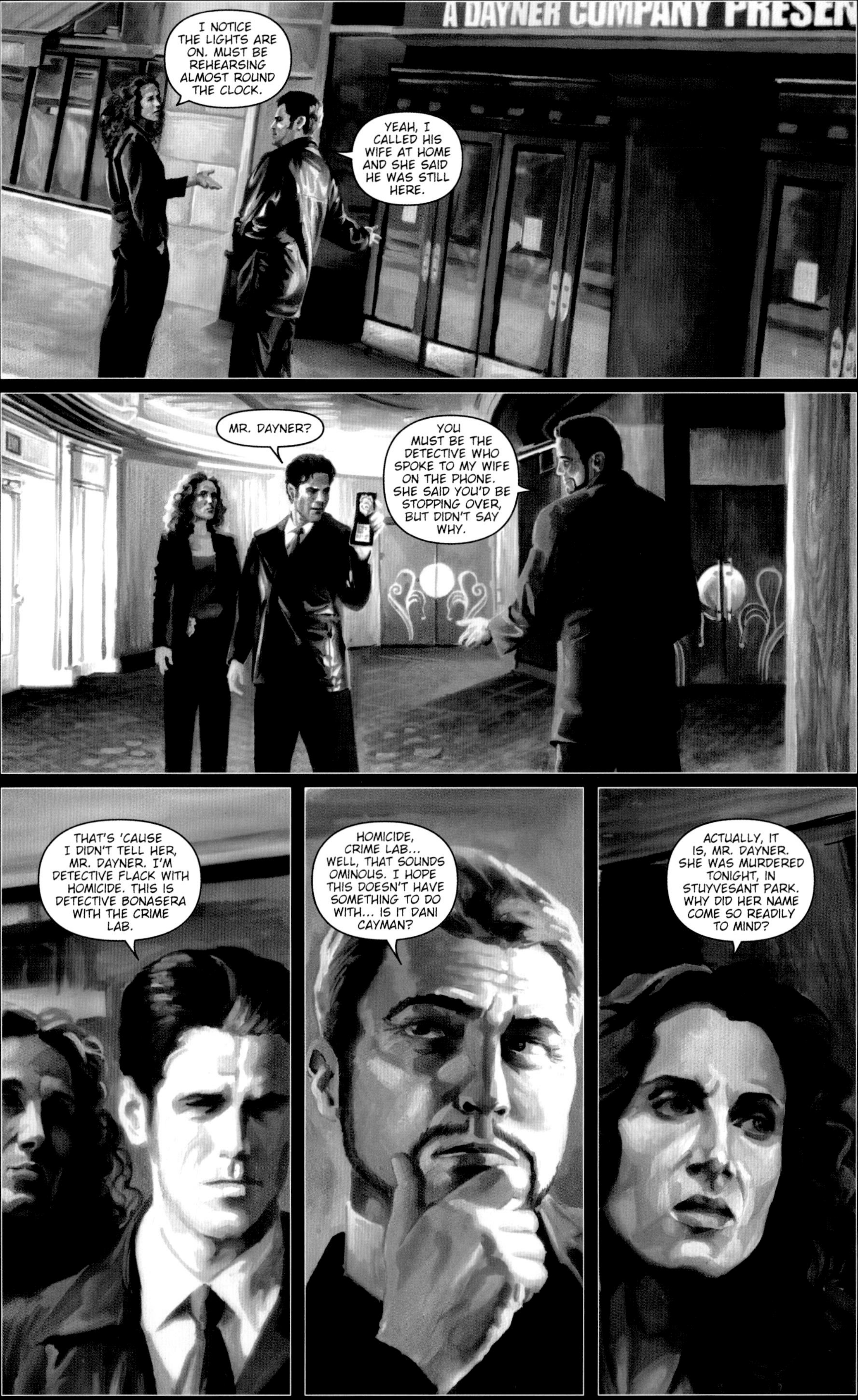
A DAYNER COMPANY PRESEN
I NOTICE THE LIGHTS ARE ON. MUST BE REHEARSING ALMOST ROUND THE CLOCK.
YEAH, I CALLED HIS WIFE AT HOME AND SHE SAID HE WAS STILL HERE.
MR. DAYNER?
YOU MUST BE THE DETECTIVE WHO SPOKE TO MY WIFE ON THE PHONE. SHE SAID YOU'D BE STOPPING OVER, BUT DIDN'T SAY WHY.
THAT'S 'CAUSE I DIDN'T TELL HER, MR. DAYNER. I'M DETECTIVE FLACK WITH HOMICIDE. THIS IS DETECTIVE BONASERA WITH THE CRIME LAB.
HOMICIDE, CRIME LAB... WELL, THAT SOUNDS OMINOUS. I HOPE THIS DOESN'T HAVE SOMETHING TO DO WITH... IS IT DANI CAYMAN?
ACTUALLY, IT IS, MR. DAYNER. SHE WAS MURDERED TONIGHT, IN STUYVESANT PARK. WHY DID HER NAME COME SO READILY TO MIND?

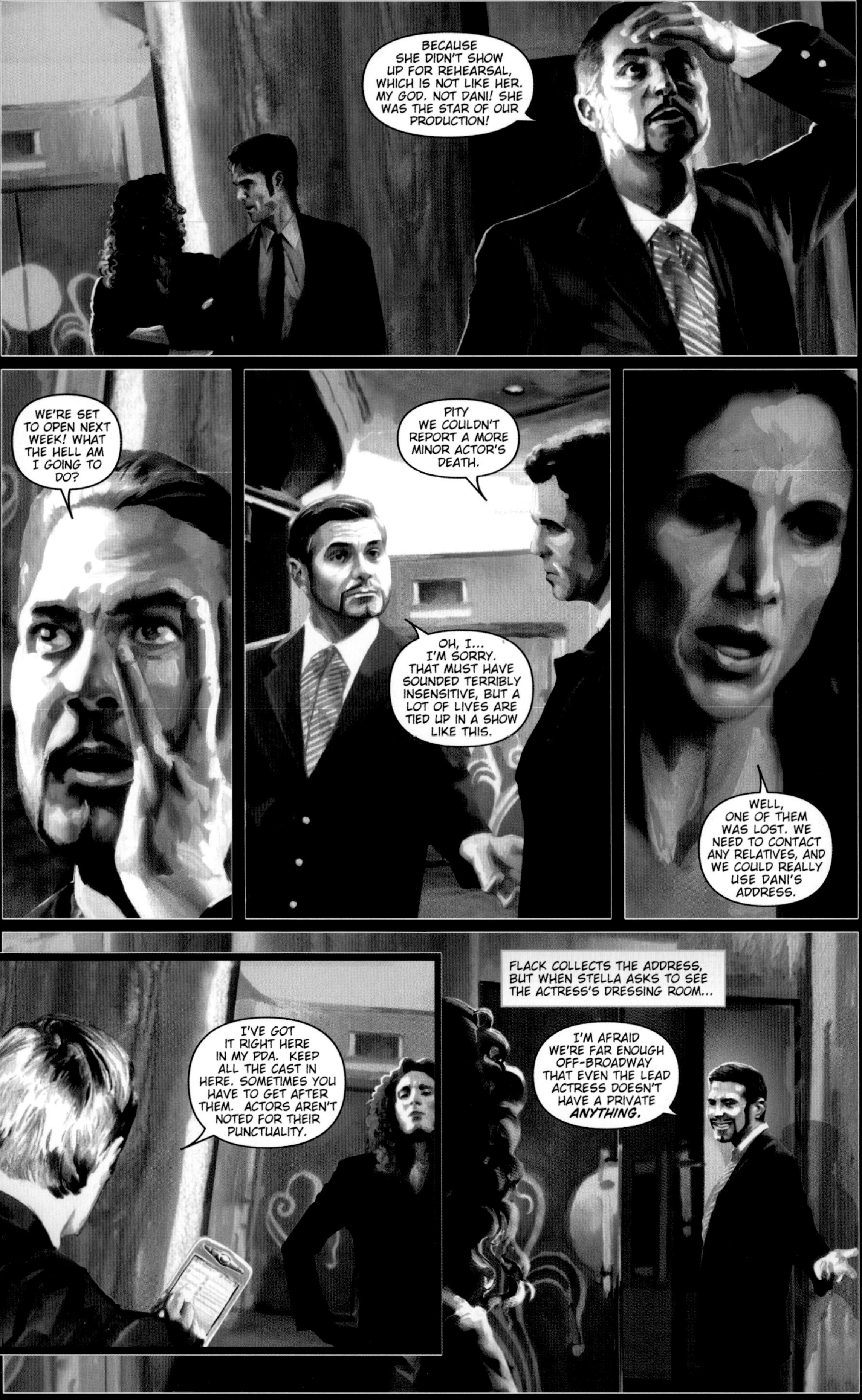
BECAUSE SHE DIDN'T SHOW UP FOR REHEARSAL, WHICH IS NOT LIKE HER. MY GOD. NOT DANI! SHE WAS THE STAR OF OUR PRODUCTION!
WE'RE SET TO OPEN NEXT WEEK! WHAT THE HELL AM I GOING TO DO?
PITY WE COULDN'T REPORT A MORE MINOR ACTOR'S DEATH.
OH, I... I'M SORRY. THAT MUST HAVE SOUNDED TERRIBLY INSENSITIVE, BUT A LOT OF LIVES ARE TIED UP IN A SHOW LIKE THIS.
WELL, ONE OF THEM WAS LOST. WE NEED TO CONTACT ANY RELATIVES, AND WE COULD REALLY USE DANI'S ADDRESS.
I'VE GOT IT RIGHT HERE IN MY PDA. KEEP ALL THE CAST IN HERE. SOMETIMES YOU HAVE TO GET AFTER THEM. ACTORS AREN'T NOTED FOR THEIR PUNCTUALITY.
FLACK COLLECTS THE ADDRESS, BUT WHEN STELLA ASKS TO SEE THE ACTRESS'S DRESSING ROOM...
I'M AFRAID WE'RE FAR ENOUGH OFF-BROADWAY THAT EVEN THE LEAD ACTRESS DOESN'T HAVE A PRIVATE ***ANYTHING.***

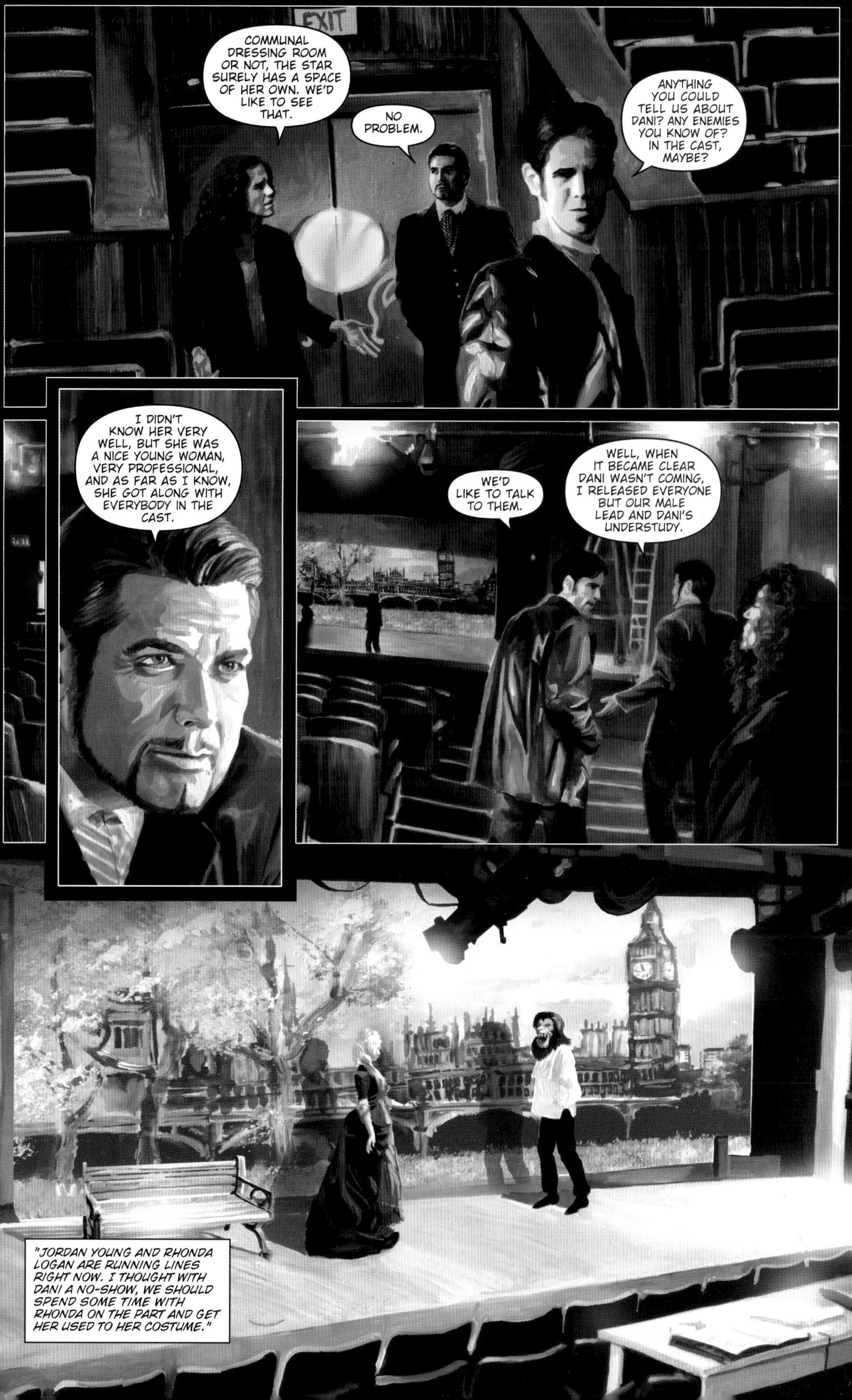

EXIT
COMMUNAL DRESSING ROOM OR NOT, THE STAR SURELY HAS A SPACE OF HER OWN. WE'D LIKE TO SEE THAT.
NO PROBLEM.
ANYTHING YOU COULD TELL US ABOUT DANI? ANY ENEMIES YOU KNOW OF? IN THE CAST, MAYBE?
I DIDN'T KNOW HER VERY WELL, BUT SHE WAS A NICE YOUNG WOMAN, VERY PROFESSIONAL, AND AS FAR AS I KNOW, SHE GOT ALONG WITH EVERYBODY IN THE CAST.
WELL, WHEN IT BECAME CLEAR DANI WASN'T COMING, I RELEASED EVERYONE BUT OUR MALE LEAD AND DANI'S UNDERSTUDY.
WE'D LIKE TO TALK TO THEM.
"JORDAN YOUNG AND RHONDA LOGAN ARE RUNNING LINES RIGHT NOW. I THOUGHT WITH DANI A NO-SHOW, WE SHOULD SPEND SOME TIME WITH RHONDA ON THE PART AND GET HER USED TO HER COSTUME."

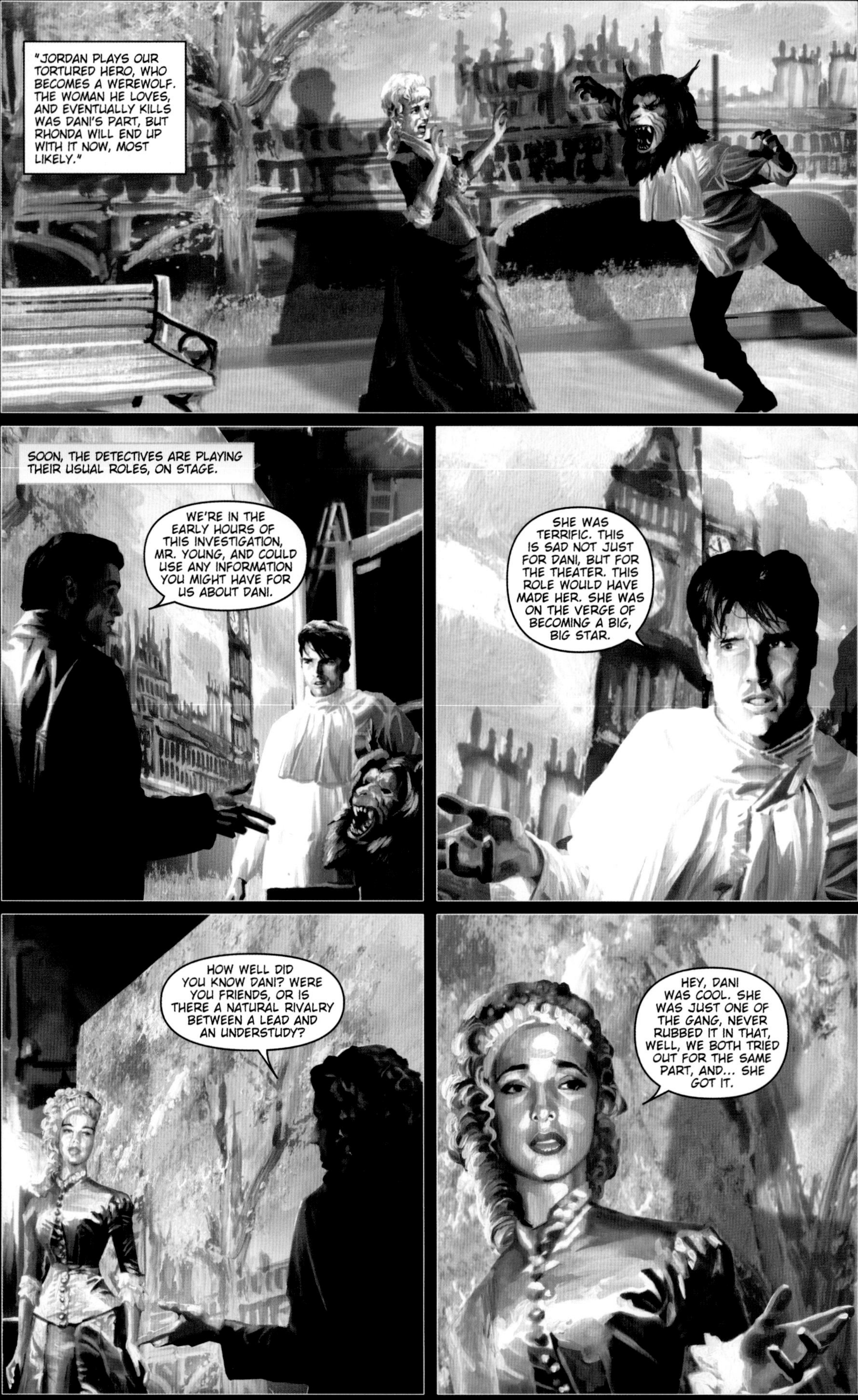
"JORDAN PLAYS OUR TORTURED HERO, WHO BECOMES A WEREWOLF. THE WOMAN HE LOVES, AND EVENTUALLY KILLS WAS DANI'S PART, BUT RHONDA WILL END UP WITH IT NOW, MOST LIKELY."
SOON, THE DETECTIVES ARE PLAYING THEIR USUAL ROLES, ON STAGE.
WE'RE IN THE EARLY HOURS OF THIS INVESTIGATION, MR. YOUNG, AND COULD USE ANY INFORMATION YOU MIGHT HAVE FOR US ABOUT DANI.
SHE WAS TERRIFIC. THIS IS SAD NOT JUST FOR DANI, BUT FOR THE THEATER. THIS ROLE WOULD HAVE MADE HER. SHE WAS ON THE VERGE OF BECOMING A BIG, BIG STAR.
HOW WELL DID YOU KNOW DANI? WERE YOU FRIENDS, OR IS THERE A NATURAL RIVALRY BETWEEN A LEAD AND AN UNDERSTUDY?
HEY, DANI WAS COOL. SHE WAS JUST ONE OF THE GANG, NEVER RUBBED IT IN THAT, WELL, WE BOTH TRIED OUT FOR THE SAME PART, AND... SHE GOT IT.

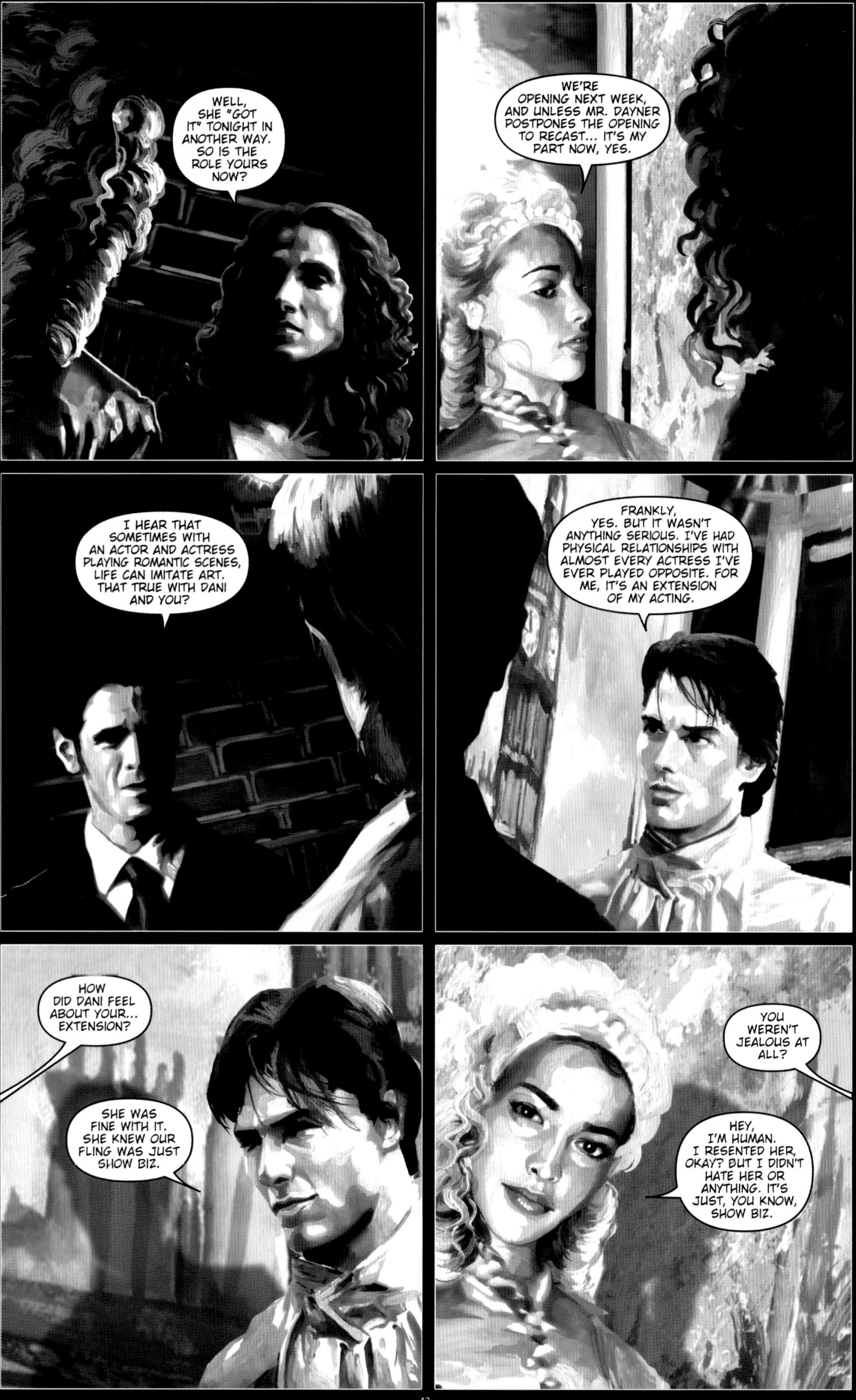
WELL, SHE "GOT IT" TONIGHT IN ANOTHER WAY. SO IS THE ROLE YOURS NOW?
WE'RE OPENING NEXT WEEK, AND UNLESS MR. DAYNER POSTPONES THE OPENING TO RECAST... IT'S MY PART NOW, YES.
I HEAR THAT SOMETIMES WITH AN ACTOR AND ACTRESS PLAYING ROMANTIC SCENES, LIFE CAN IMITATE ART. THAT TRUE WITH DANI AND YOU?
FRANKLY, YES. BUT IT WASN'T ANYTHING SERIOUS. I'VE HAD PHYSICAL RELATIONSHIPS WITH ALMOST EVERY ACTRESS I'VE EVER PLAYED OPPOSITE. FOR ME, IT'S AN EXTENSION OF MY ACTING.
HOW DID DANI FEEL ABOUT YOUR... EXTENSION?
SHE WAS FINE WITH IT. SHE KNEW OUR FLING WAS JUST SHOW BIZ.
YOU WEREN'T JEALOUS AT ALL?
HEY, I'M HUMAN. I RESENTED HER, OKAY? BUT I DIDN'T HATE HER OR ANYTHING. IT'S JUST, YOU KNOW, SHOW BIZ.

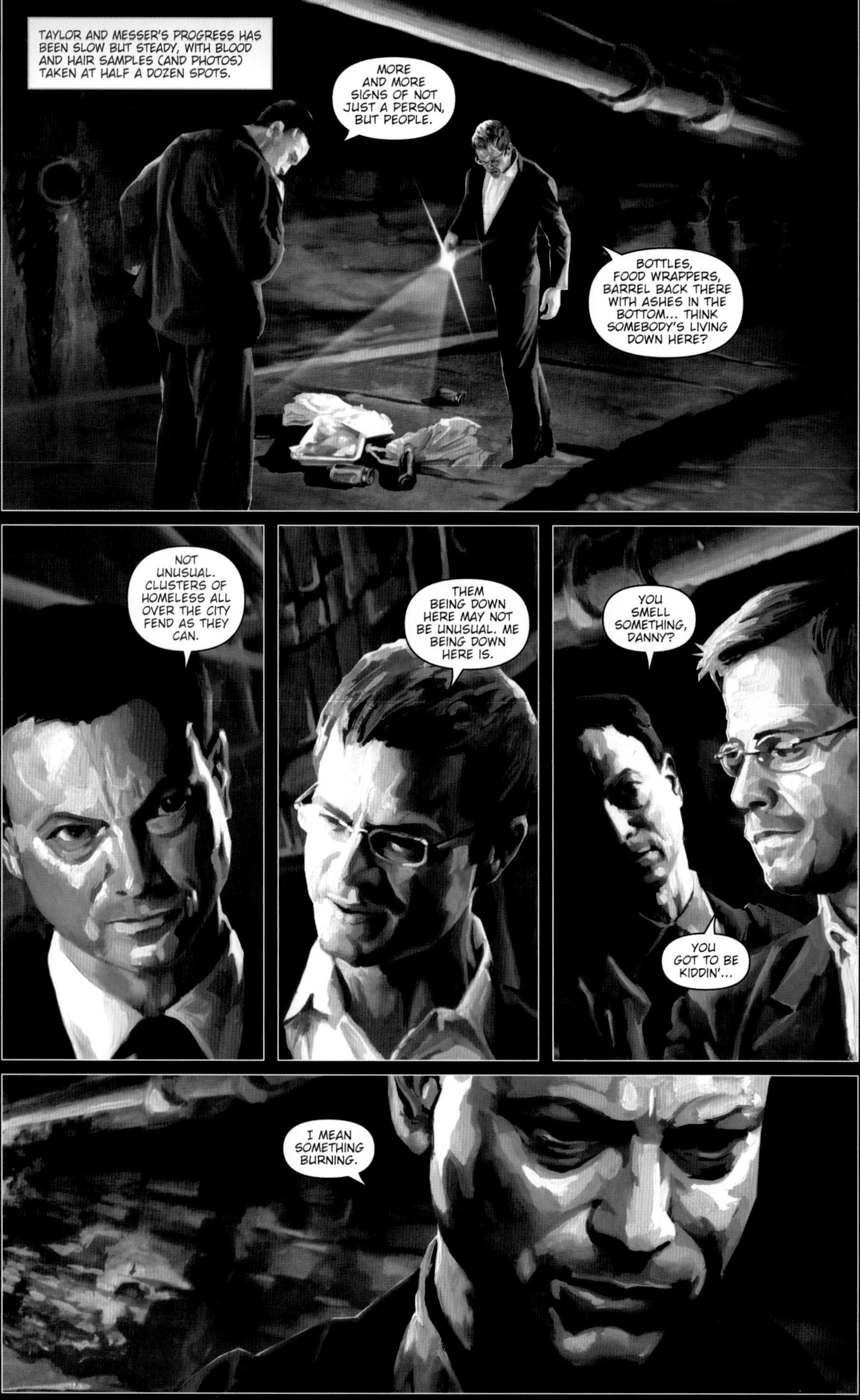
TAYLOR AND MESSER'S PROGRESS HAS BEEN SLOW BUT STEADY, WITH BLOOD AND HAIR SAMPLES (AND PHOTOS) TAKEN AT HALF A DOZEN SPOTS.
MORE AND MORE SIGNS OF NOT JUST A PERSON, BUT PEOPLE.
BOTTLES, FOOD WRAPPERS, BARREL BACK THERE WITH ASHES IN THE BOTTOM... THINK SOMEBODY'S LIVING DOWN HERE?
NOT UNUSUAL. CLUSTERS OF HOMELESS ALL OVER THE CITY FEND AS THEY CAN.
THEM BEING DOWN HERE MAY NOT BE UNUSUAL. ME BEING DOWN HERE IS.
YOU SMELL SOMETHING, DANNY?
YOU GOT TO BE KIDDIN'...
I MEAN SOMETHING BURNING.

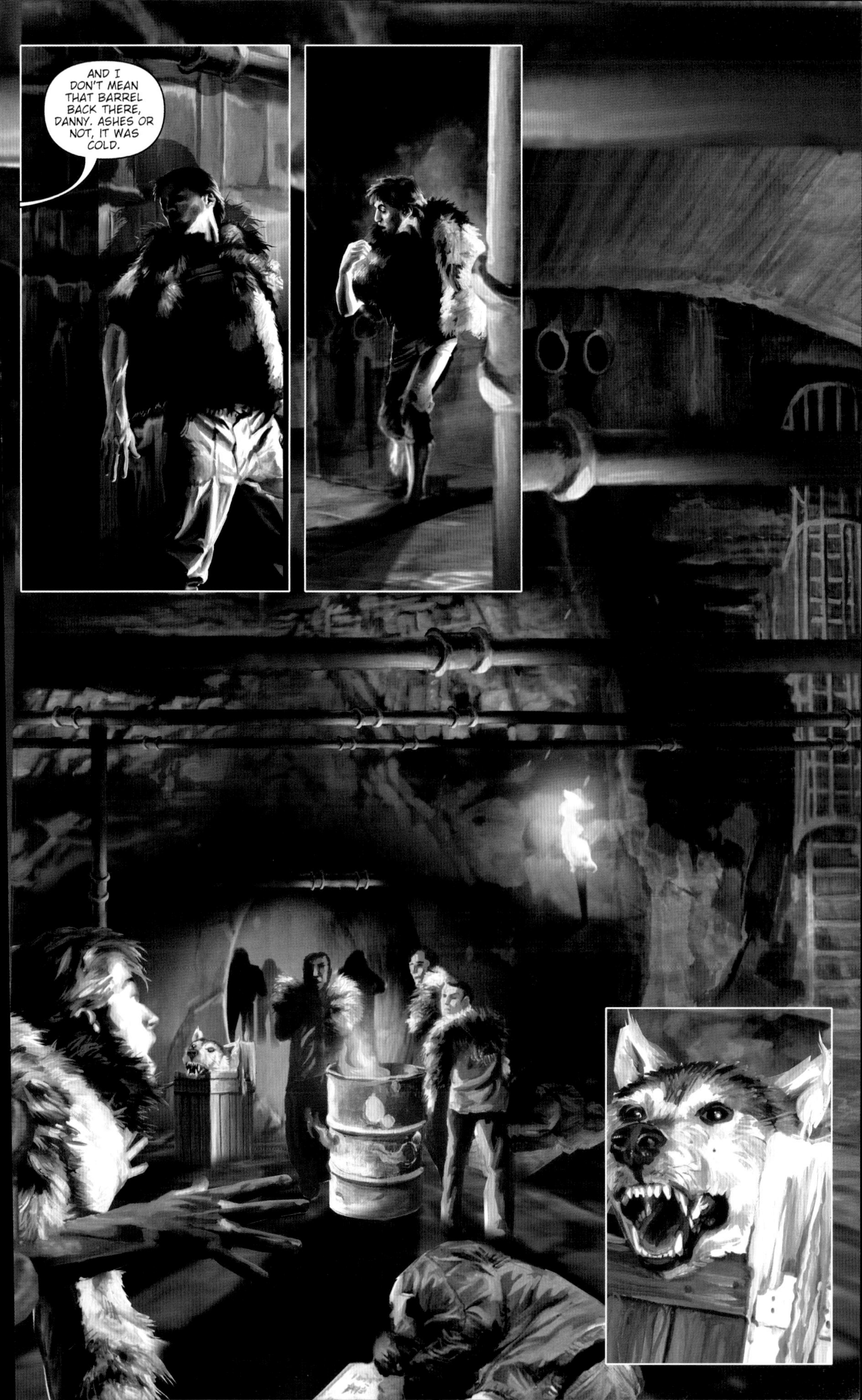
AND I DON'T MEAN THAT BARREL BACK THERE, DANNY. ASHES OR NOT, IT WAS COLD.

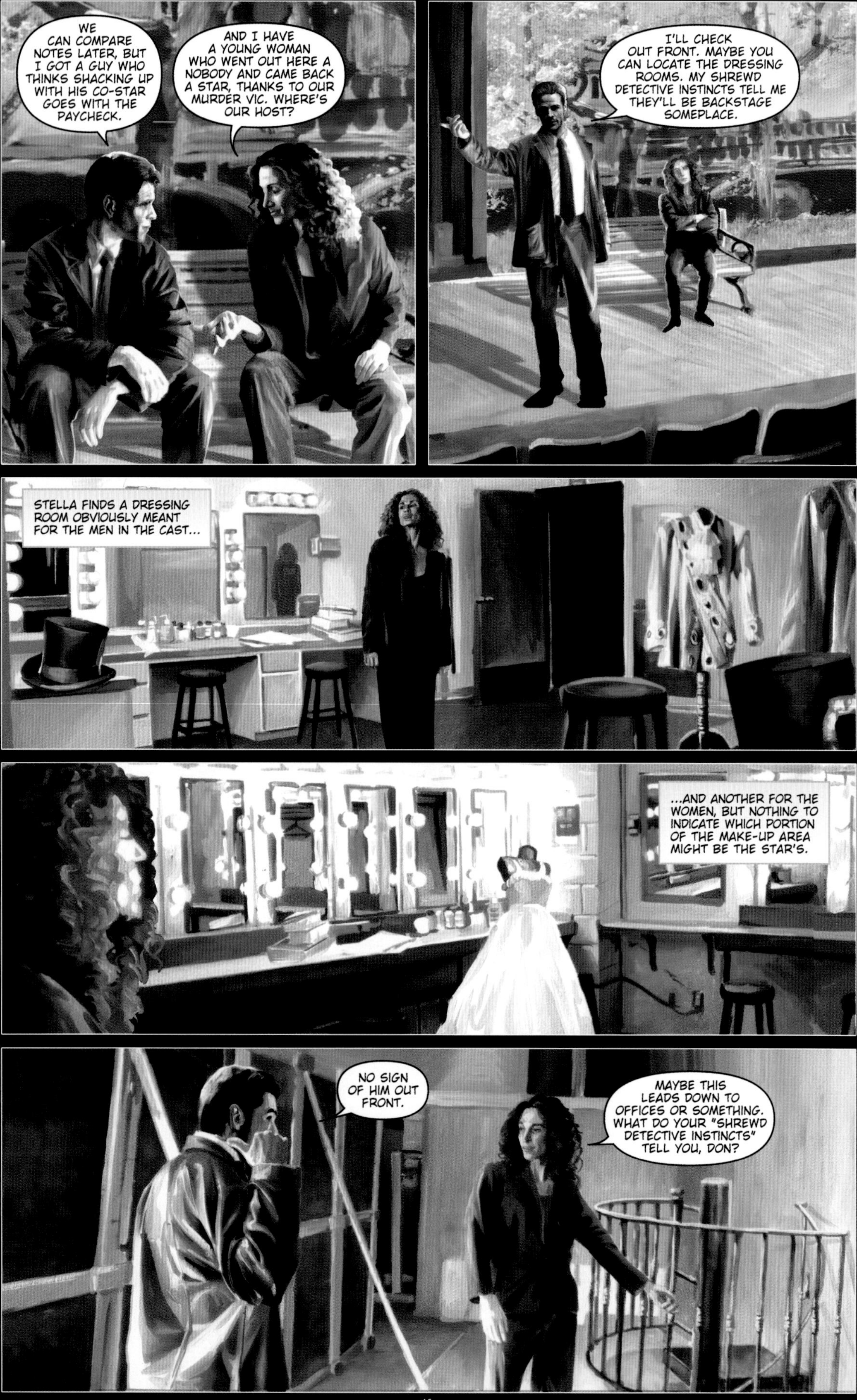
WE CAN COMPARE NOTES LATER, BUT I GOT A GUY WHO THINKS SHACKING UP WITH HIS CO-STAR GOES WITH THE PAYCHECK.
AND I HAVE A YOUNG WOMAN WHO WENT OUT HERE A NOBODY AND CAME BACK A STAR, THANKS TO OUR MURDER VIC. WHERE'S OUR HOST?
I'LL CHECK OUT FRONT. MAYBE YOU CAN LOCATE THE DRESSING ROOMS. MY SHREWD DETECTIVE INSTINCTS TELL ME THEY'LL BE BACKSTAGE SOMEPLACE.
STELLA FINDS A DRESSING ROOM OBVIOUSLY MEANT FOR THE MEN IN THE CAST...
...AND ANOTHER FOR THE WOMEN, BUT NOTHING TO INDICATE WHICH PORTION OF THE MAKE-UP AREA MIGHT BE THE STAR'S.
NO SIGN OF HIM OUT FRONT.
MAYBE THIS LEADS DOWN TO OFFICES OR SOMETHING. WHAT DO YOUR "SHREWD DETECTIVE INSTINCTS" TELL YOU, DON?

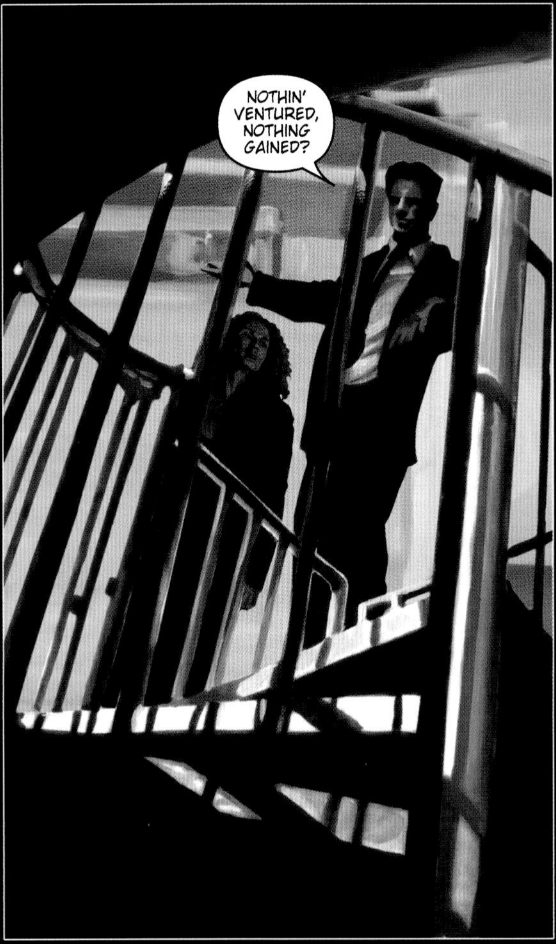
NOTHIN' VENTURED, NOTHING GAINED?

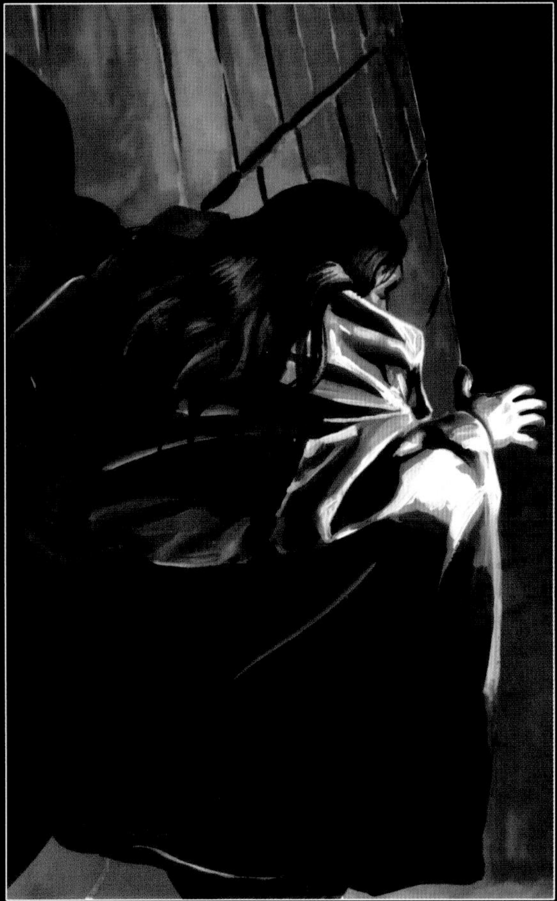

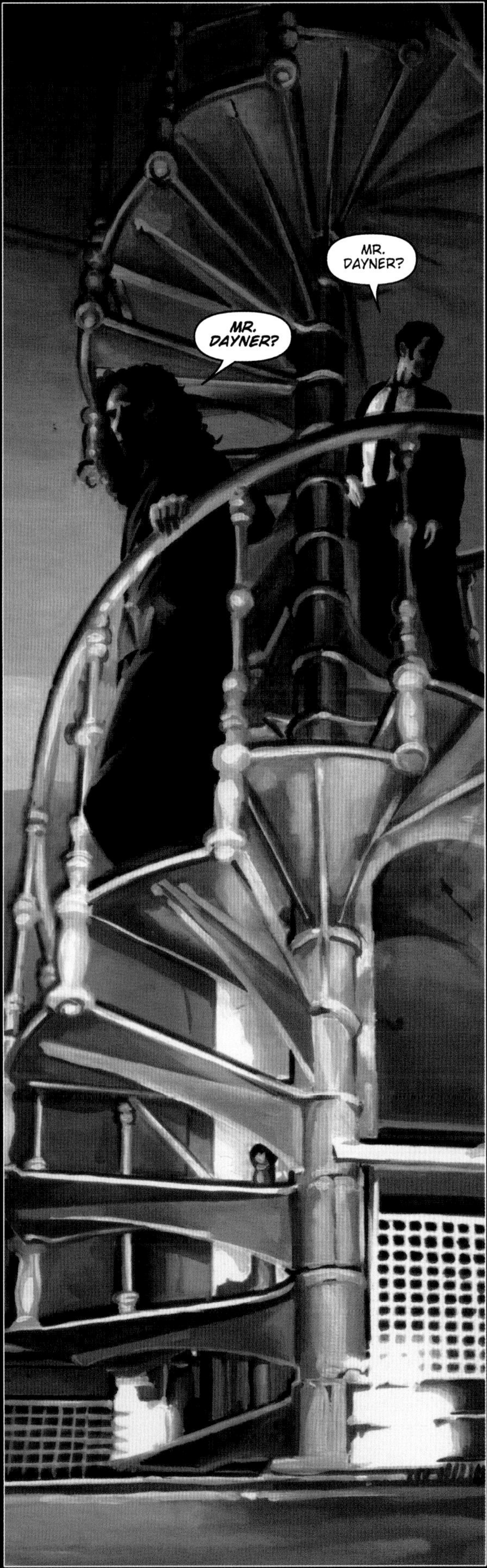
MR. DAYNER?
MR. DAYNER?

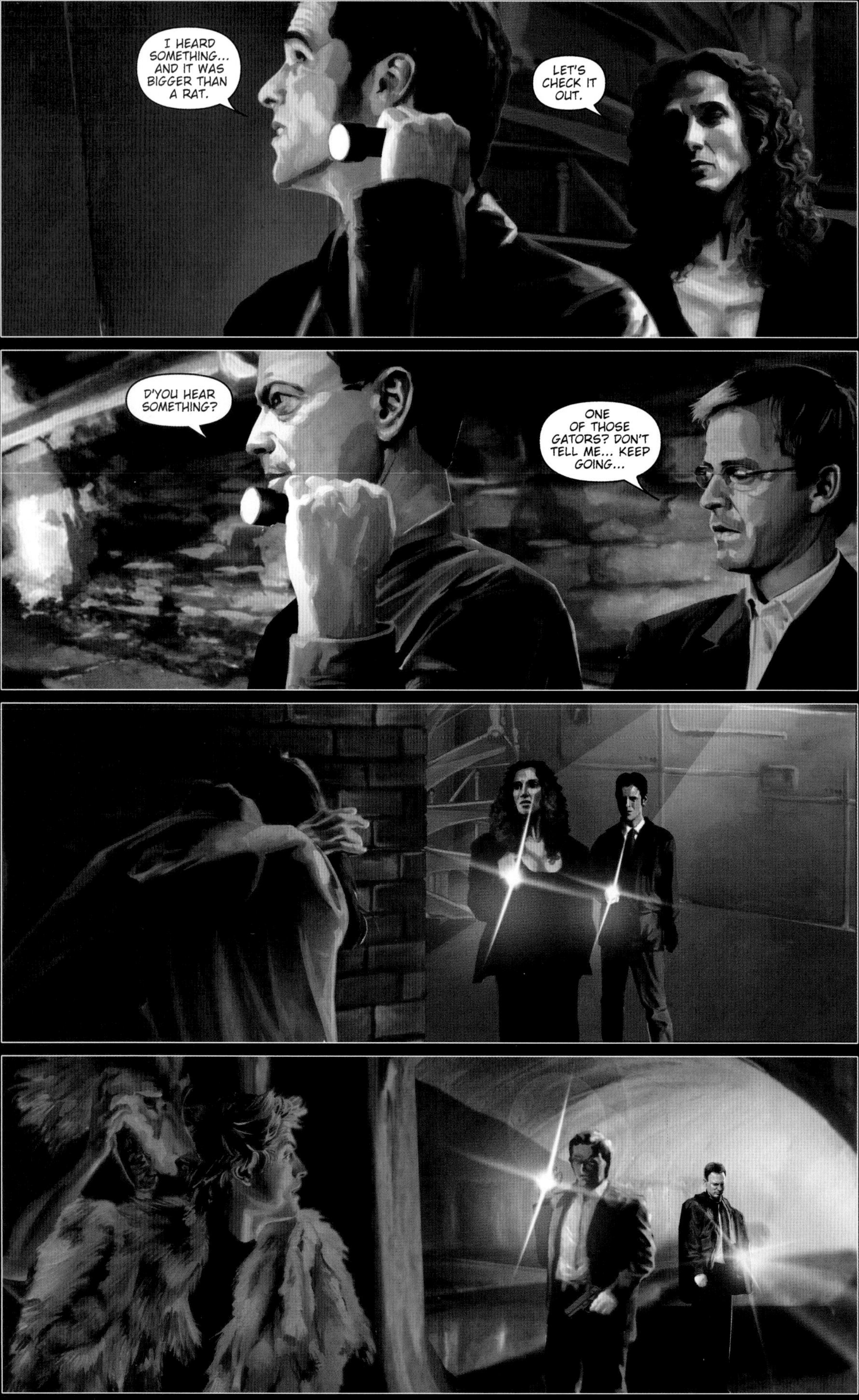
I HEARD SOMETHING... AND IT WAS BIGGER THAN A RAT.
LET'S CHECK IT OUT.
D'YOU HEAR SOMETHING?
ONE OF THOSE GATORS? DON'T TELL ME... KEEP GOING...

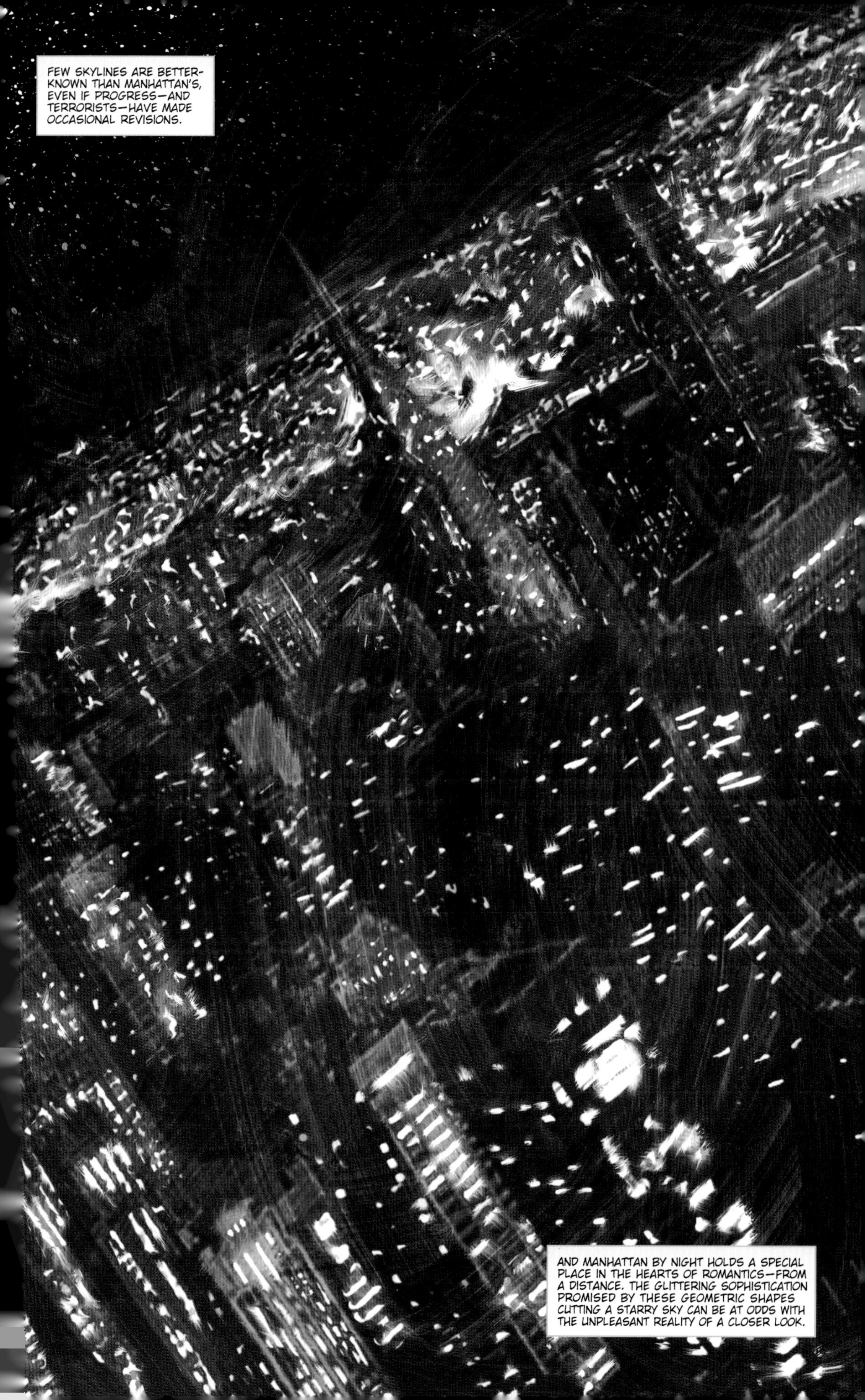
FEW SKYLINES ARE BETTER-KNOWN THAN MANHATTAN'S, EVEN IF PROGRESS—AND TERRORISTS—HAVE MADE OCCASIONAL REVISIONS.
AND MANHATTAN BY NIGHT HOLDS A SPECIAL PLACE IN THE HEARTS OF ROMANTICS—FROM A DISTANCE. THE GLITTERING SOPHISTICATION PROMISED BY THESE GEOMETRIC SHAPES CUTTING A STARRY SKY CAN BE AT ODDS WITH THE UNPLEASANT REALITY OF A CLOSER LOOK.

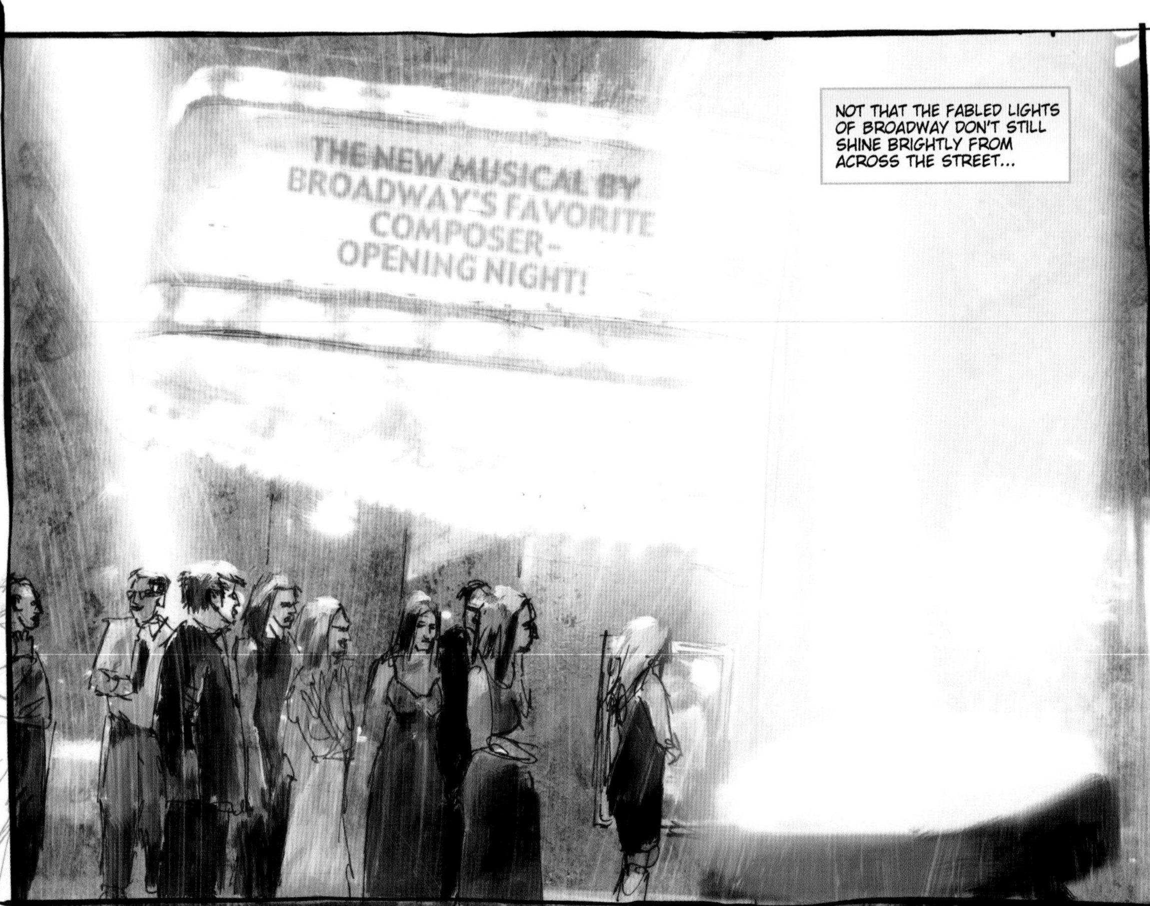
THE NEW MUSICAL BY
BROADWAY'S FAVORITE
COMPOSER–
OPENING NIGHT!
NOT THAT THE FABLED LIGHTS OF BROADWAY DON'T STILL SHINE BRIGHTLY FROM ACROSS THE STREET...

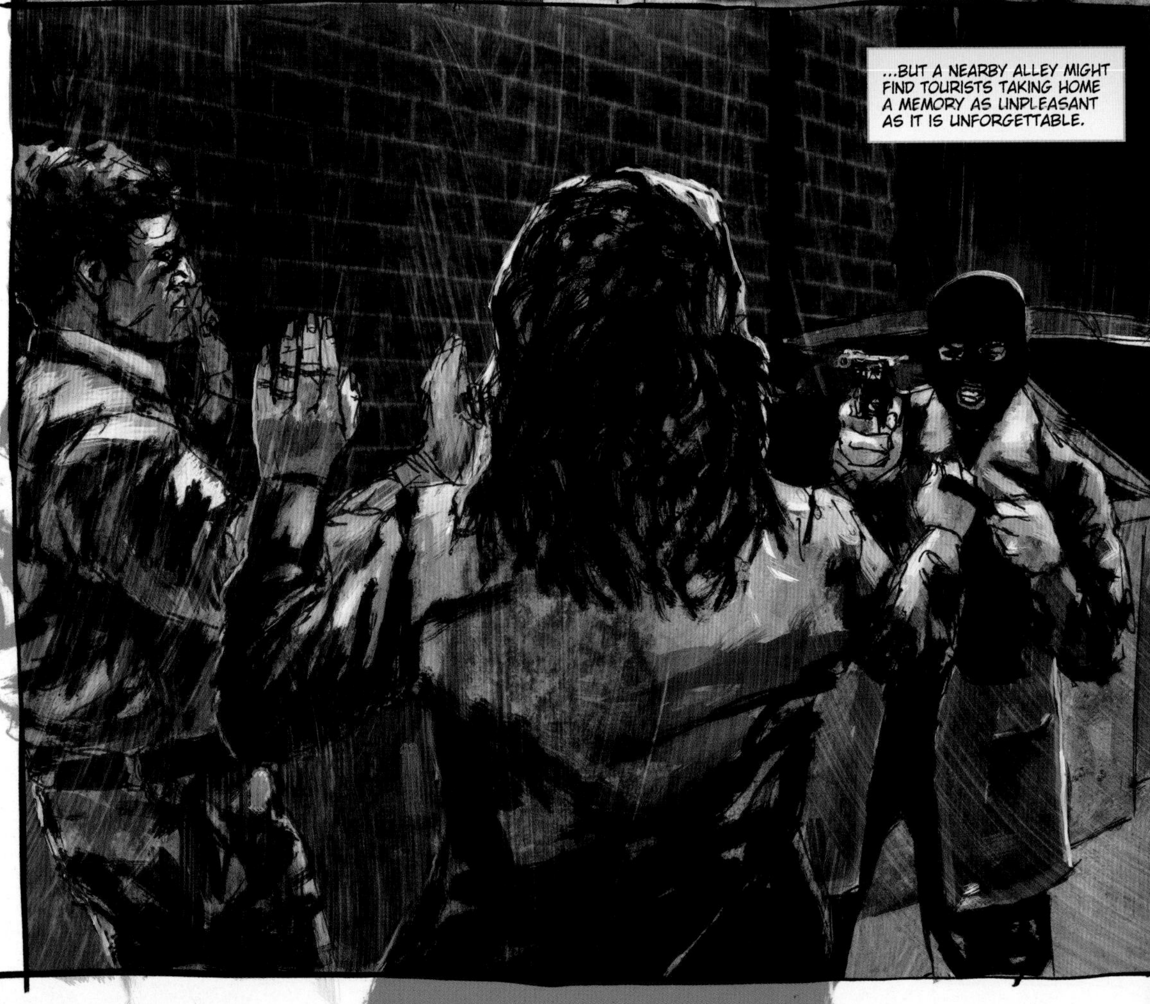
...BUT A NEARBY ALLEY MIGHT FIND TOURISTS TAKING HOME A MEMORY AS UNPLEASANT AS IT IS UNFORGETTABLE.

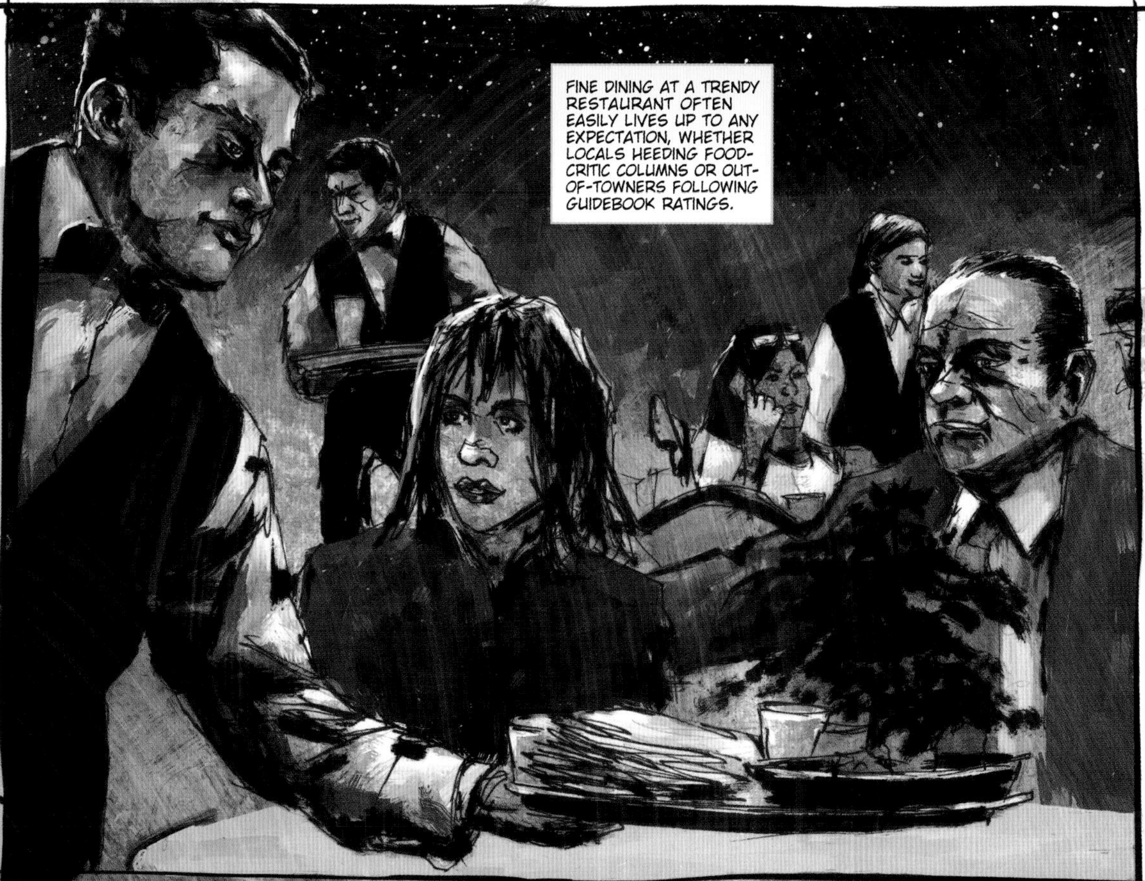
FINE DINING AT A TRENDY RESTAURANT OFTEN EASILY LIVES UP TO ANY EXPECTATION, WHETHER LOCALS HEEDING FOOD-CRITIC COLUMNS OR OUT-OF-TOWNERS FOLLOWING GUIDEBOOK RATINGS.

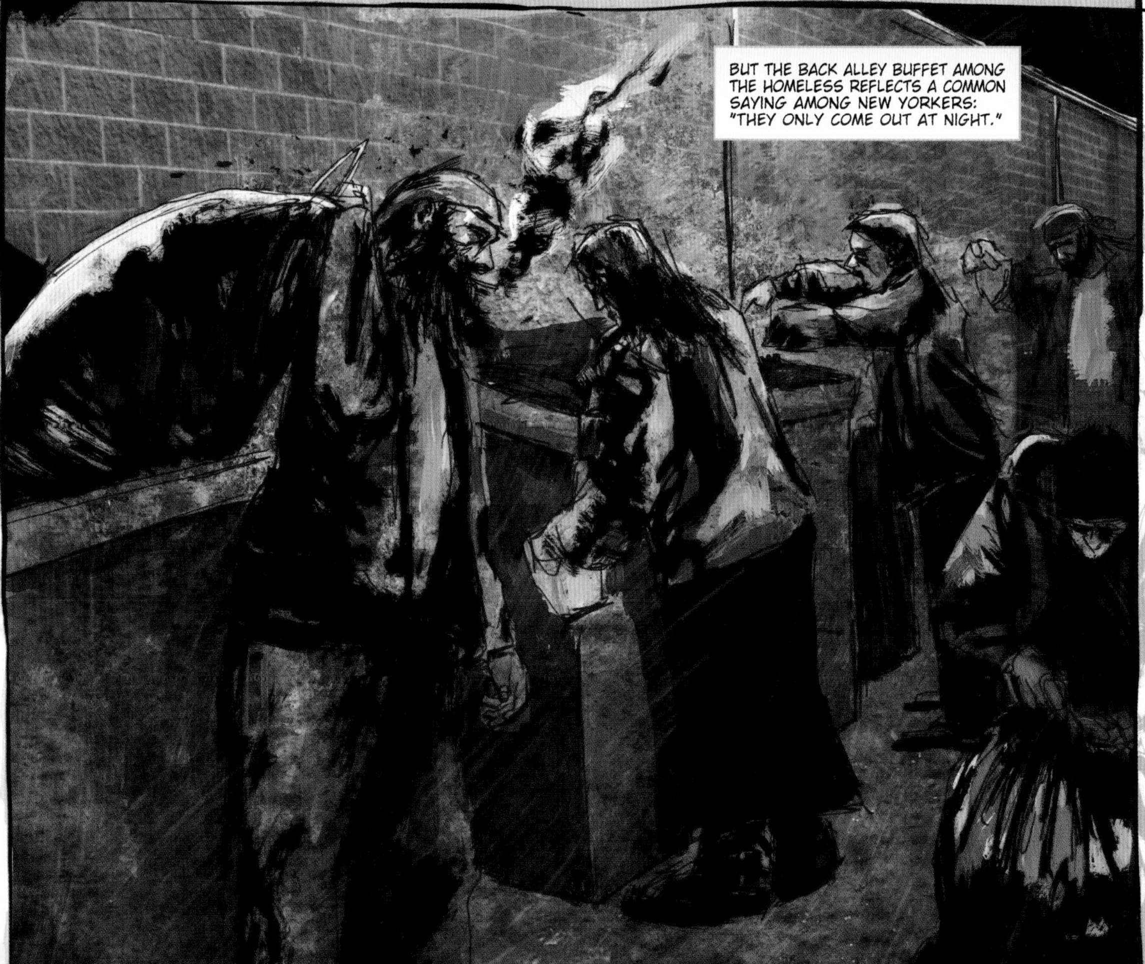
BUT THE BACK ALLEY BUFFET AMONG THE HOMELESS REFLECTS A COMMON SAYING AMONG NEW YORKERS: "THEY ONLY COME OUT AT NIGHT."

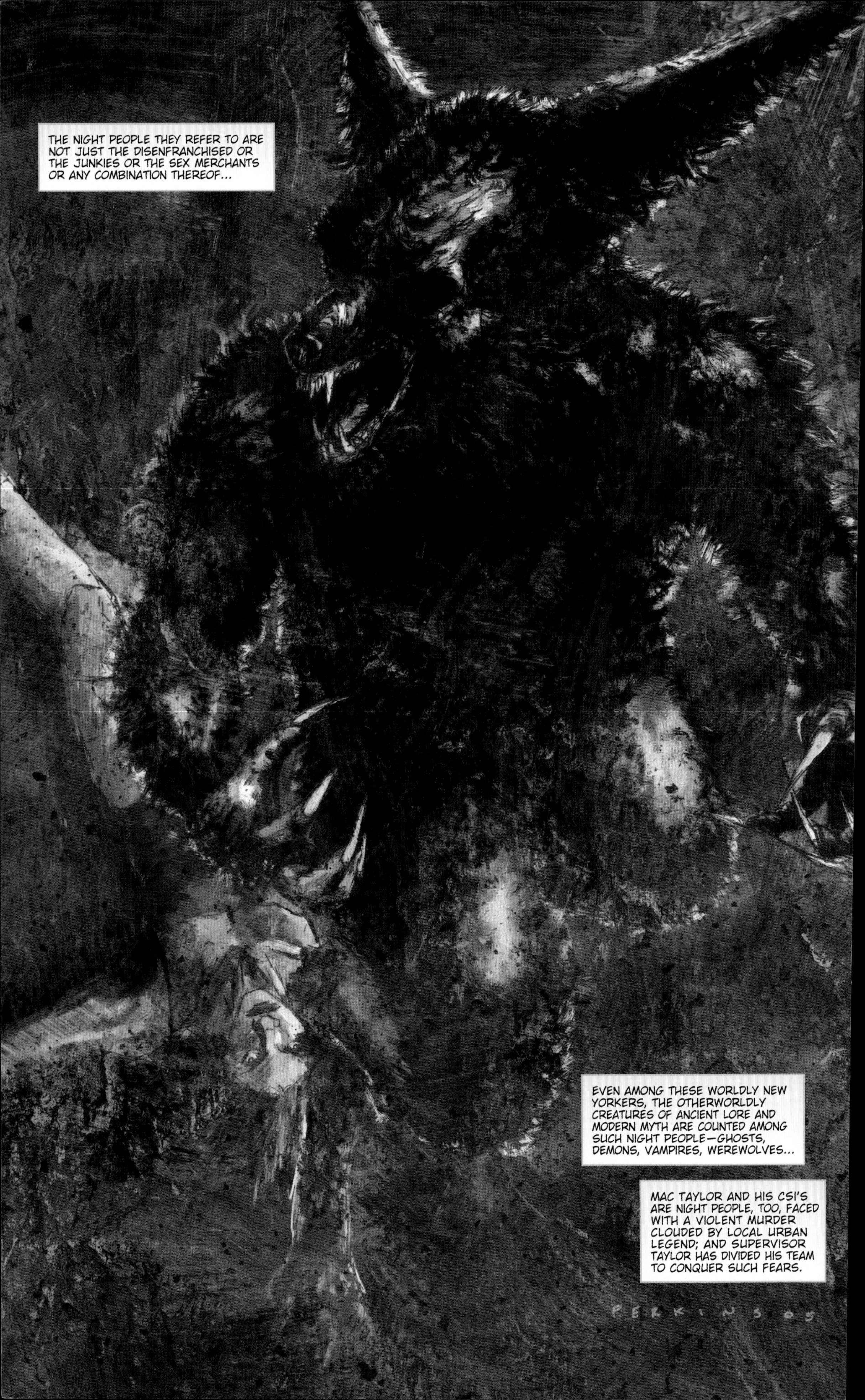
THE NIGHT PEOPLE THEY REFER TO ARE NOT JUST THE DISENFRANCHISED OR THE JUNKIES OR THE SEX MERCHANTS OR ANY COMBINATION THEREOF...
EVEN AMONG THESE WORLDLY NEW YORKERS, THE OTHERWORLDLY CREATURES OF ANCIENT LORE AND MODERN MYTH ARE COUNTED AMONG SUCH NIGHT PEOPLE—GHOSTS, DEMONS, VAMPIRES, WEREWOLVES...
MAC TAYLOR AND HIS CSI'S ARE NIGHT PEOPLE, TOO, FACED WITH A VIOLENT MURDER CLOUDED BY LOCAL URBAN LEGEND; AND SUPERVISOR TAYLOR HAS DIVIDED HIS TEAM TO CONQUER SUCH FEARS.
PERKINS 05

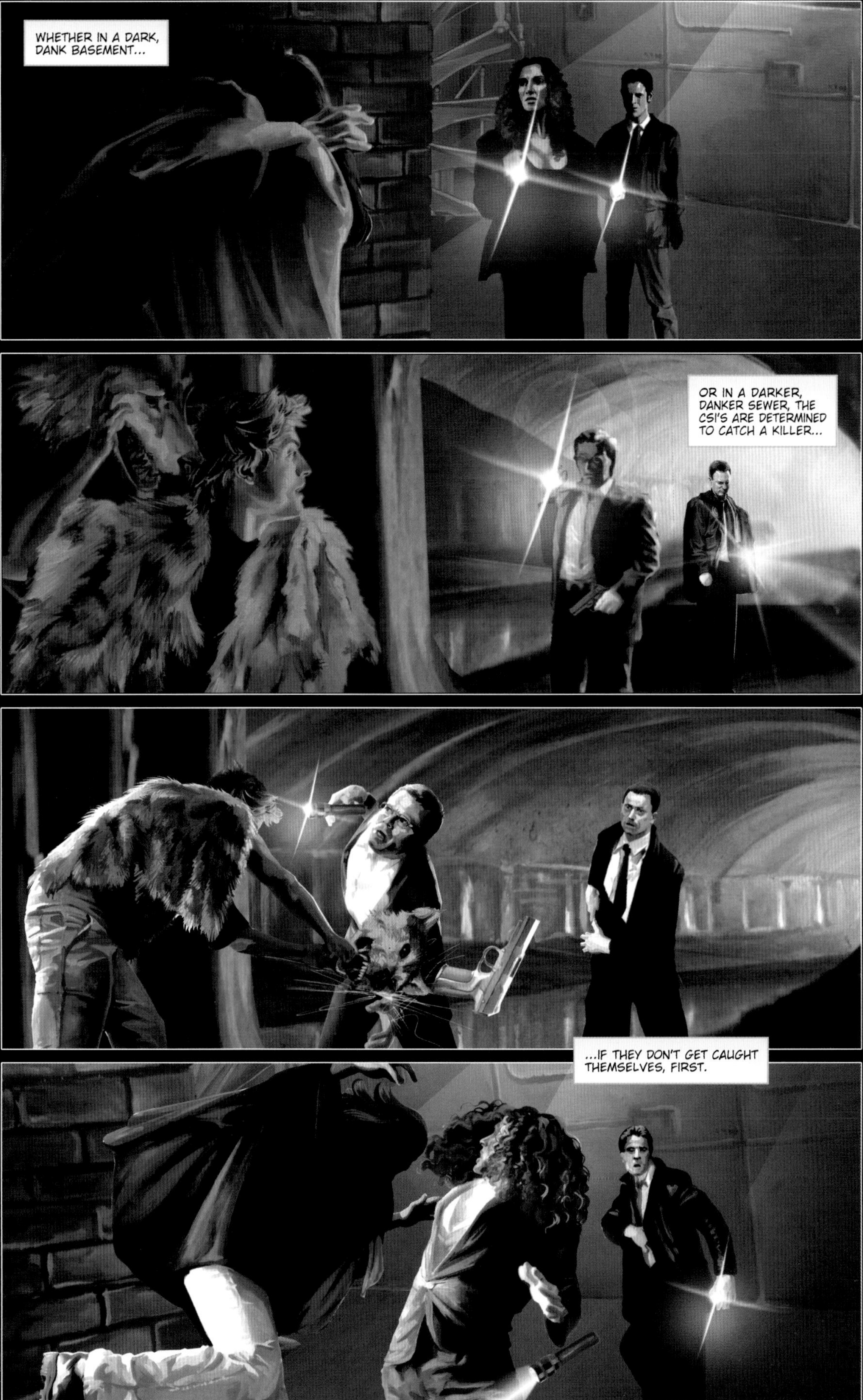
WHETHER IN A DARK, DANK BASEMENT...
OR IN A DARKER, DANKER SEWER, THE CSI'S ARE DETERMINED TO CATCH A KILLER...
...IF THEY DON'T GET CAUGHT THEMSELVES, FIRST.

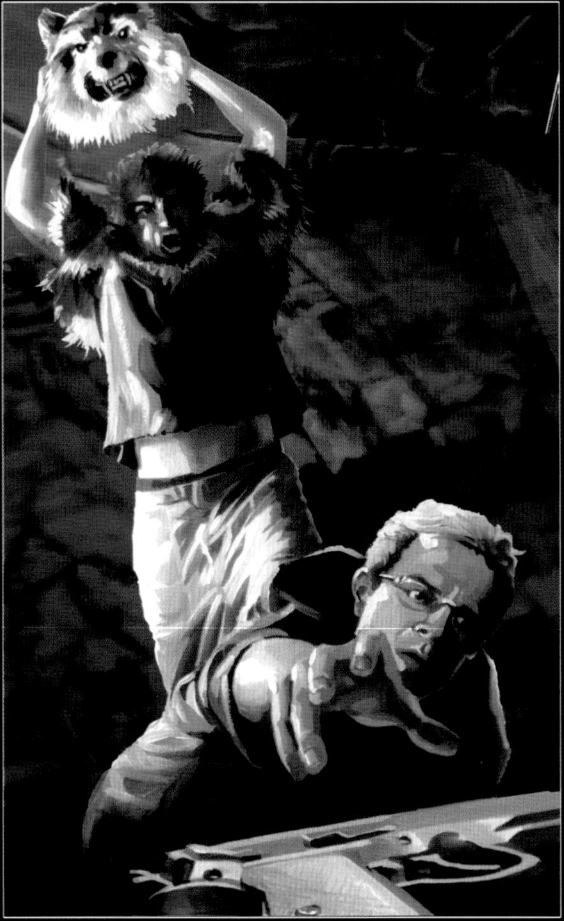

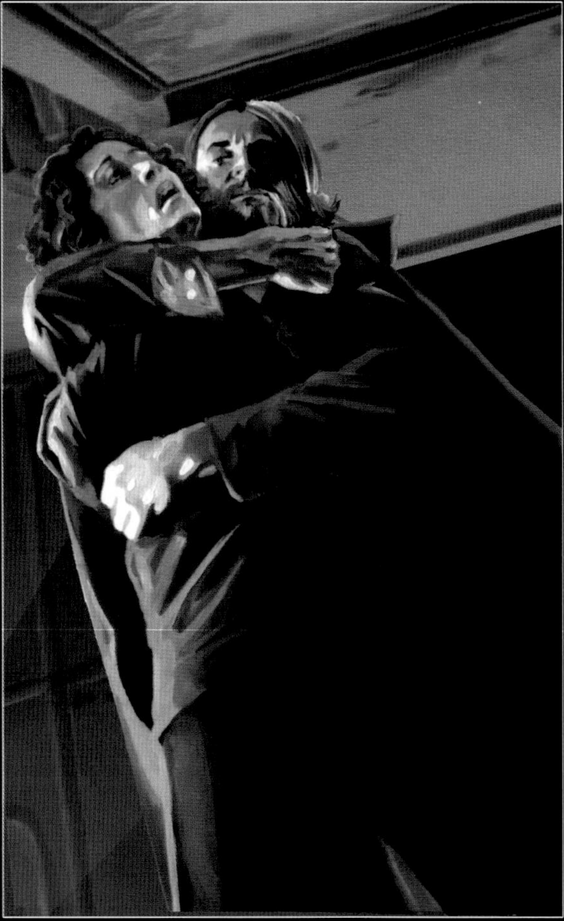

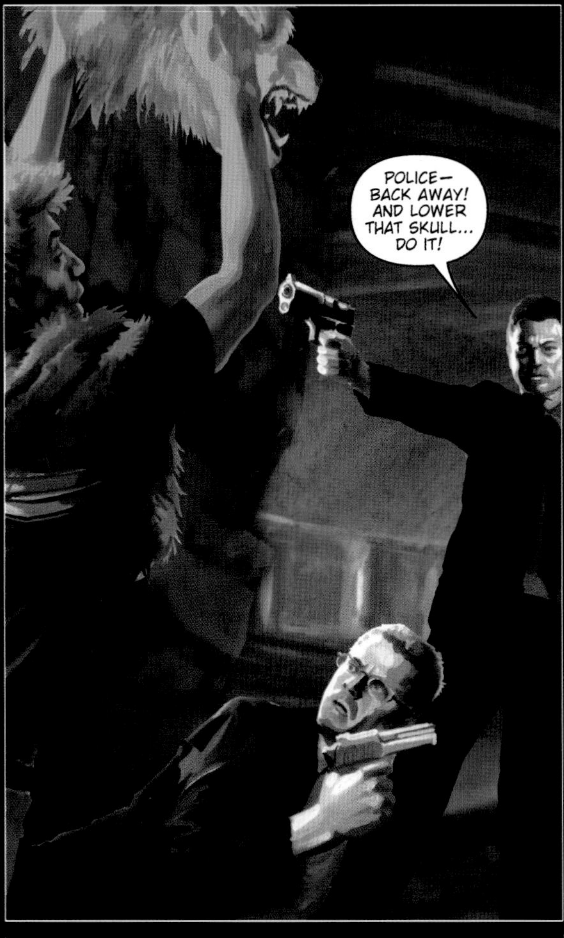
POLICE—
BACK AWAY!
AND LOWER
THAT SKULL...
DO IT!

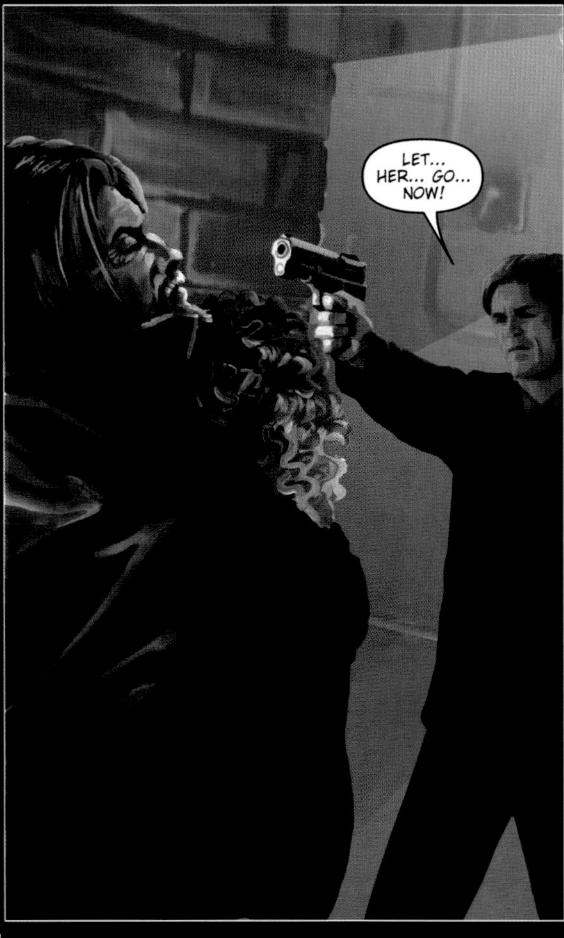
LET...
HER... GO...
NOW!

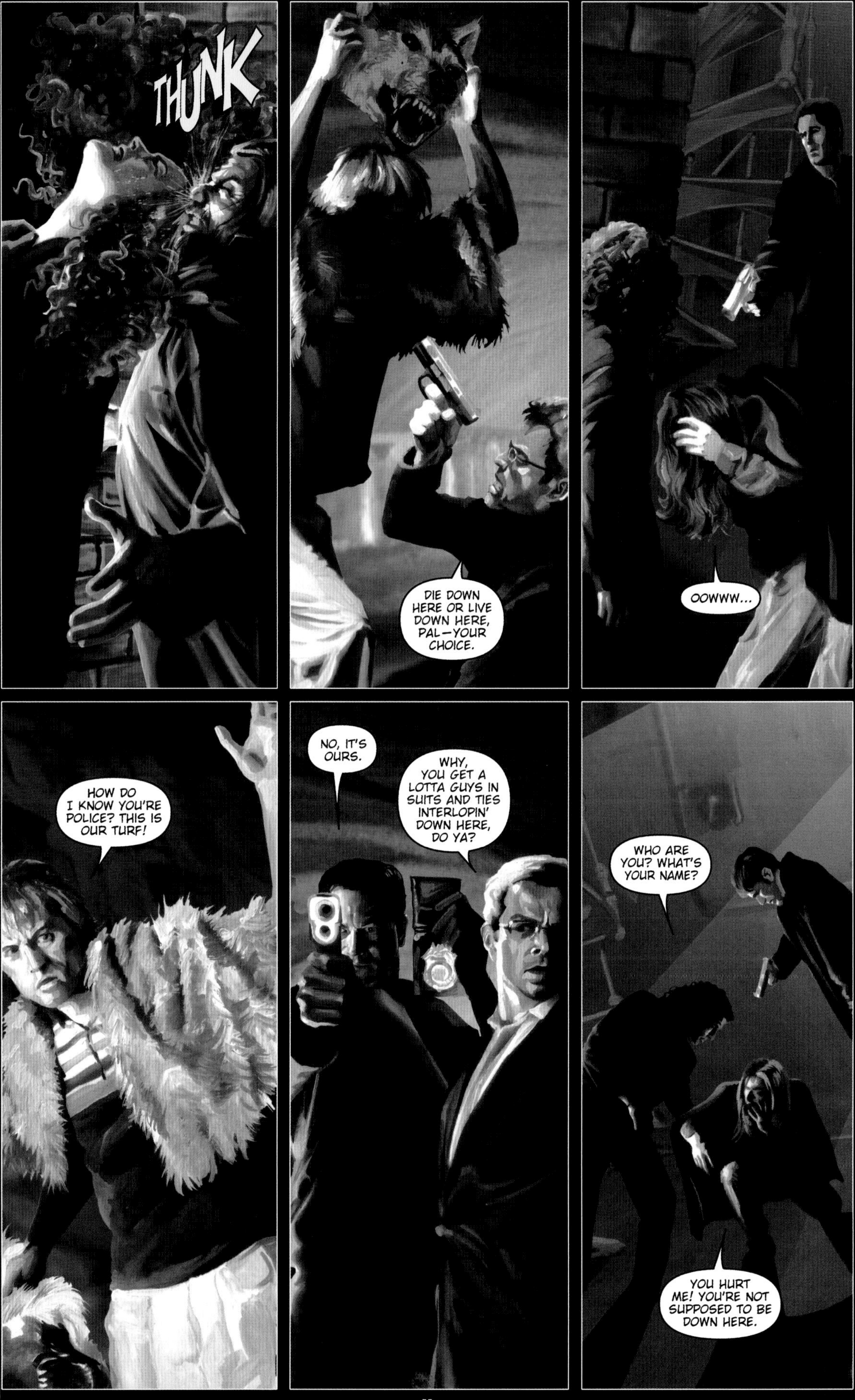
THUNK
DIE DOWN HERE OR LIVE DOWN HERE, PAL—YOUR CHOICE.
OOWWW...
HOW DO I KNOW YOU'RE POLICE? THIS IS OUR TURF!
NO, IT'S OURS.
WHY, YOU GET A LOTTA GUYS IN SUITS AND TIES INTERLOPIN' DOWN HERE, DO YA?
WHO ARE YOU? WHAT'S YOUR NAME?
YOU HURT ME! YOU'RE NOT SUPPOSED TO BE DOWN HERE.

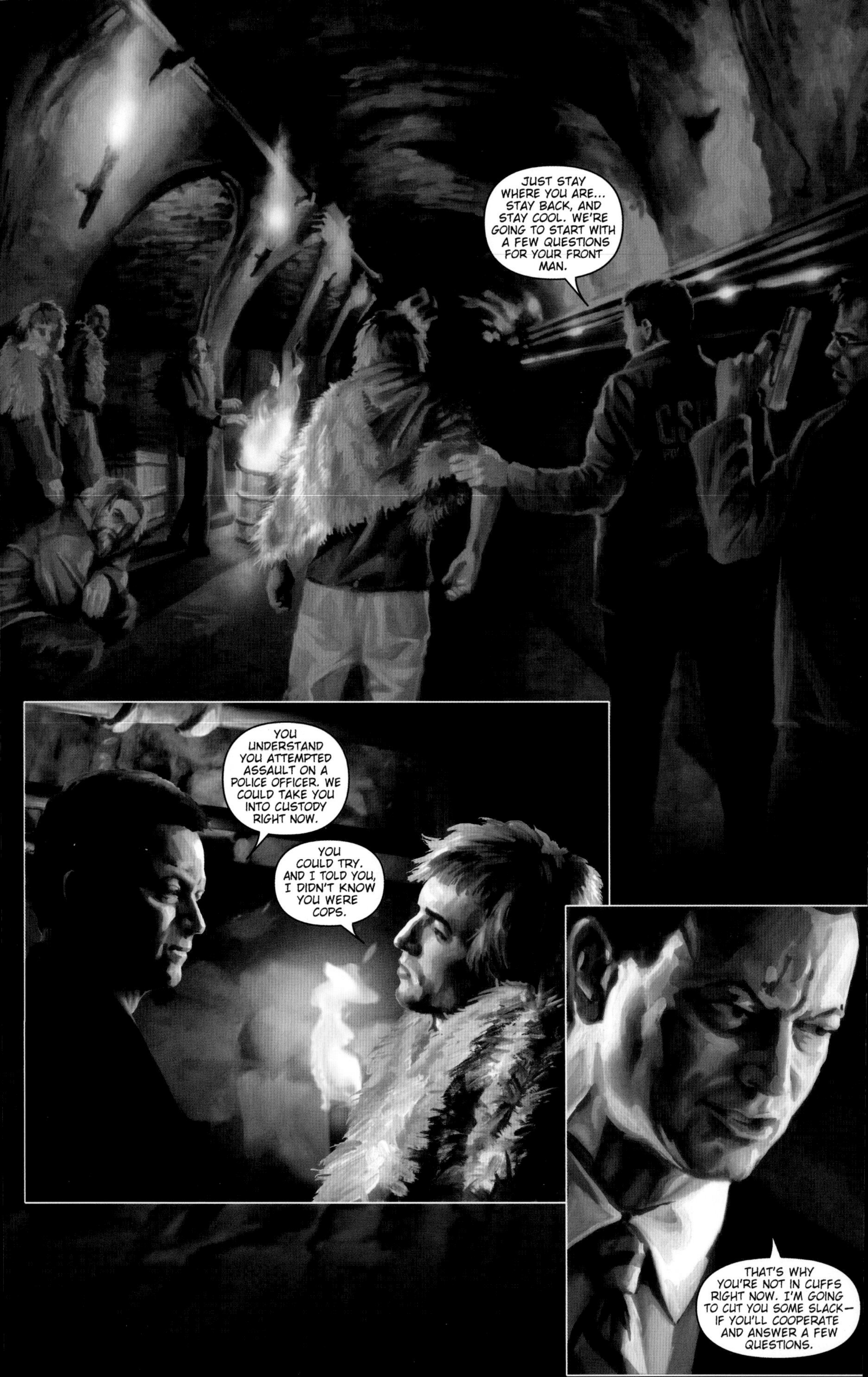
JUST STAY WHERE YOU ARE... STAY BACK, AND STAY COOL. WE'RE GOING TO START WITH A FEW QUESTIONS FOR YOUR FRONT MAN.
YOU UNDERSTAND YOU ATTEMPTED ASSAULT ON A POLICE OFFICER. WE COULD TAKE YOU INTO CUSTODY RIGHT NOW.
YOU COULD TRY. AND I TOLD YOU, I DIDN'T KNOW YOU WERE COPS.
THAT'S WHY YOU'RE NOT IN CUFFS RIGHT NOW. I'M GOING TO CUT YOU SOME SLACK— IF YOU'LL COOPERATE AND ANSWER A FEW QUESTIONS.

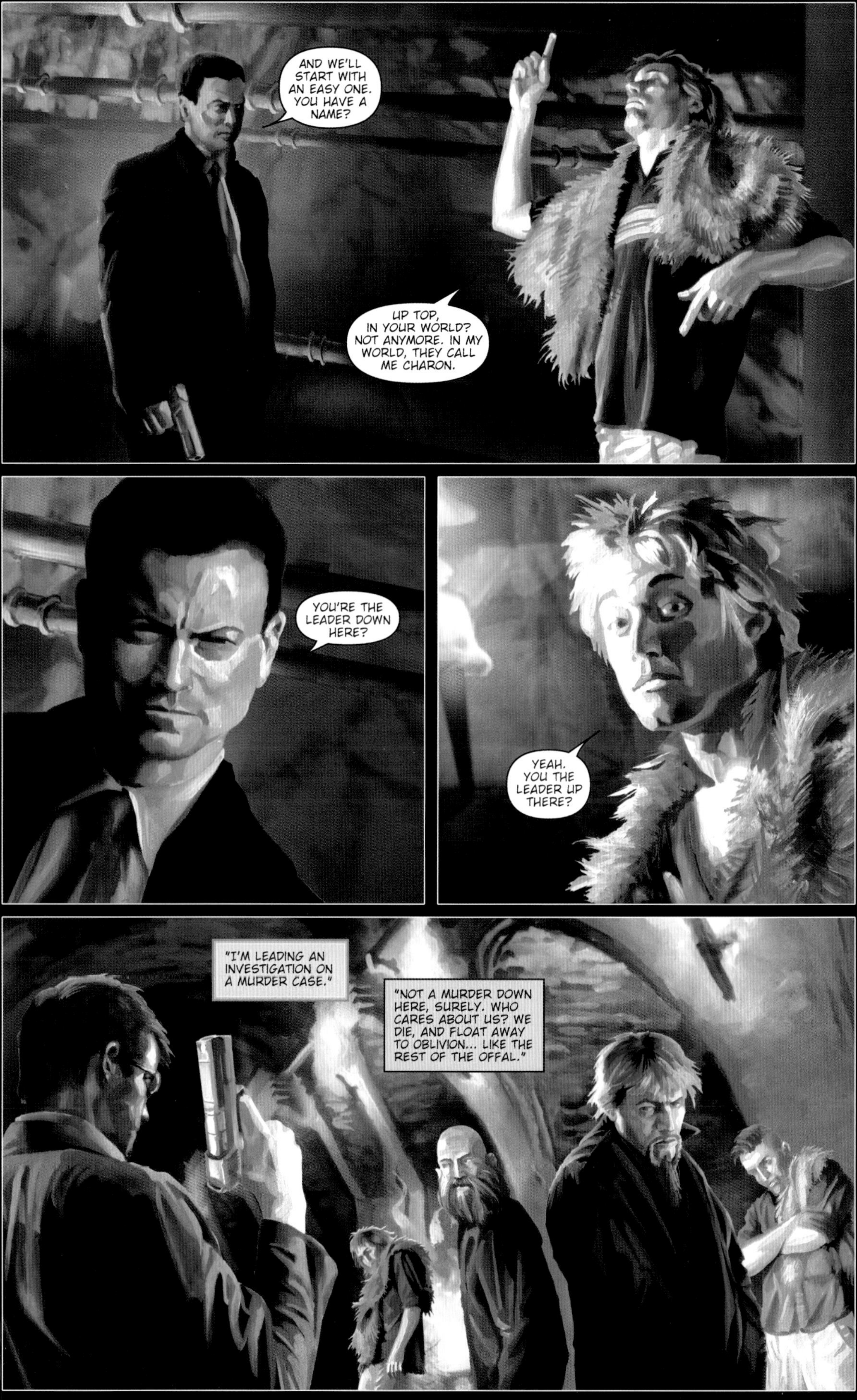
AND WE'LL START WITH AN EASY ONE. YOU HAVE A NAME?
UP TOP, IN YOUR WORLD? NOT ANYMORE. IN MY WORLD, THEY CALL ME CHARON.
YOU'RE THE LEADER DOWN HERE?
YEAH. YOU THE LEADER UP THERE?
"I'M LEADING AN INVESTIGATION ON A MURDER CASE."
"NOT A MURDER DOWN HERE, SURELY. WHO CARES ABOUT US? WE DIE, AND FLOAT AWAY TO OBLIVION... LIKE THE REST OF THE OFFAL."

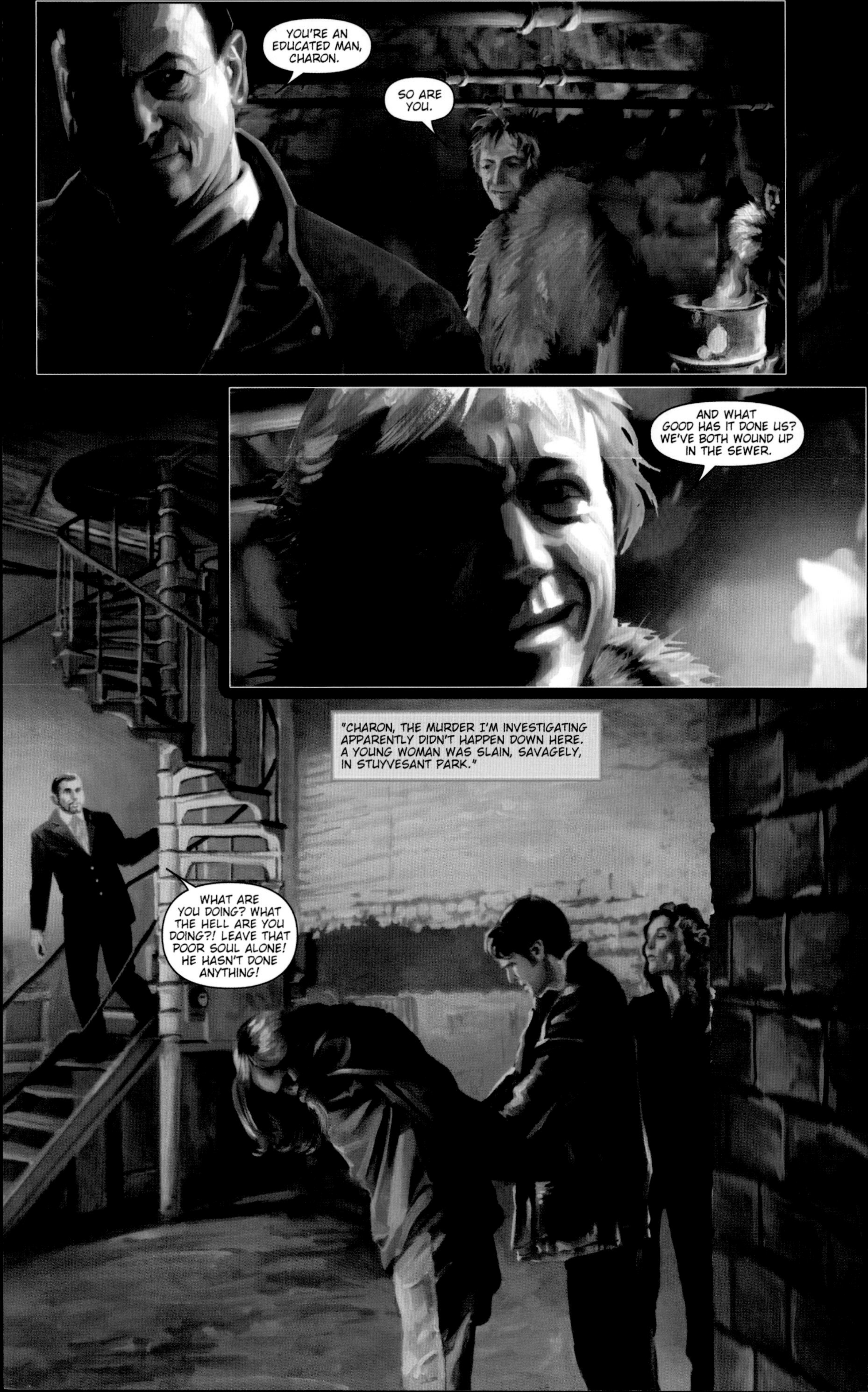
YOU'RE AN EDUCATED MAN, CHARON.
SO ARE YOU.
AND WHAT GOOD HAS IT DONE US? WE'VE BOTH WOUND UP IN THE SEWER.
"CHARON, THE MURDER I'M INVESTIGATING APPARENTLY DIDN'T HAPPEN DOWN HERE. A YOUNG WOMAN WAS SLAIN, SAVAGELY, IN STUYVESANT PARK."
WHAT ARE YOU DOING? WHAT THE HELL ARE YOU DOING?! LEAVE THAT POOR SOUL ALONE! HE HASN'T DONE ANYTHING!

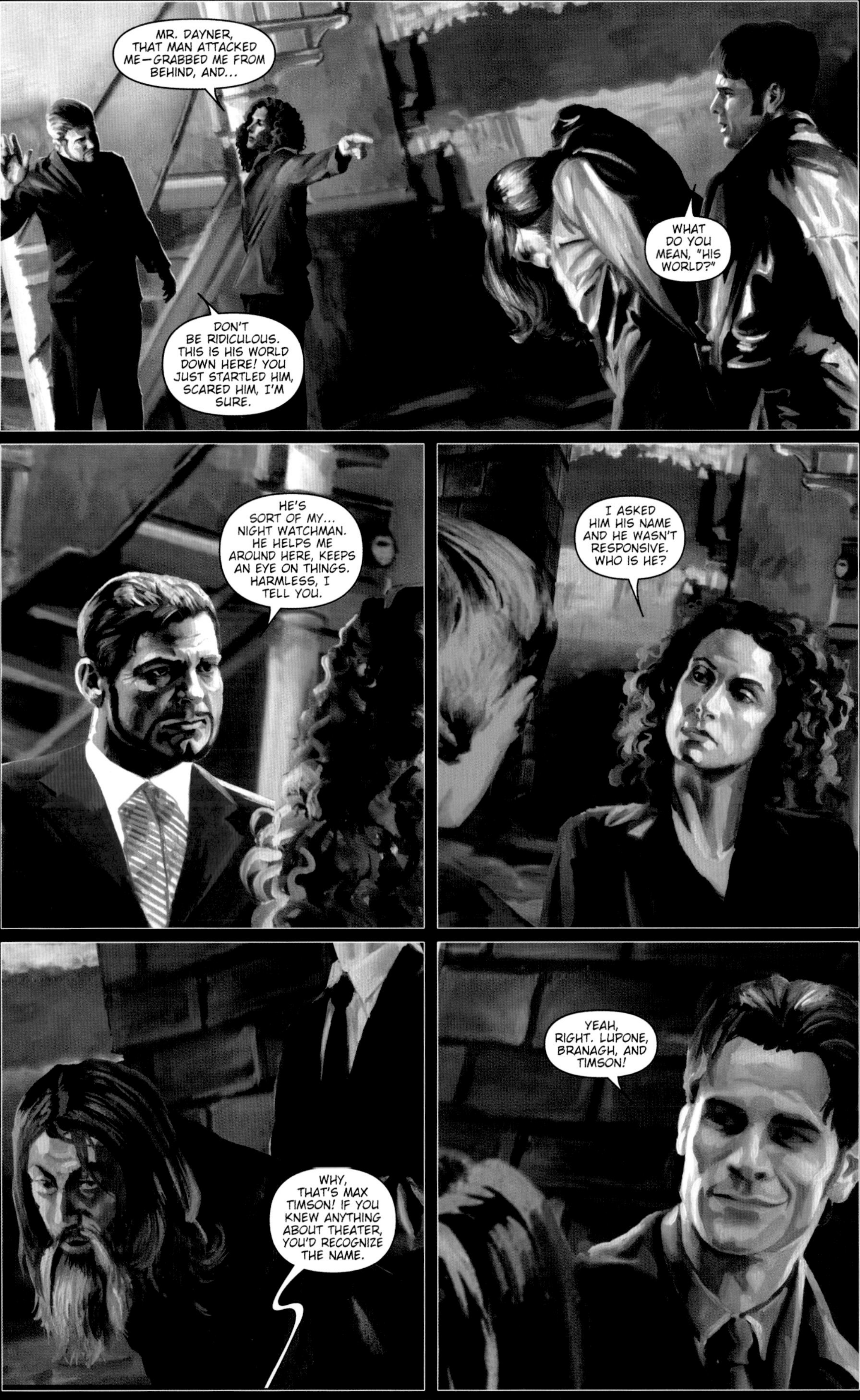
MR. DAYNER, THAT MAN ATTACKED ME—GRABBED ME FROM BEHIND, AND...
DON'T BE RIDICULOUS. THIS IS HIS WORLD DOWN HERE! YOU JUST STARTLED HIM, SCARED HIM, I'M SURE.
WHAT DO YOU MEAN, "HIS WORLD?"
HE'S SORT OF MY... NIGHT WATCHMAN. HE HELPS ME AROUND HERE, KEEPS AN EYE ON THINGS. HARMLESS, I TELL YOU.
I ASKED HIM HIS NAME AND HE WASN'T RESPONSIVE. WHO IS HE?
WHY, THAT'S MAX TIMSON! IF YOU KNEW ANYTHING ABOUT THEATER, YOU'D RECOGNIZE THE NAME.
YEAH, RIGHT. LUPONE, BRANAGH, AND TIMSON!

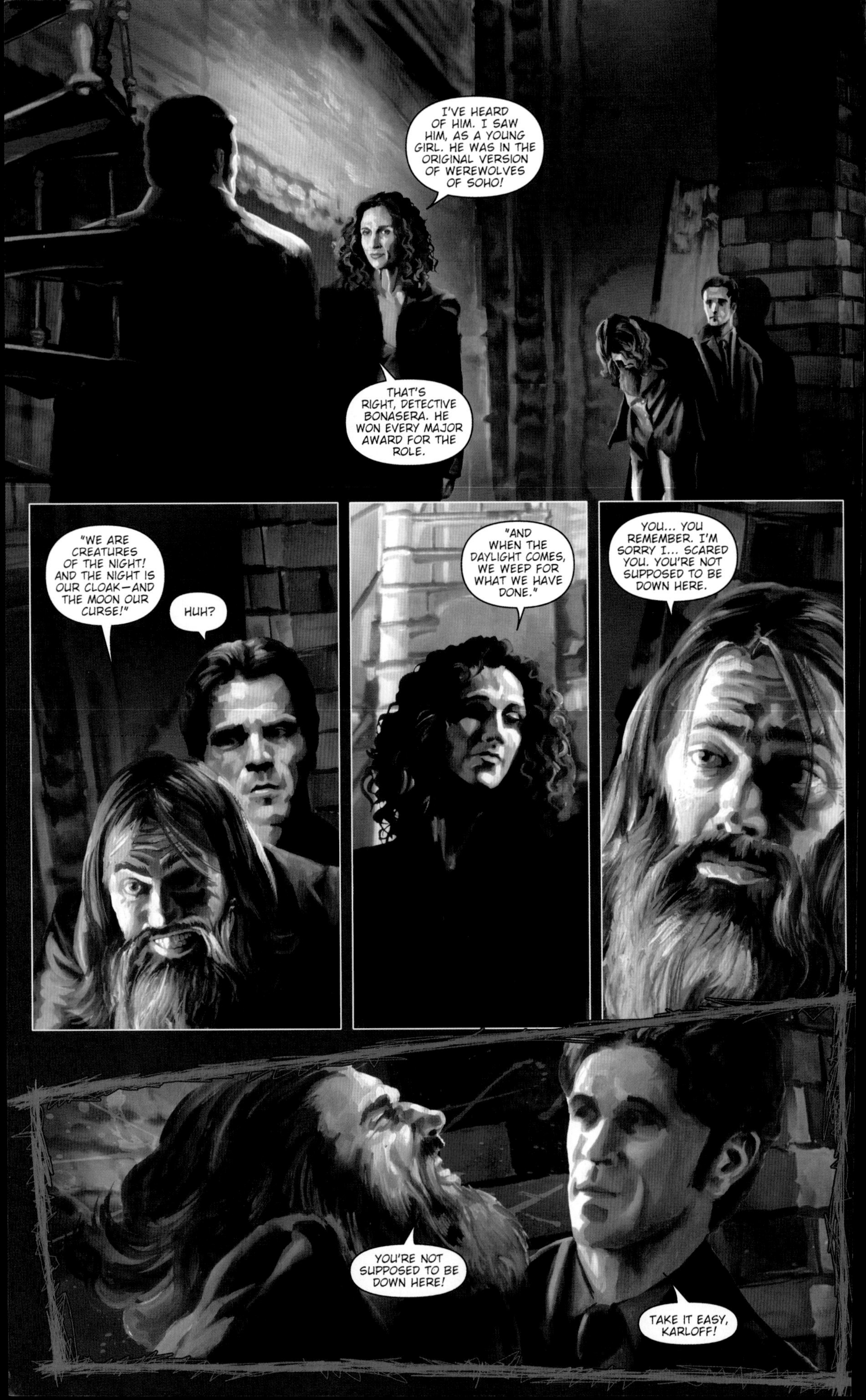
I'VE HEARD OF HIM. I SAW HIM, AS A YOUNG GIRL. HE WAS IN THE ORIGINAL VERSION OF WEREWOLVES OF SOHO!
THAT'S RIGHT, DETECTIVE BONASERA. HE WON EVERY MAJOR AWARD FOR THE ROLE.
"WE ARE CREATURES OF THE NIGHT! AND THE NIGHT IS OUR CLOAK—AND THE MOON OUR CURSE!"
HUH?
"AND WHEN THE DAYLIGHT COMES, WE WEEP FOR WHAT WE HAVE DONE."
YOU... YOU REMEMBER. I'M SORRY I... SCARED YOU. YOU'RE NOT SUPPOSED TO BE DOWN HERE.
YOU'RE NOT SUPPOSED TO BE DOWN HERE!
TAKE IT EASY, KARLOFF!

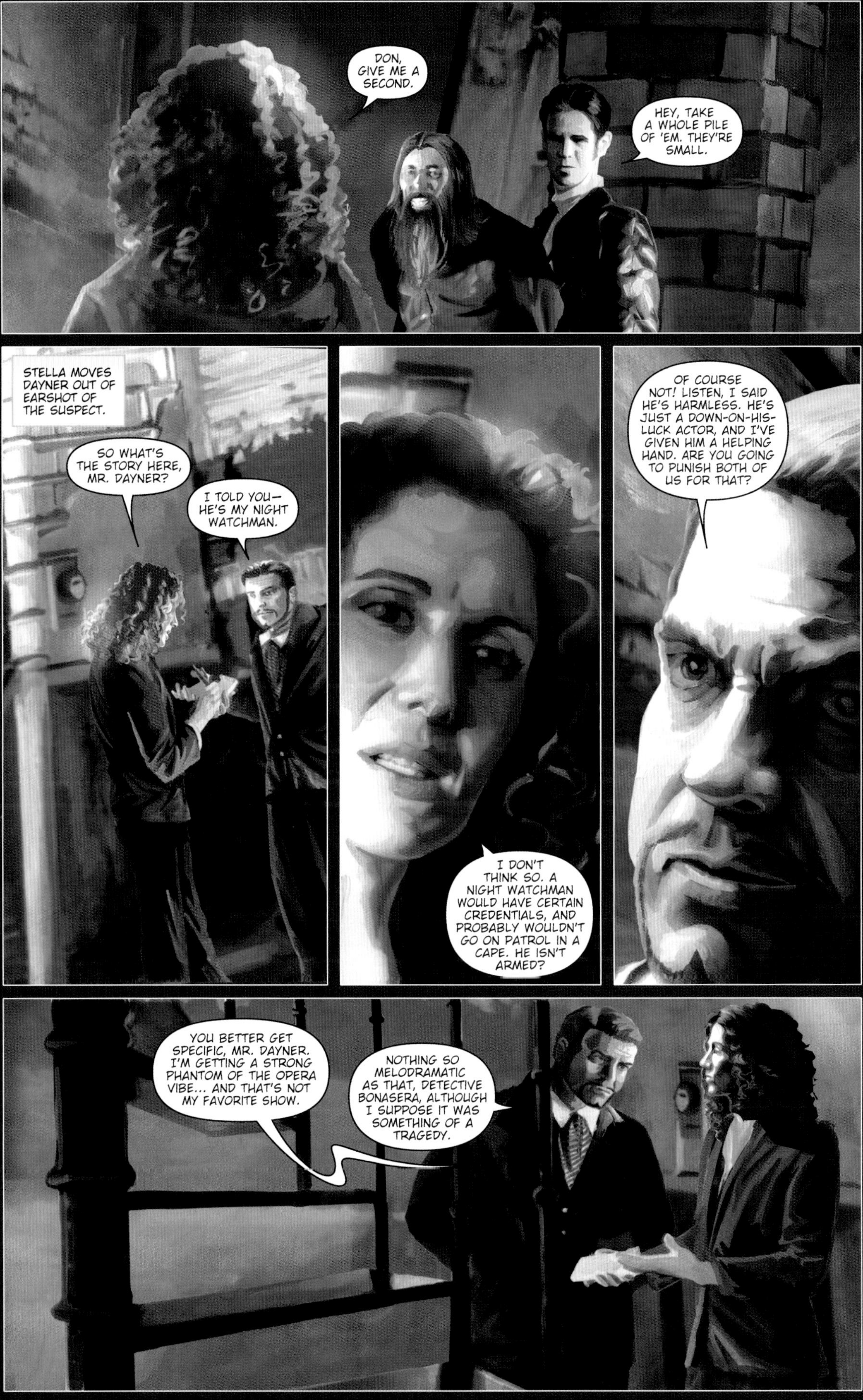

DON, GIVE ME A SECOND.
HEY, TAKE A WHOLE PILE OF 'EM. THEY'RE SMALL.
STELLA MOVES DAYNER OUT OF EARSHOT OF THE SUSPECT.
SO WHAT'S THE STORY HERE, MR. DAYNER?
I TOLD YOU— HE'S MY NIGHT WATCHMAN.
I DON'T THINK SO. A NIGHT WATCHMAN WOULD HAVE CERTAIN CREDENTIALS, AND PROBABLY WOULDN'T GO ON PATROL IN A CAPE. HE ISN'T ARMED?
OF COURSE NOT! LISTEN, I SAID HE'S HARMLESS. HE'S JUST A DOWN-ON-HIS-LUCK ACTOR, AND I'VE GIVEN HIM A HELPING HAND. ARE YOU GOING TO PUNISH BOTH OF US FOR THAT?
YOU BETTER GET SPECIFIC, MR. DAYNER. I'M GETTING A STRONG PHANTOM OF THE OPERA VIBE... AND THAT'S NOT MY FAVORITE SHOW.
NOTHING SO MELODRAMATIC AS THAT, DETECTIVE BONASERA, ALTHOUGH I SUPPOSE IT WAS SOMETHING OF A TRAGEDY.

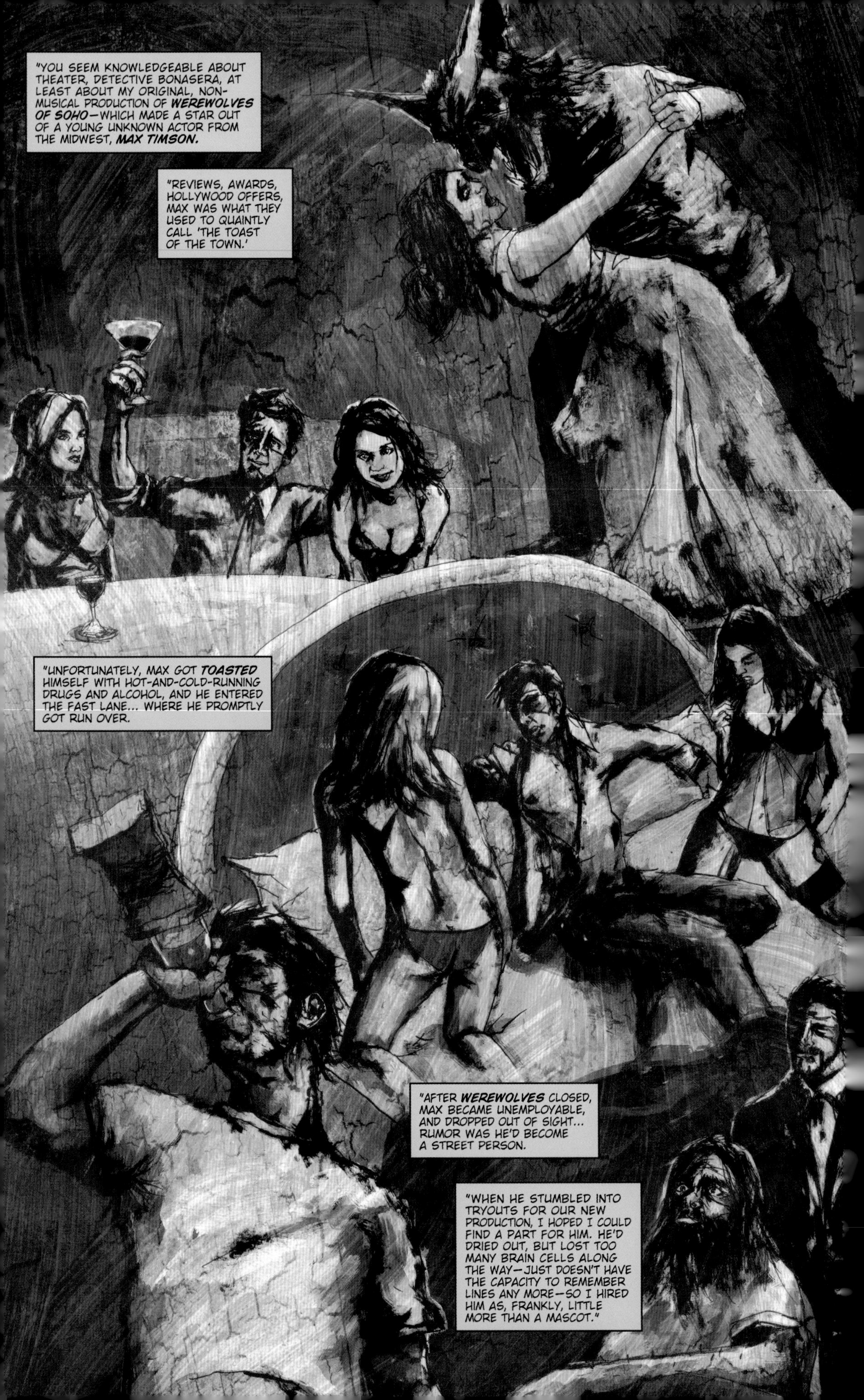
"YOU SEEM KNOWLEDGEABLE ABOUT THEATER, DETECTIVE BONASERA, AT LEAST ABOUT MY ORIGINAL, NON-MUSICAL PRODUCTION OF ***WEREWOLVES OF SOHO***—WHICH MADE A STAR OUT OF A YOUNG UNKNOWN ACTOR FROM THE MIDWEST, ***MAX TIMSON.***
"REVIEWS, AWARDS, HOLLYWOOD OFFERS, MAX WAS WHAT THEY USED TO QUAINTLY CALL 'THE TOAST OF THE TOWN.'
"UNFORTUNATELY, MAX GOT ***TOASTED*** HIMSELF WITH HOT-AND-COLD-RUNNING DRUGS AND ALCOHOL, AND HE ENTERED THE FAST LANE... WHERE HE PROMPTLY GOT RUN OVER.
"AFTER ***WEREWOLVES*** CLOSED, MAX BECAME UNEMPLOYABLE, AND DROPPED OUT OF SIGHT... RUMOR WAS HE'D BECOME A STREET PERSON.
"WHEN HE STUMBLED INTO TRYOUTS FOR OUR NEW PRODUCTION, I HOPED I COULD FIND A PART FOR HIM. HE'D DRIED OUT, BUT LOST TOO MANY BRAIN CELLS ALONG THE WAY—JUST DOESN'T HAVE THE CAPACITY TO REMEMBER LINES ANY MORE—SO I HIRED HIM AS, FRANKLY, LITTLE MORE THAN A MASCOT."

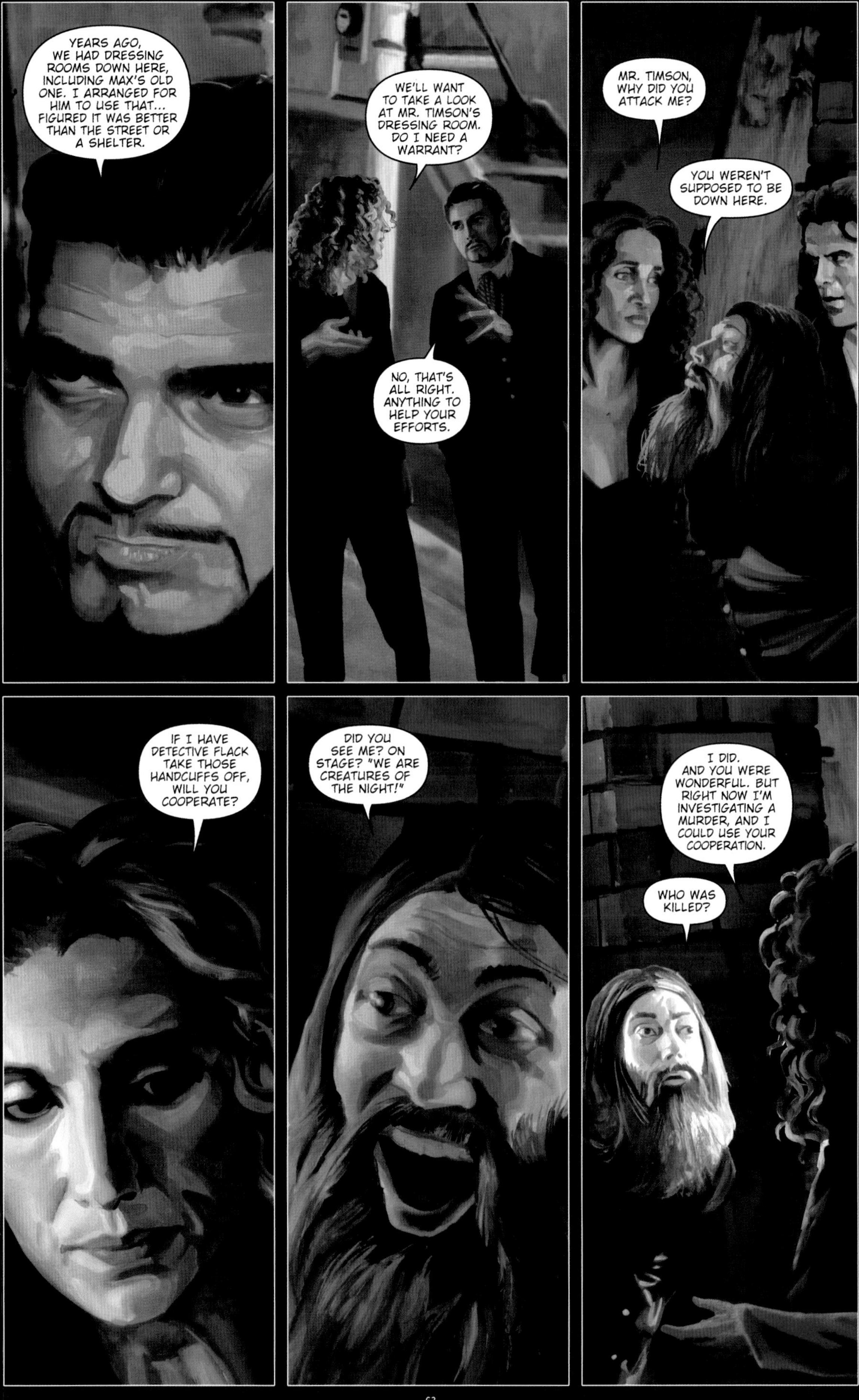
YEARS AGO, WE HAD DRESSING ROOMS DOWN HERE, INCLUDING MAX'S OLD ONE. I ARRANGED FOR HIM TO USE THAT... FIGURED IT WAS BETTER THAN THE STREET OR A SHELTER.
WE'LL WANT TO TAKE A LOOK AT MR. TIMSON'S DRESSING ROOM. DO I NEED A WARRANT?
NO, THAT'S ALL RIGHT. ANYTHING TO HELP YOUR EFFORTS.
MR. TIMSON, WHY DID YOU ATTACK ME?
YOU WEREN'T SUPPOSED TO BE DOWN HERE.
IF I HAVE DETECTIVE FLACK TAKE THOSE HANDCUFFS OFF, WILL YOU COOPERATE?
DID YOU SEE ME? ON STAGE? "WE ARE CREATURES OF THE NIGHT!"
I DID. AND YOU WERE WONDERFUL. BUT RIGHT NOW I'M INVESTIGATING A MURDER, AND I COULD USE YOUR COOPERATION.
WHO WAS KILLED?

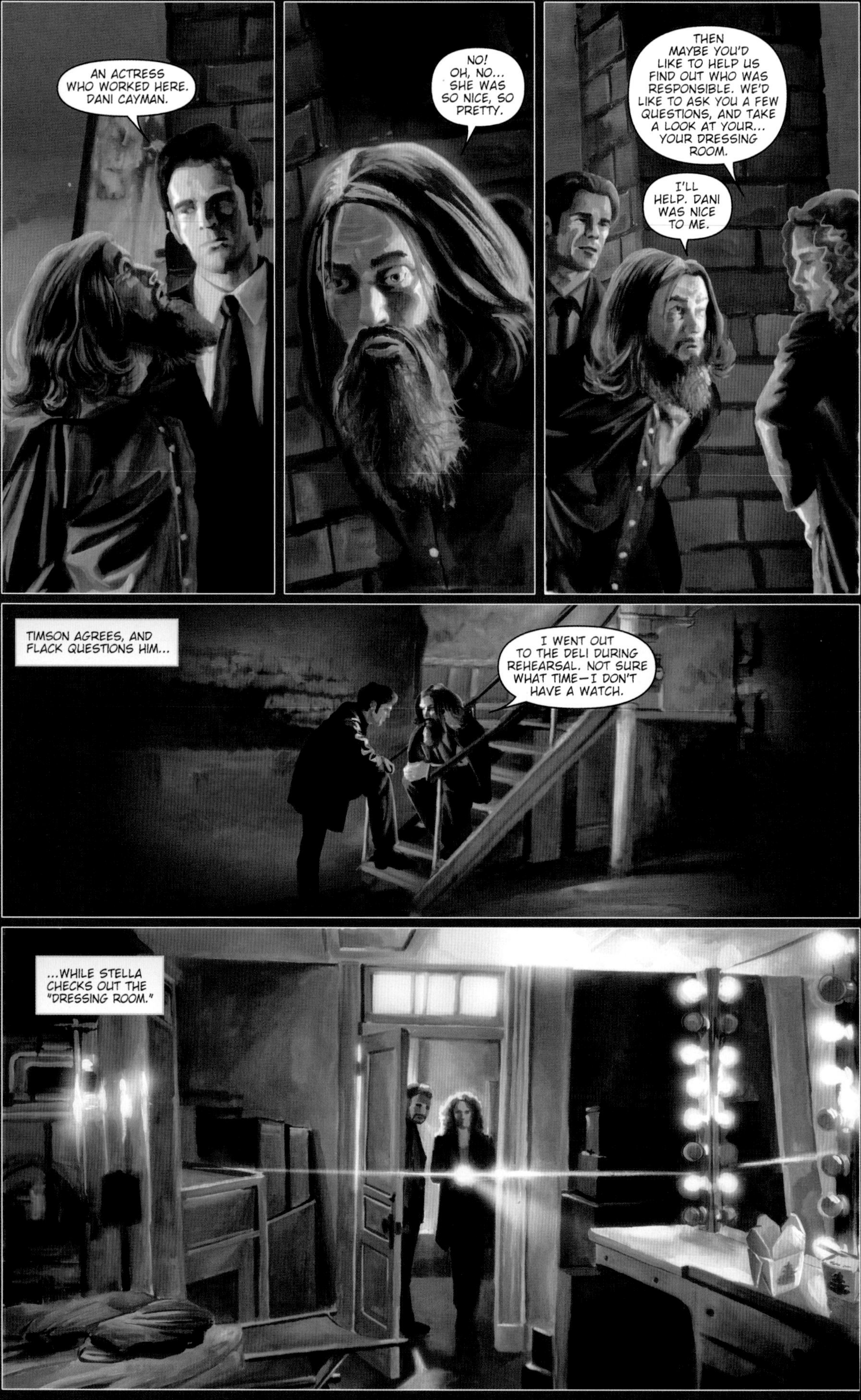
AN ACTRESS WHO WORKED HERE. DANI CAYMAN.
NO! OH, NO... SHE WAS SO NICE, SO PRETTY.
THEN MAYBE YOU'D LIKE TO HELP US FIND OUT WHO WAS RESPONSIBLE. WE'D LIKE TO ASK YOU A FEW QUESTIONS, AND TAKE A LOOK AT YOUR... YOUR DRESSING ROOM.
I'LL HELP. DANI WAS NICE TO ME.
TIMSON AGREES, AND FLACK QUESTIONS HIM...
I WENT OUT TO THE DELI DURING REHEARSAL. NOT SURE WHAT TIME—I DON'T HAVE A WATCH.
...WHILE STELLA CHECKS OUT THE "DRESSING ROOM."

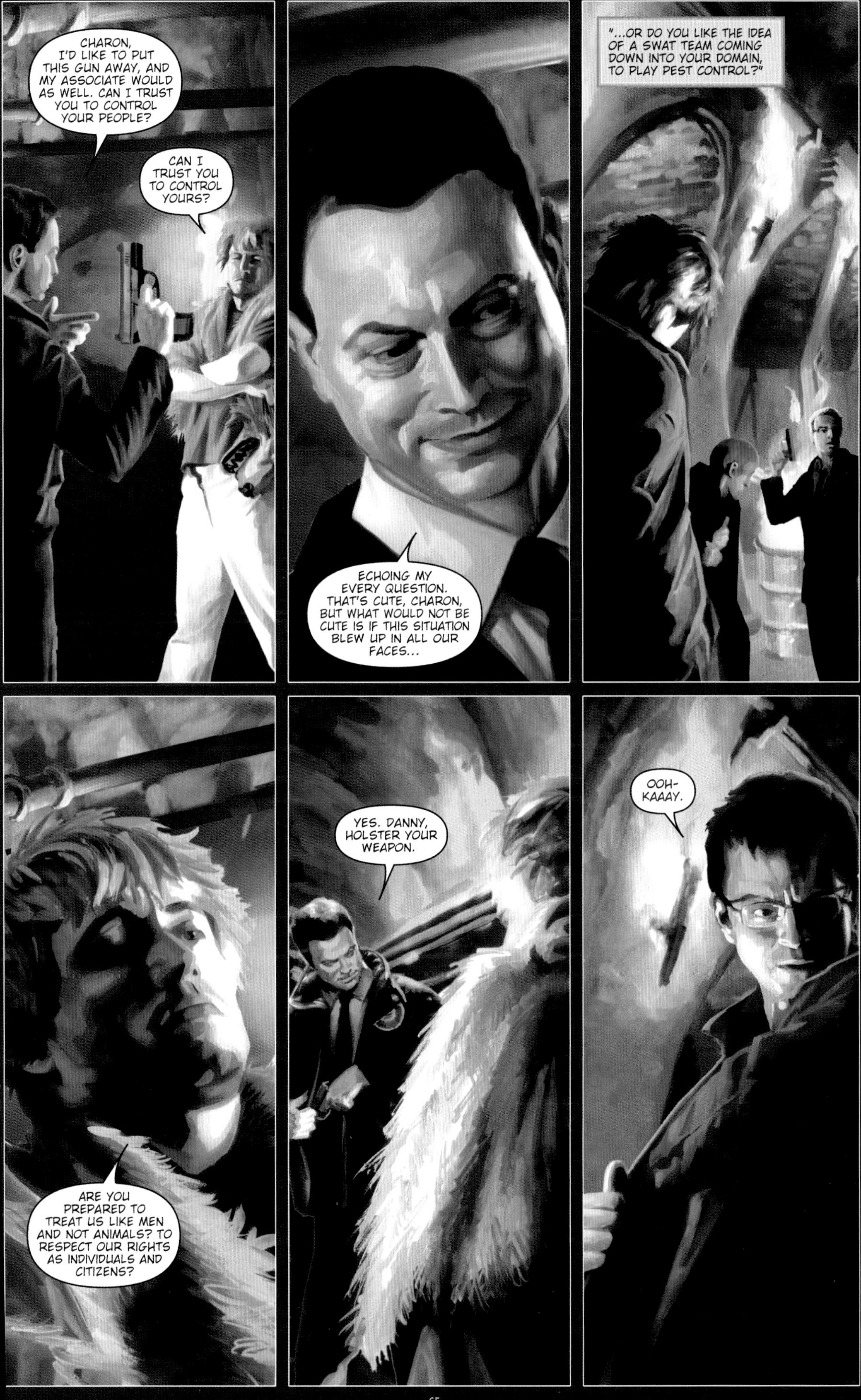
CHARON, I'D LIKE TO PUT THIS GUN AWAY, AND MY ASSOCIATE WOULD AS WELL. CAN I TRUST YOU TO CONTROL YOUR PEOPLE?
CAN I TRUST YOU TO CONTROL YOURS?
ECHOING MY EVERY QUESTION. THAT'S CUTE, CHARON, BUT WHAT WOULD NOT BE CUTE IS IF THIS SITUATION BLEW UP IN ALL OUR FACES...
"...OR DO YOU LIKE THE IDEA OF A SWAT TEAM COMING DOWN INTO YOUR DOMAIN, TO PLAY PEST CONTROL?"
ARE YOU PREPARED TO TREAT US LIKE MEN AND NOT ANIMALS? TO RESPECT OUR RIGHTS AS INDIVIDUALS AND CITIZENS?
YES. DANNY, HOLSTER YOUR WEAPON.
OOH-KAAAY.

WERE YOU IN STUYVESANT PARK TONIGHT, CHARON?

DID YOU TAKE THAT TALISMAN WITH YOU?

HEY, WE'RE NO WOLF CULT. DON'T BELIEVE THE NONSENSE YOU HEAR. I JUST PICKED THIS UP TONIGHT FOR A DECORATING TOUCH.

I WAS. WE ALL WERE.

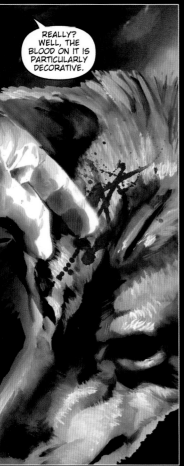

REALLY? WELL, THE BLOOD ON IT IS PARTICULARLY DECORATIVE.

LOOK, DETECTIVE, I FOUND THIS IN A DUMPSTER BEHIND A DELI AT FIRST AND FIFTEENTH. IT JUST SEEMED LIKE A FUNKY SOUVENIR.

IN THE PARK—YOU SAW THE DEAD WOMAN?

WE SAW HER. WE DID NOT KILL HER.

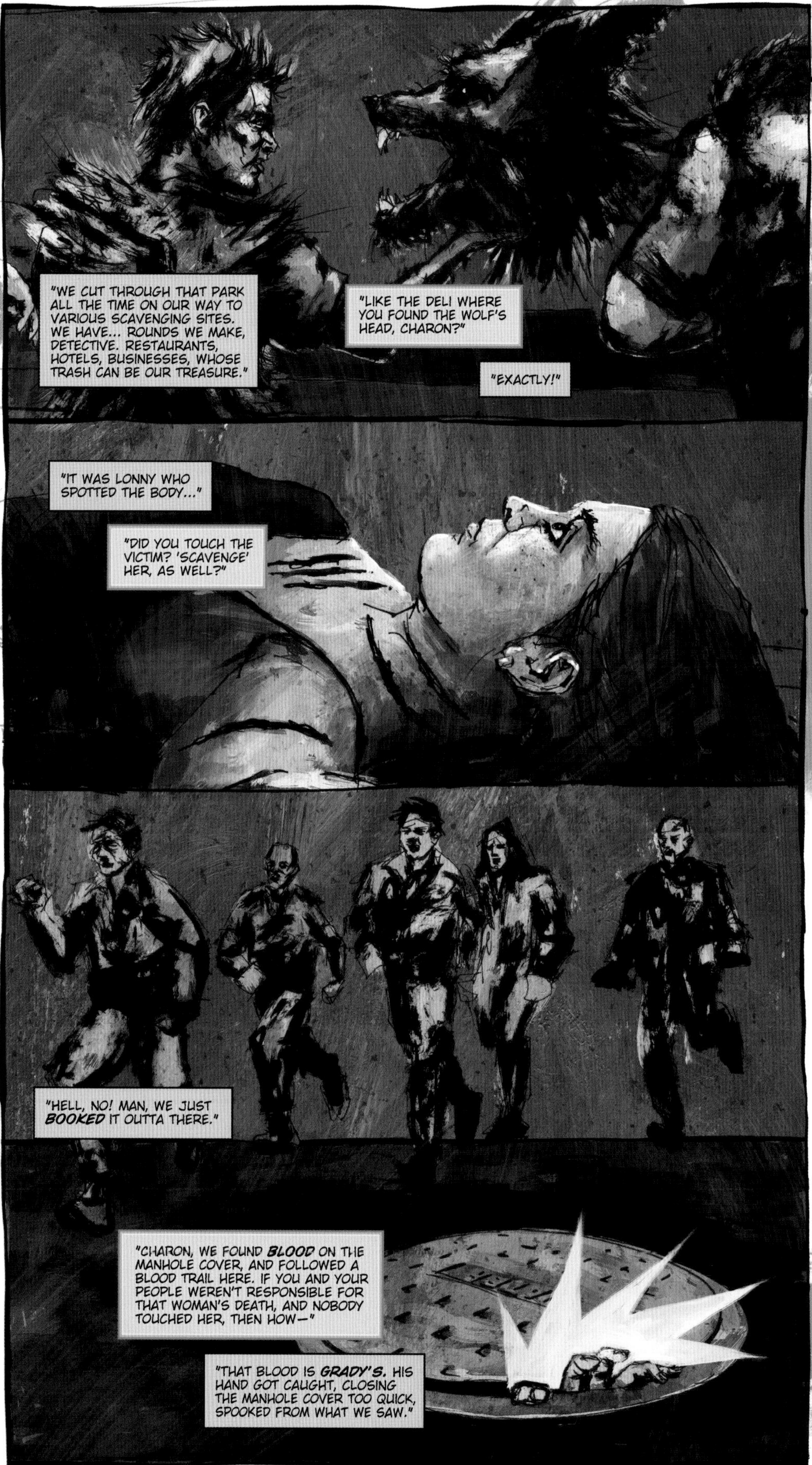
"WE CUT THROUGH THAT PARK ALL THE TIME ON OUR WAY TO VARIOUS SCAVENGING SITES. WE HAVE... ROUNDS WE MAKE, DETECTIVE. RESTAURANTS, HOTELS, BUSINESSES, WHOSE TRASH CAN BE OUR TREASURE."
"LIKE THE DELI WHERE YOU FOUND THE WOLF'S HEAD, CHARON?"
"EXACTLY!"
"IT WAS LONNY WHO SPOTTED THE BODY..."
"DID YOU TOUCH THE VICTIM? 'SCAVENGE' HER, AS WELL?"
"HELL, NO! MAN, WE JUST **BOOKED** IT OUTTA THERE."
"CHARON, WE FOUND **BLOOD** ON THE MANHOLE COVER, AND FOLLOWED A BLOOD TRAIL HERE. IF YOU AND YOUR PEOPLE WEREN'T RESPONSIBLE FOR THAT WOMAN'S DEATH, AND NOBODY TOUCHED HER, THEN HOW—"
"THAT BLOOD IS **GRADY'S.** HIS HAND GOT CAUGHT, CLOSING THE MANHOLE COVER TOO QUICK, SPOOKED FROM WHAT WE SAW."

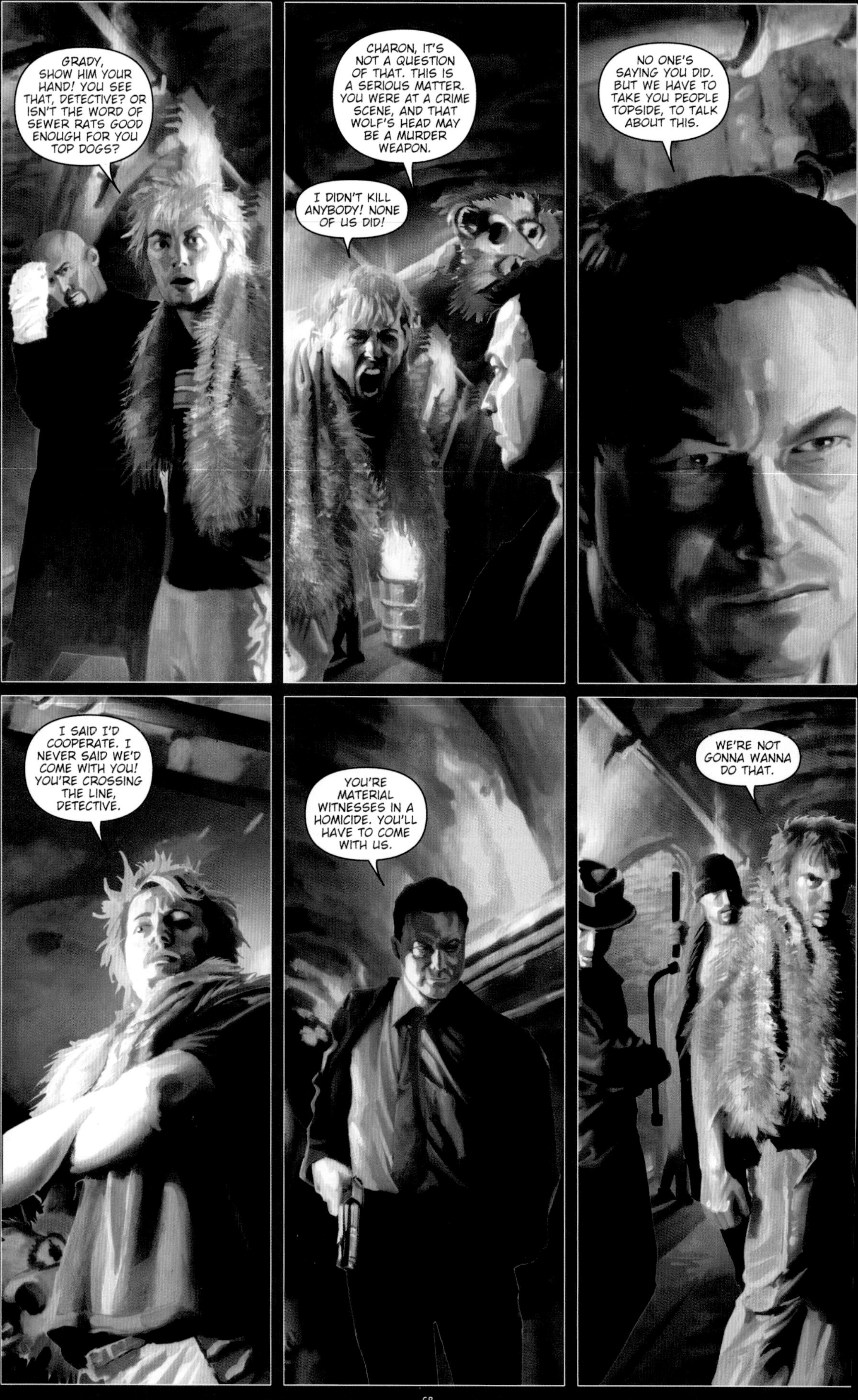
GRADY, SHOW HIM YOUR HAND! YOU SEE THAT, DETECTIVE? OR ISN'T THE WORD OF SEWER RATS GOOD ENOUGH FOR YOU TOP DOGS?
CHARON, IT'S NOT A QUESTION OF THAT. THIS IS A SERIOUS MATTER. YOU WERE AT A CRIME SCENE, AND THAT WOLF'S HEAD MAY BE A MURDER WEAPON.
I DIDN'T KILL ANYBODY! NONE OF US DID!
NO ONE'S SAYING YOU DID. BUT WE HAVE TO TAKE YOU PEOPLE TOPSIDE, TO TALK ABOUT THIS.
I SAID I'D COOPERATE. I NEVER SAID WE'D COME WITH YOU! YOU'RE CROSSING THE LINE, DETECTIVE.
YOU'RE MATERIAL WITNESSES IN A HOMICIDE. YOU'LL HAVE TO COME WITH US.
WE'RE NOT GONNA WANNA DO THAT.

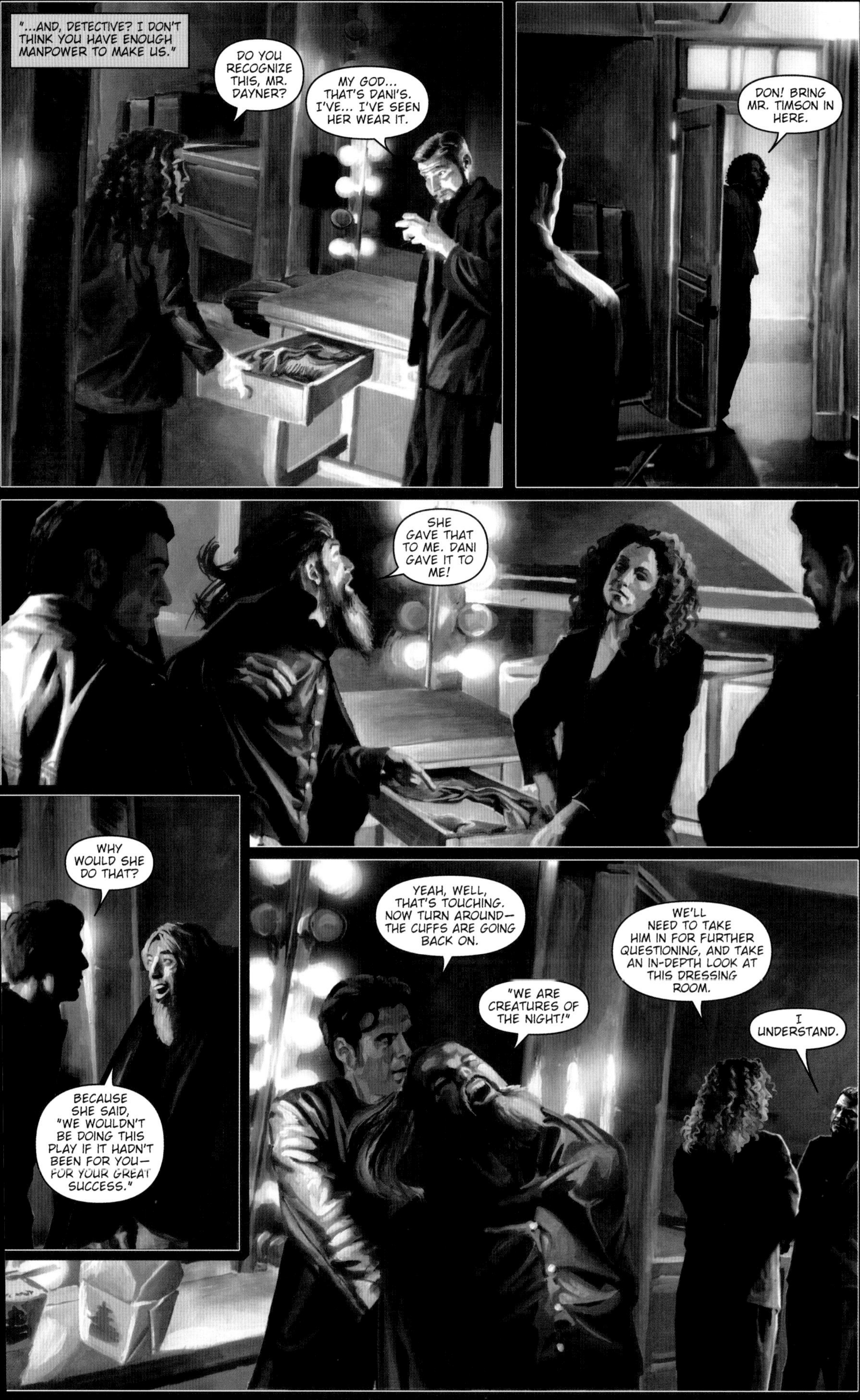
"...AND, DETECTIVE? I DON'T THINK YOU HAVE ENOUGH MANPOWER TO MAKE US."
DO YOU RECOGNIZE THIS, MR. DAYNER?
MY GOD... THAT'S DANI'S. I'VE... I'VE SEEN HER WEAR IT.
DON! BRING MR. TIMSON IN HERE.
SHE GAVE THAT TO ME. DANI GAVE IT TO ME!
WHY WOULD SHE DO THAT?
BECAUSE SHE SAID, "WE WOULDN'T BE DOING THIS PLAY IF IT HADN'T BEEN FOR YOU— FOR YOUR GREAT SUCCESS."
YEAH, WELL, THAT'S TOUCHING. NOW TURN AROUND— THE CUFFS ARE GOING BACK ON.
"WE ARE CREATURES OF THE NIGHT!"
WE'LL NEED TO TAKE HIM IN FOR FURTHER QUESTIONING, AND TAKE AN IN-DEPTH LOOK AT THIS DRESSING ROOM.
I UNDERSTAND.

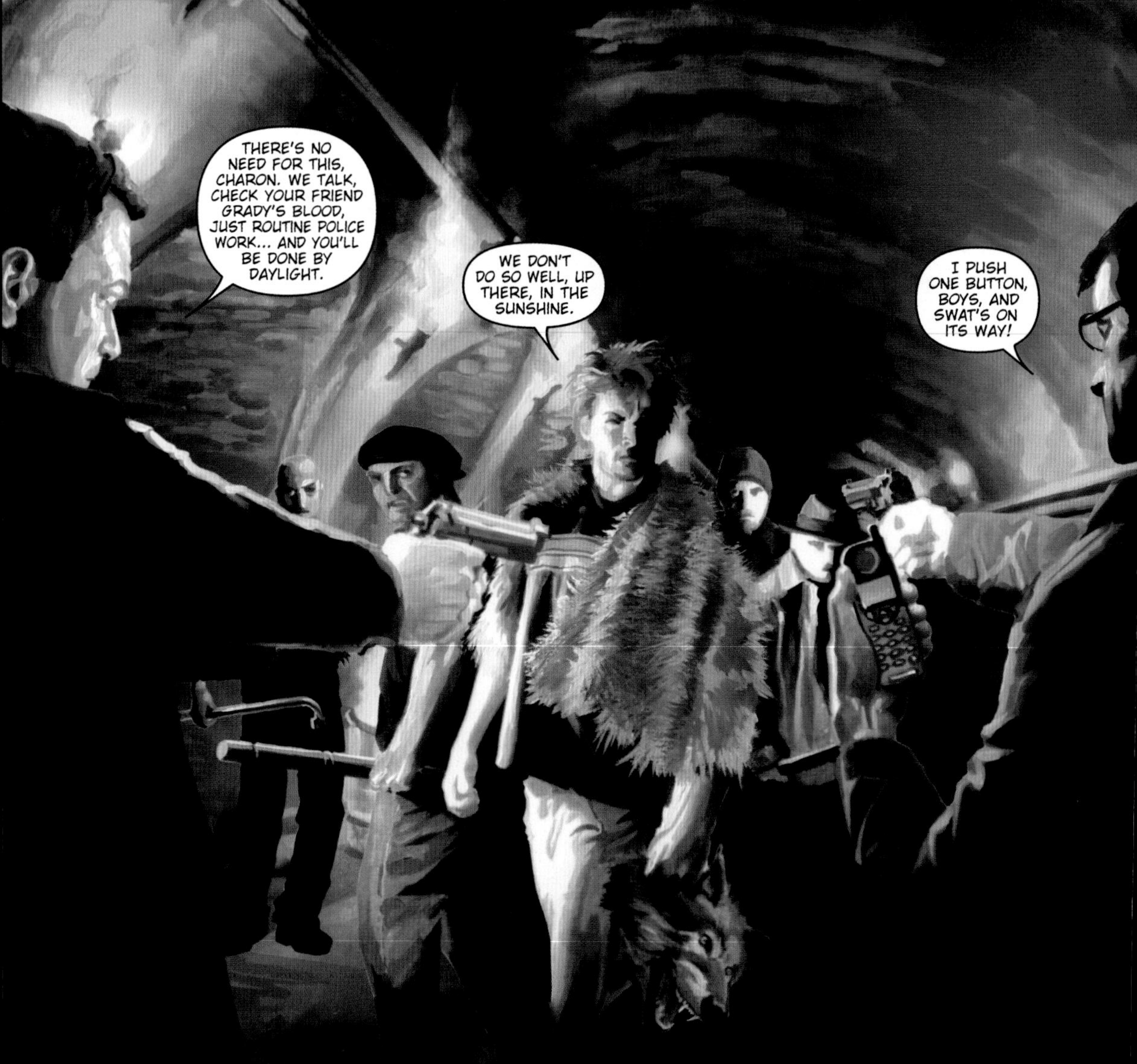
THERE'S NO NEED FOR THIS, CHARON. WE TALK, CHECK YOUR FRIEND GRADY'S BLOOD, JUST ROUTINE POLICE WORK... AND YOU'LL BE DONE BY DAYLIGHT.
WE DON'T DO SO WELL, UP THERE, IN THE SUNSHINE.
I PUSH ONE BUTTON, BOYS, AND SWAT'S ON ITS WAY!

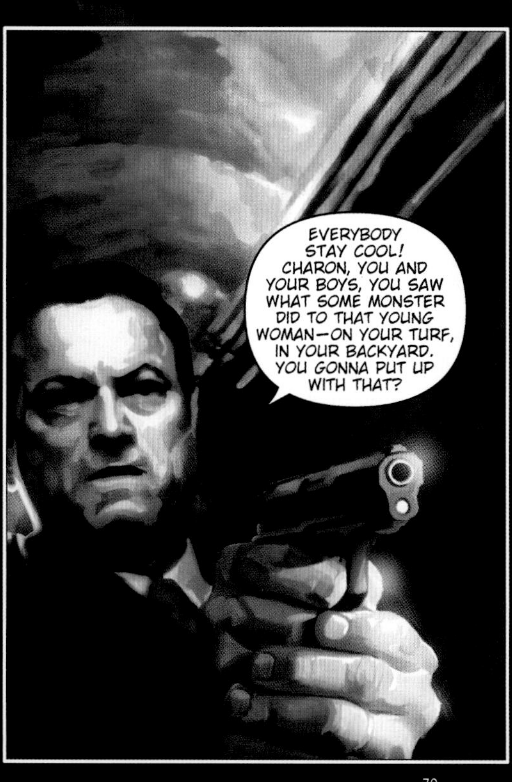
EVERYBODY STAY COOL! CHARON, YOU AND YOUR BOYS, YOU SAW WHAT SOME MONSTER DID TO THAT YOUNG WOMAN—ON YOUR TURF, IN YOUR BACKYARD. YOU GONNA PUT UP WITH THAT?

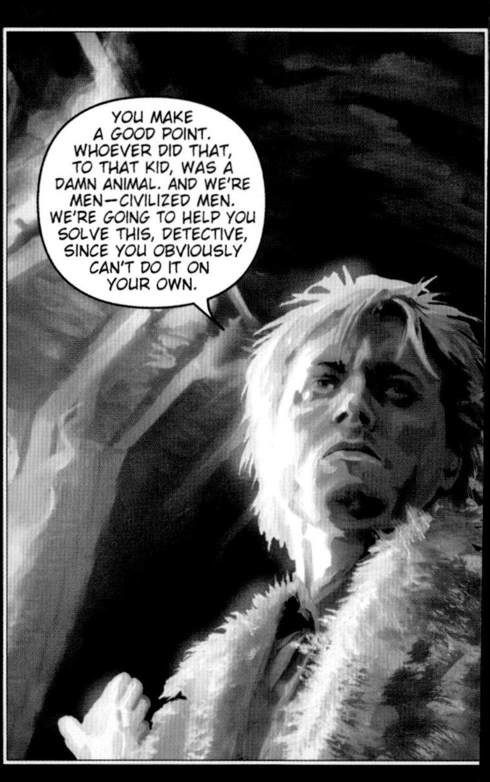
YOU MAKE A GOOD POINT. WHOEVER DID THAT, TO THAT KID, WAS A DAMN ANIMAL. AND WE'RE MEN—CIVILIZED MEN. WE'RE GOING TO HELP YOU SOLVE THIS, DETECTIVE, SINCE YOU OBVIOUSLY CAN'T DO IT ON YOUR OWN.

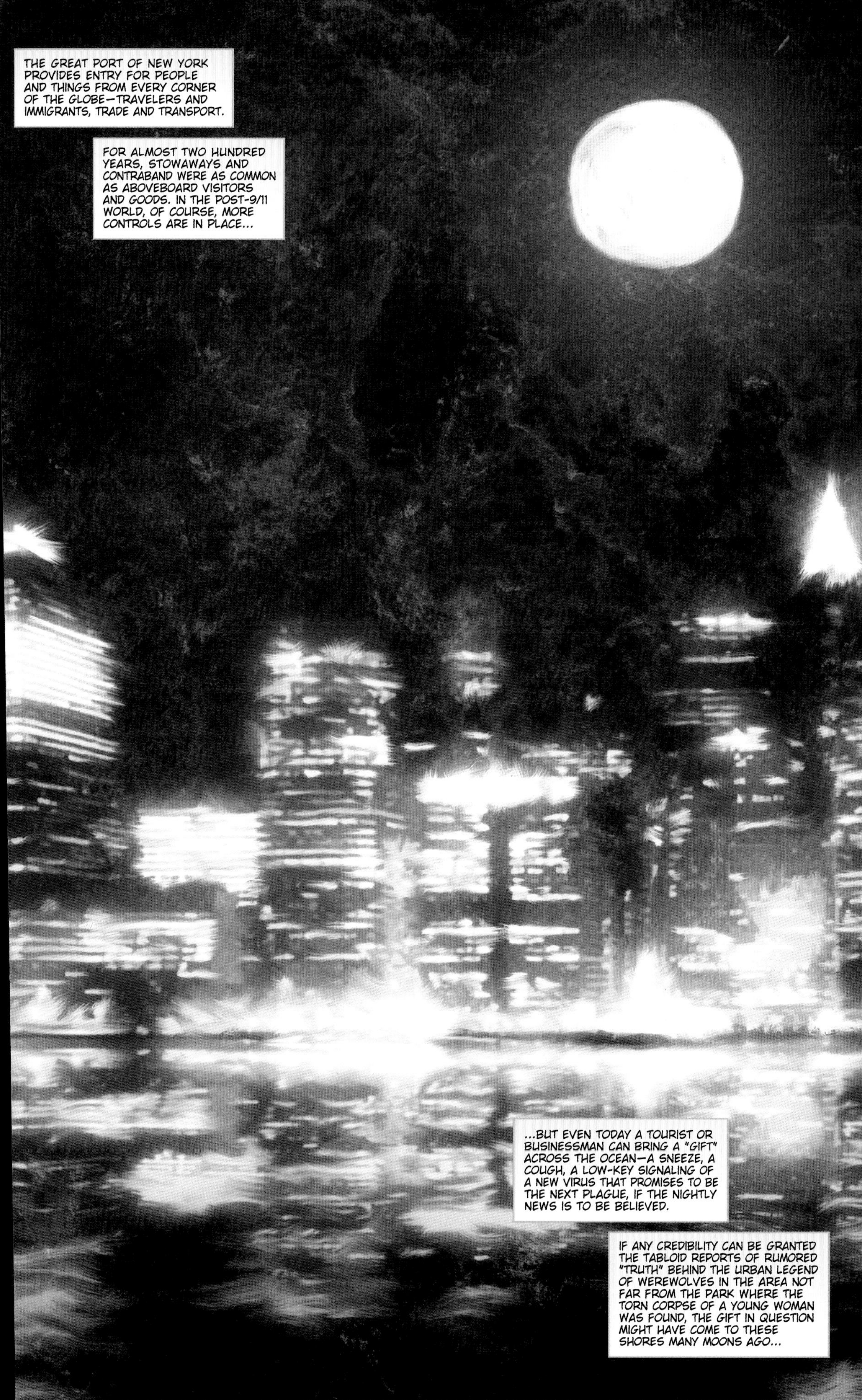
THE GREAT PORT OF NEW YORK PROVIDES ENTRY FOR PEOPLE AND THINGS FROM EVERY CORNER OF THE GLOBE—TRAVELERS AND IMMIGRANTS, TRADE AND TRANSPORT.
FOR ALMOST TWO HUNDRED YEARS, STOWAWAYS AND CONTRABAND WERE AS COMMON AS ABOVEBOARD VISITORS AND GOODS. IN THE POST-9/11 WORLD, OF COURSE, MORE CONTROLS ARE IN PLACE...
...BUT EVEN TODAY A TOURIST OR BUSINESSMAN CAN BRING A "GIFT" ACROSS THE OCEAN—A SNEEZE, A COUGH, A LOW-KEY SIGNALING OF A NEW VIRUS THAT PROMISES TO BE THE NEXT PLAGUE, IF THE NIGHTLY NEWS IS TO BE BELIEVED.
IF ANY CREDIBILITY CAN BE GRANTED THE TABLOID REPORTS OF RUMORED "TRUTH" BEHIND THE URBAN LEGEND OF WEREWOLVES IN THE AREA NOT FAR FROM THE PARK WHERE THE TORN CORPSE OF A YOUNG WOMAN WAS FOUND, THE GIFT IN QUESTION MIGHT HAVE COME TO THESE SHORES MANY MOONS AGO...

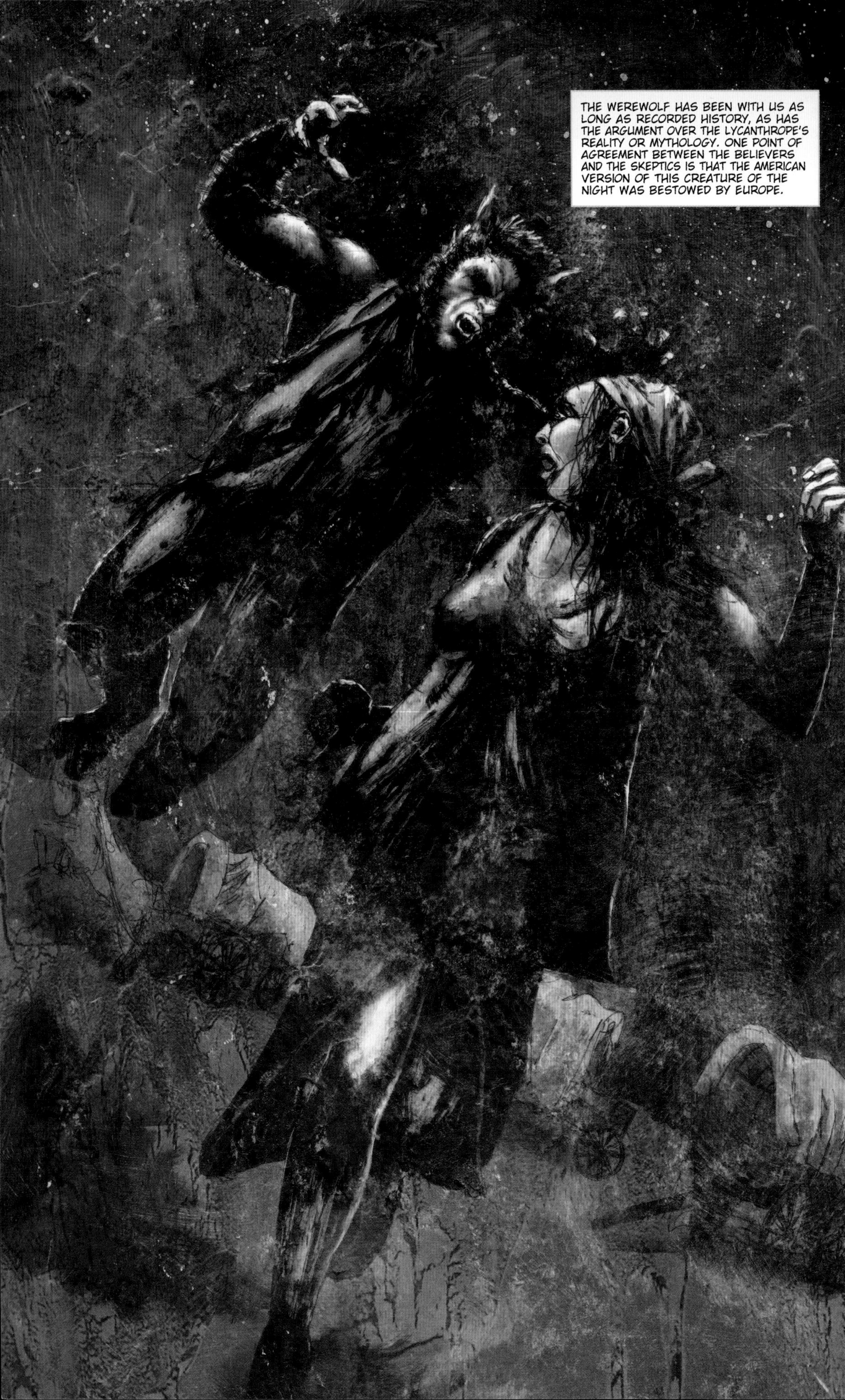
THE WEREWOLF HAS BEEN WITH US AS LONG AS RECORDED HISTORY, AS HAS THE ARGUMENT OVER THE LYCANTHROPE'S REALITY OR MYTHOLOGY. ONE POINT OF AGREEMENT BETWEEN THE BELIEVERS AND THE SKEPTICS IS THAT THE AMERICAN VERSION OF THIS CREATURE OF THE NIGHT WAS BESTOWED BY EUROPE.

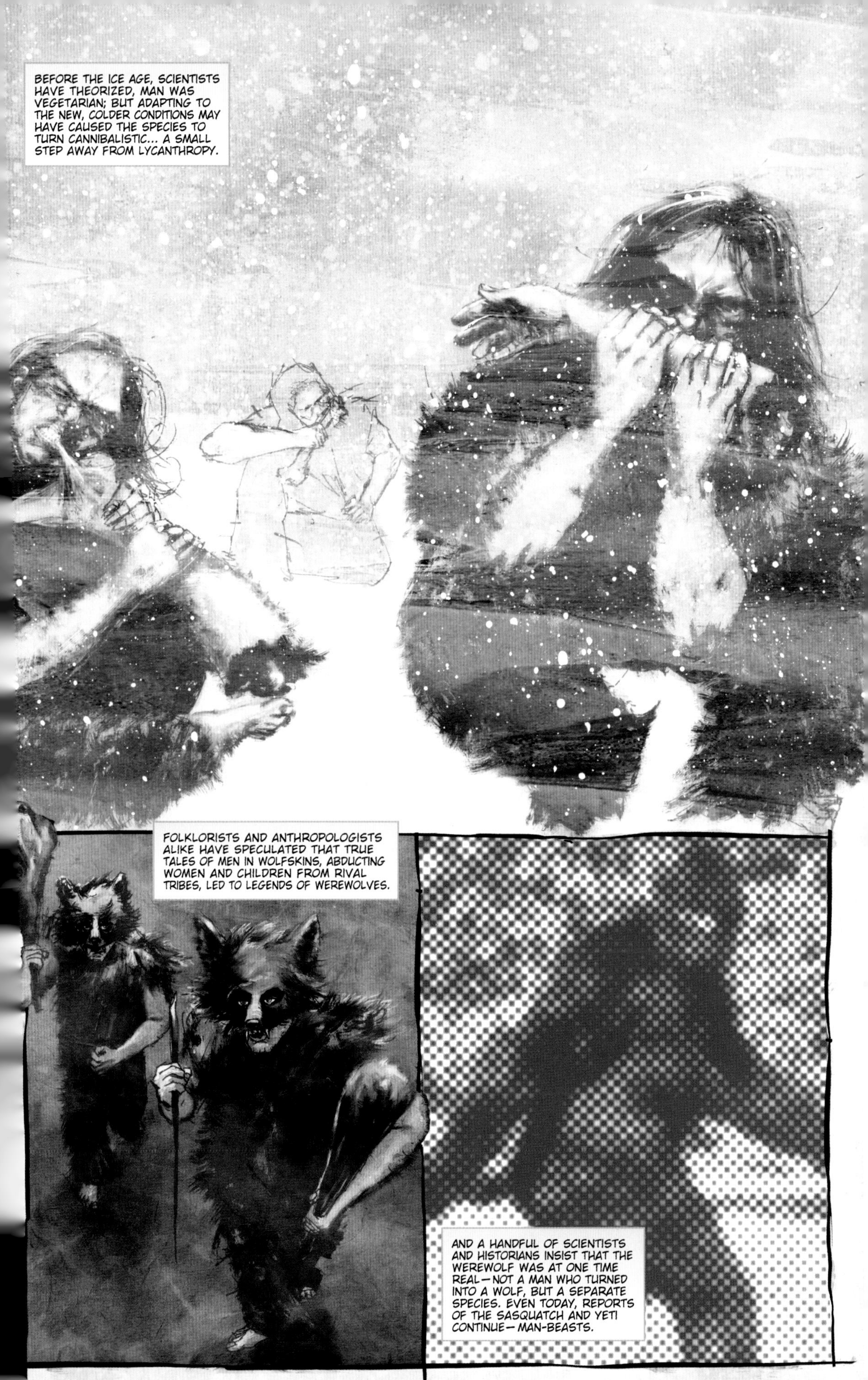
BEFORE THE ICE AGE, SCIENTISTS HAVE THEORIZED, MAN WAS VEGETARIAN; BUT ADAPTING TO THE NEW, COLDER CONDITIONS MAY HAVE CAUSED THE SPECIES TO TURN CANNIBALISTIC... A SMALL STEP AWAY FROM LYCANTHROPY.
FOLKLORISTS AND ANTHROPOLOGISTS ALIKE HAVE SPECULATED THAT TRUE TALES OF MEN IN WOLFSKINS, ABDUCTING WOMEN AND CHILDREN FROM RIVAL TRIBES, LED TO LEGENDS OF WEREWOLVES.
AND A HANDFUL OF SCIENTISTS AND HISTORIANS INSIST THAT THE WEREWOLF WAS AT ONE TIME REAL—NOT A MAN WHO TURNED INTO A WOLF, BUT A SEPARATE SPECIES. EVEN TODAY, REPORTS OF THE SASQUATCH AND YETI CONTINUE—MAN-BEASTS.

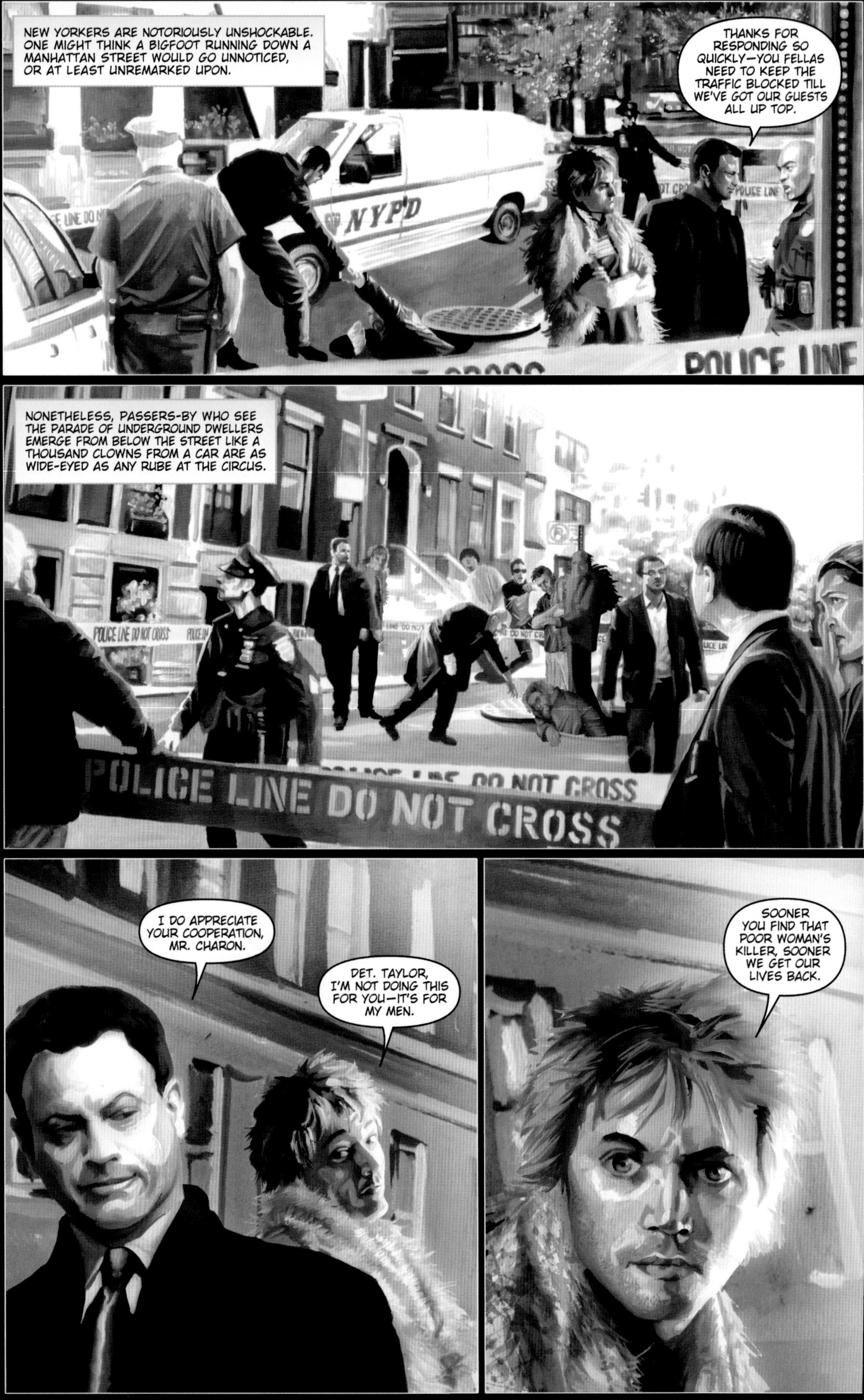
NEW YORKERS ARE NOTORIOUSLY UNSHOCKABLE. ONE MIGHT THINK A BIGFOOT RUNNING DOWN A MANHATTAN STREET WOULD GO UNNOTICED, OR AT LEAST UNREMARKED UPON.
THANKS FOR RESPONDING SO QUICKLY—YOU FELLAS NEED TO KEEP THE TRAFFIC BLOCKED TILL WE'VE GOT OUR GUESTS ALL UP TOP.
NYPD
POLICE LINE
NONETHELESS, PASSERS-BY WHO SEE THE PARADE OF UNDERGROUND DWELLERS EMERGE FROM BELOW THE STREET LIKE A THOUSAND CLOWNS FROM A CAR ARE AS WIDE-EYED AS ANY RUBE AT THE CIRCUS.
POLICE LINE DO NOT CROSS
POLICE LINE DO NOT CROSS
I DO APPRECIATE YOUR COOPERATION, MR. CHARON.
DET. TAYLOR, I'M NOT DOING THIS FOR YOU—IT'S FOR MY MEN.
SOONER YOU FIND THAT POOR WOMAN'S KILLER, SOONER WE GET OUR LIVES BACK.

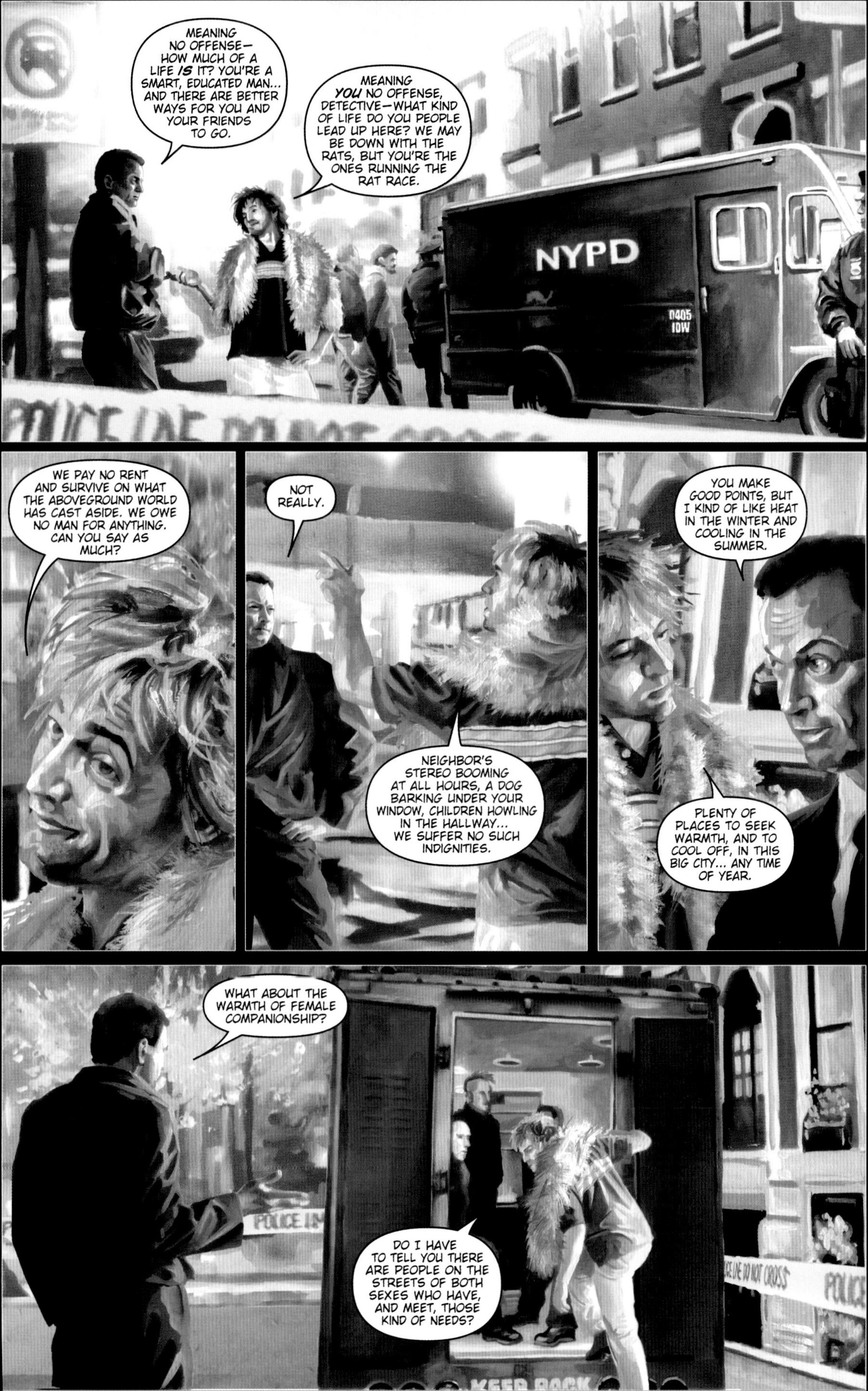
MEANING NO OFFENSE— HOW MUCH OF A LIFE *IS* IT? YOU'RE A SMART, EDUCATED MAN... AND THERE ARE BETTER WAYS FOR YOU AND YOUR FRIENDS TO GO.
MEANING *YOU* NO OFFENSE, DETECTIVE—WHAT KIND OF LIFE DO YOU PEOPLE LEAD UP HERE? WE MAY BE DOWN WITH THE RATS, BUT YOU'RE THE ONES RUNNING THE RAT RACE.
NYPD
0405 IDW
WE PAY NO RENT AND SURVIVE ON WHAT THE ABOVEGROUND WORLD HAS CAST ASIDE. WE OWE NO MAN FOR ANYTHING. CAN YOU SAY AS MUCH?
NOT REALLY.
NEIGHBOR'S STEREO BOOMING AT ALL HOURS, A DOG BARKING UNDER YOUR WINDOW, CHILDREN HOWLING IN THE HALLWAY... WE SUFFER NO SUCH INDIGNITIES.
YOU MAKE GOOD POINTS, BUT I KIND OF LIKE HEAT IN THE WINTER AND COOLING IN THE SUMMER.
PLENTY OF PLACES TO SEEK WARMTH, AND TO COOL OFF, IN THIS BIG CITY... ANY TIME OF YEAR.
WHAT ABOUT THE WARMTH OF FEMALE COMPANIONSHIP?
DO I HAVE TO TELL YOU THERE ARE PEOPLE ON THE STREETS OF BOTH SEXES WHO HAVE, AND MEET, THOSE KIND OF NEEDS?

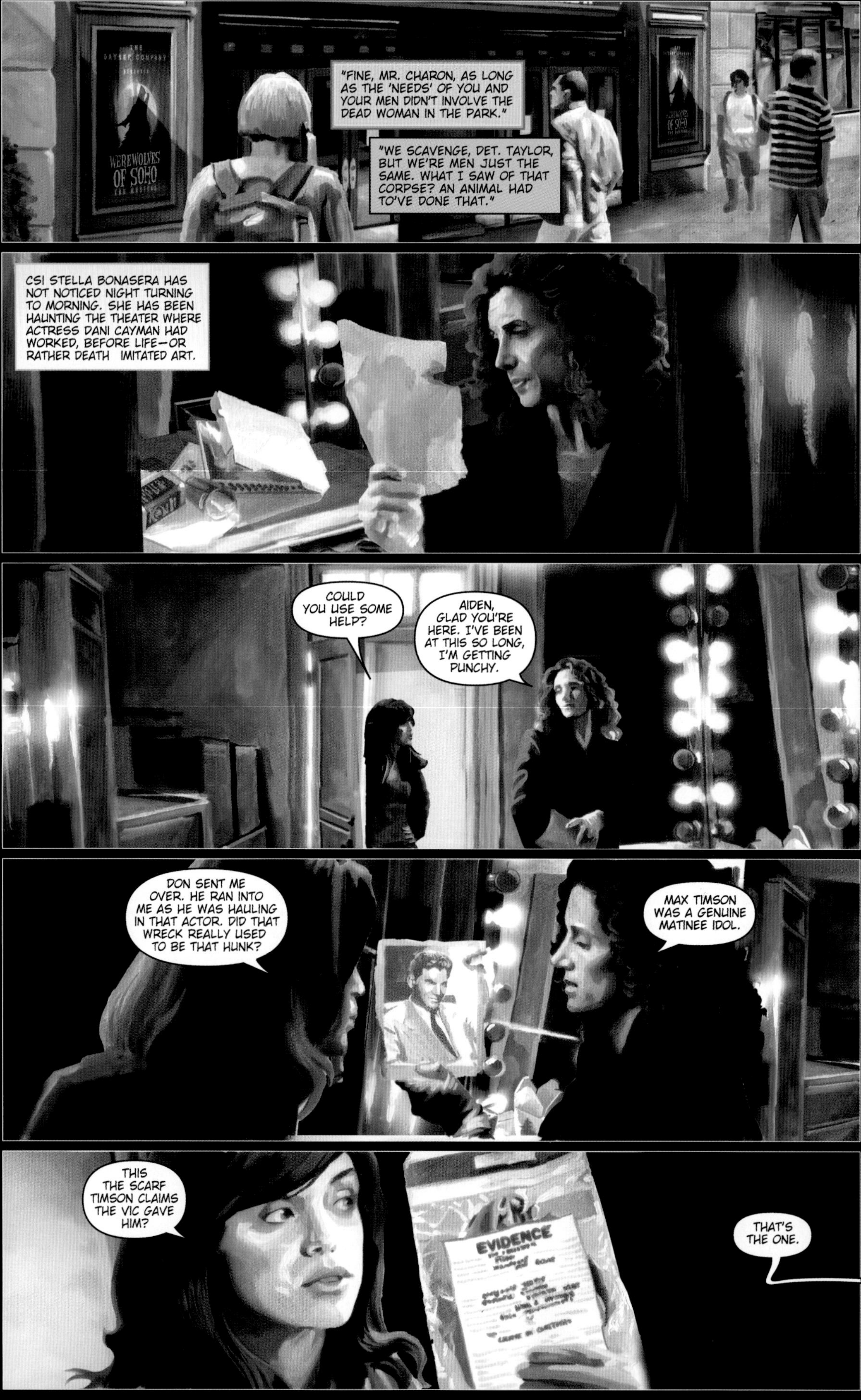
WEREWOLVES OF SOHO
"FINE, MR. CHARON, AS LONG AS THE 'NEEDS' OF YOU AND YOUR MEN DIDN'T INVOLVE THE DEAD WOMAN IN THE PARK."
"WE SCAVENGE, DET. TAYLOR, BUT WE'RE MEN JUST THE SAME. WHAT I SAW OF THAT CORPSE? AN ANIMAL HAD TO'VE DONE THAT."
CSI STELLA BONASERA HAS NOT NOTICED NIGHT TURNING TO MORNING. SHE HAS BEEN HAUNTING THE THEATER WHERE ACTRESS DANI CAYMAN HAD WORKED, BEFORE LIFE—OR RATHER DEATH IMITATED ART.
COULD YOU USE SOME HELP?
AIDEN, GLAD YOU'RE HERE. I'VE BEEN AT THIS SO LONG, I'M GETTING PUNCHY.
DON SENT ME OVER. HE RAN INTO ME AS HE WAS HAULING IN THAT ACTOR. DID THAT WRECK REALLY USED TO BE THAT HUNK?
MAX TIMSON WAS A GENUINE MATINEE IDOL.
THIS THE SCARF TIMSON CLAIMS THE VIC GAVE HIM?
EVIDENCE
THAT'S THE ONE.

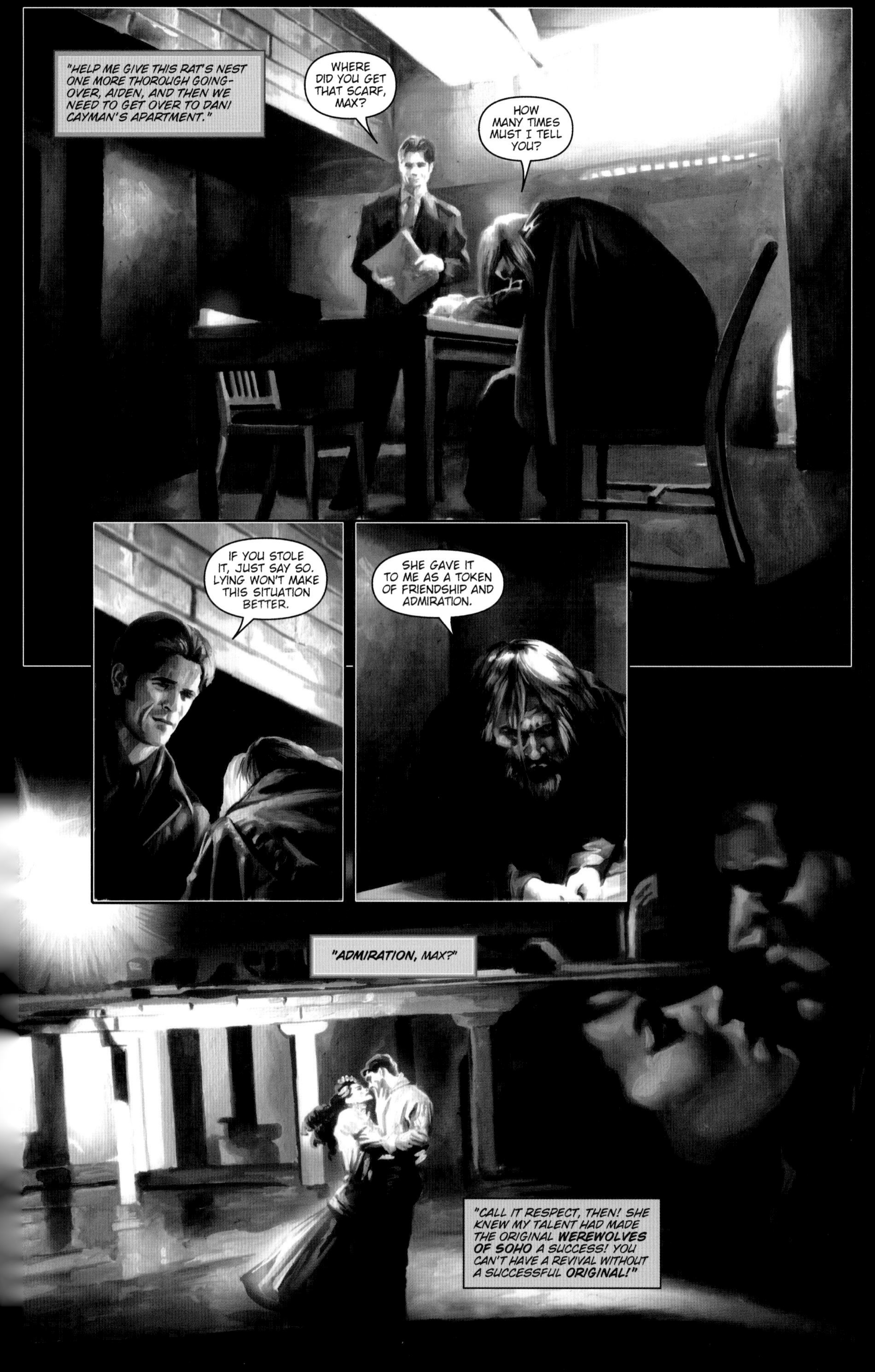
"HELP ME GIVE THIS RAT'S NEST ONE MORE THOROUGH GOING-OVER, AIDEN, AND THEN WE NEED TO GET OVER TO DANI CAYMAN'S APARTMENT."
WHERE DID YOU GET THAT SCARF, MAX?
HOW MANY TIMES MUST I TELL YOU?
IF YOU STOLE IT, JUST SAY SO. LYING WON'T MAKE THIS SITUATION BETTER.
SHE GAVE IT TO ME AS A TOKEN OF FRIENDSHIP AND ADMIRATION.
"ADMIRATION, MAX?"
"CALL IT RESPECT, THEN! SHE KNEW MY TALENT HAD MADE THE ORIGINAL WEREWOLVES OF SOHO A SUCCESS! YOU CAN'T HAVE A REVIVAL WITHOUT A SUCCESSFUL ORIGINAL!"

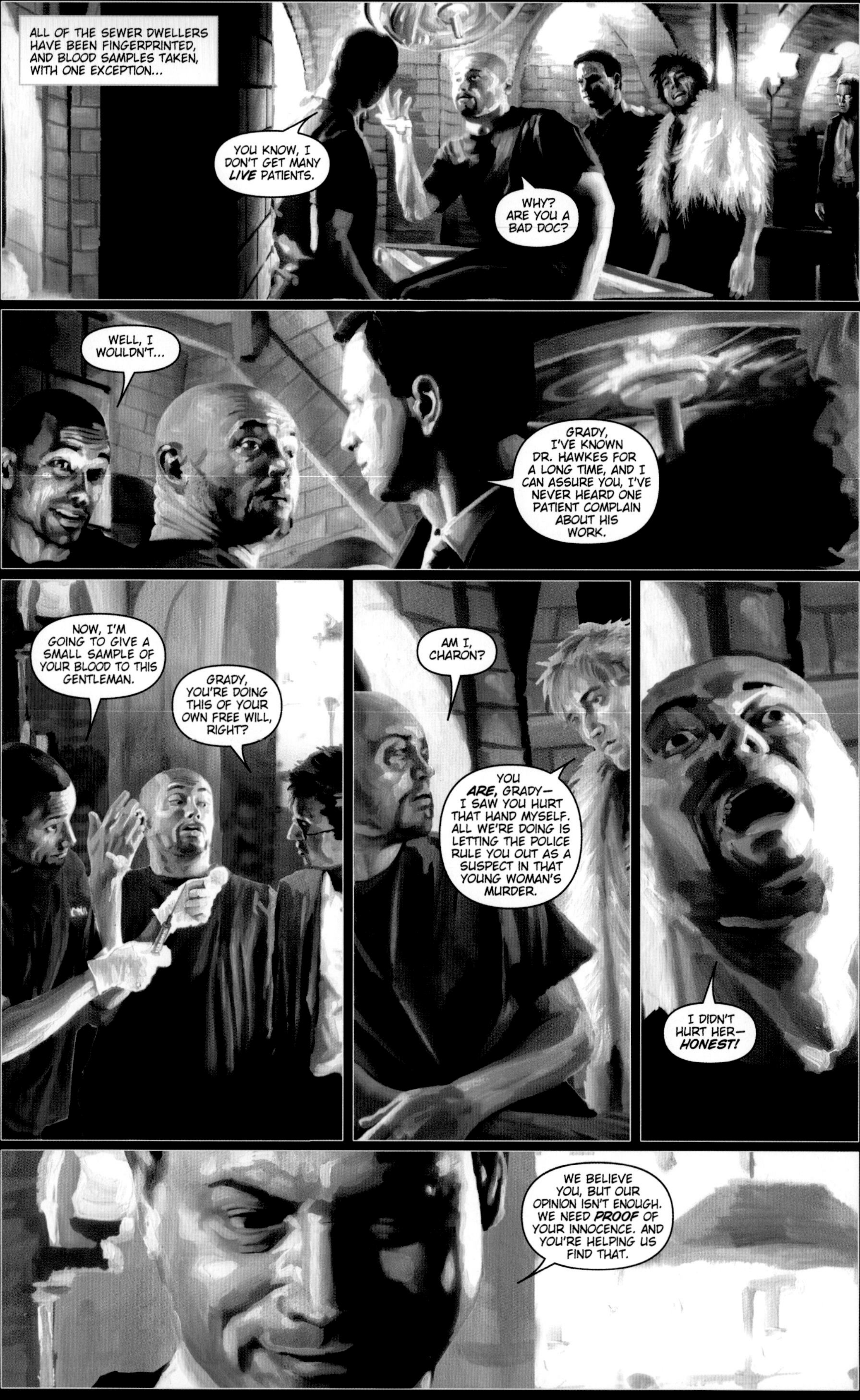
ALL OF THE SEWER DWELLERS HAVE BEEN FINGERPRINTED, AND BLOOD SAMPLES TAKEN, WITH ONE EXCEPTION...
YOU KNOW, I DON'T GET MANY *LIVE* PATIENTS.
WHY? ARE YOU A BAD DOC?
WELL, I WOULDN'T...
GRADY, I'VE KNOWN DR. HAWKES FOR A LONG TIME, AND I CAN ASSURE YOU, I'VE NEVER HEARD ONE PATIENT COMPLAIN ABOUT HIS WORK.
NOW, I'M GOING TO GIVE A SMALL SAMPLE OF YOUR BLOOD TO THIS GENTLEMAN.
GRADY, YOU'RE DOING THIS OF YOUR OWN FREE WILL, RIGHT?
AM I, CHARON?
YOU *ARE,* GRADY— I SAW YOU HURT THAT HAND MYSELF. ALL WE'RE DOING IS LETTING THE POLICE RULE YOU OUT AS A SUSPECT IN THAT YOUNG WOMAN'S MURDER.
I DIDN'T HURT HER— *HONEST!*
WE BELIEVE YOU, BUT OUR OPINION ISN'T ENOUGH. WE NEED *PROOF* OF YOUR INNOCENCE. AND YOU'RE HELPING US FIND THAT.

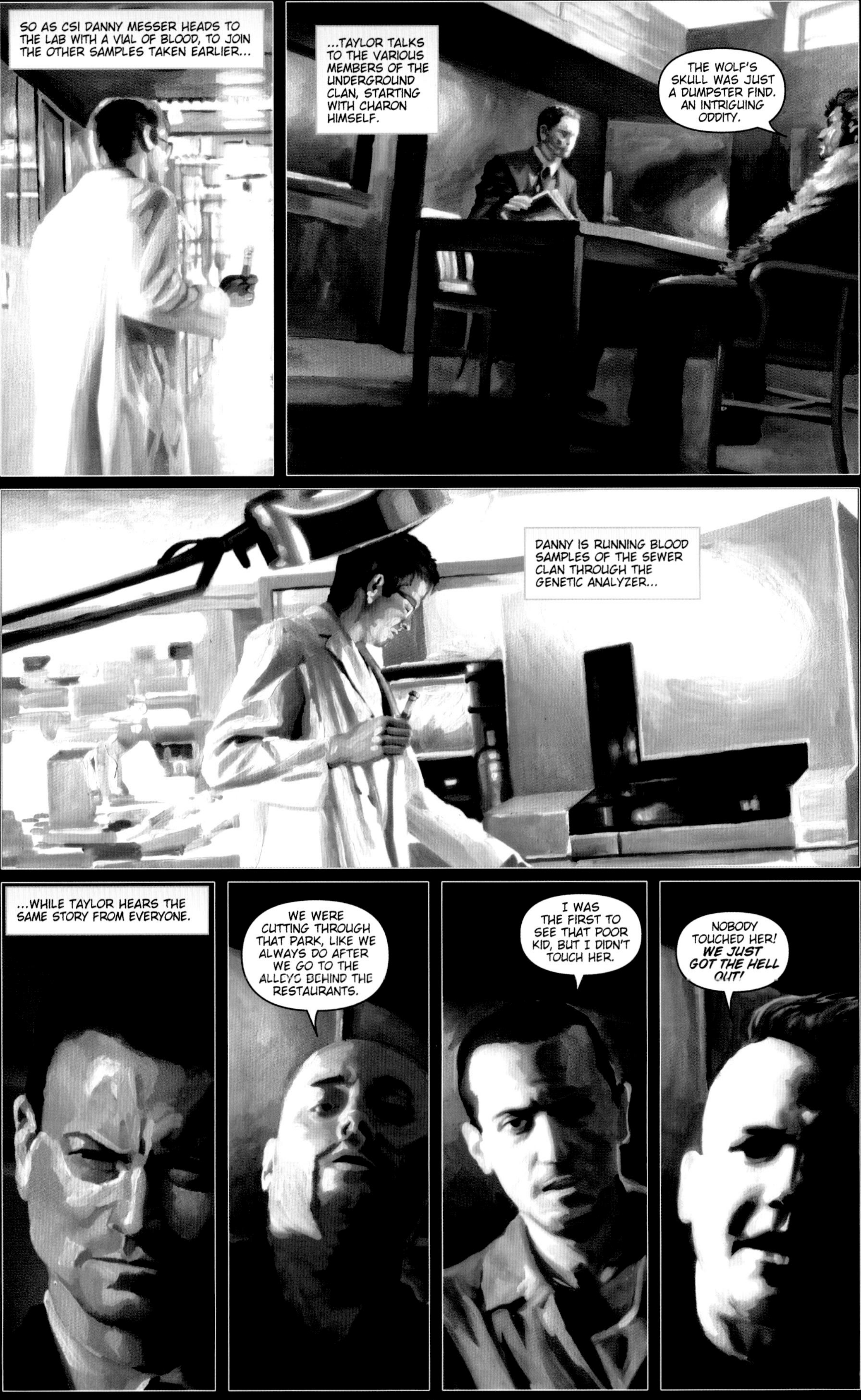
SO AS CSI DANNY MESSER HEADS TO THE LAB WITH A VIAL OF BLOOD, TO JOIN THE OTHER SAMPLES TAKEN EARLIER...
...TAYLOR TALKS TO THE VARIOUS MEMBERS OF THE UNDERGROUND CLAN, STARTING WITH CHARON HIMSELF.
THE WOLF'S SKULL WAS JUST A DUMPSTER FIND. AN INTRIGUING ODDITY.
DANNY IS RUNNING BLOOD SAMPLES OF THE SEWER CLAN THROUGH THE GENETIC ANALYZER...
...WHILE TAYLOR HEARS THE SAME STORY FROM EVERYONE.
WE WERE CUTTING THROUGH THAT PARK, LIKE WE ALWAYS DO AFTER WE GO TO THE ALLEYS BEHIND THE RESTAURANTS.
I WAS THE FIRST TO SEE THAT POOR KID, BUT I DIDN'T TOUCH HER.
NOBODY TOUCHED HER! WE JUST GOT THE HELL OUT!

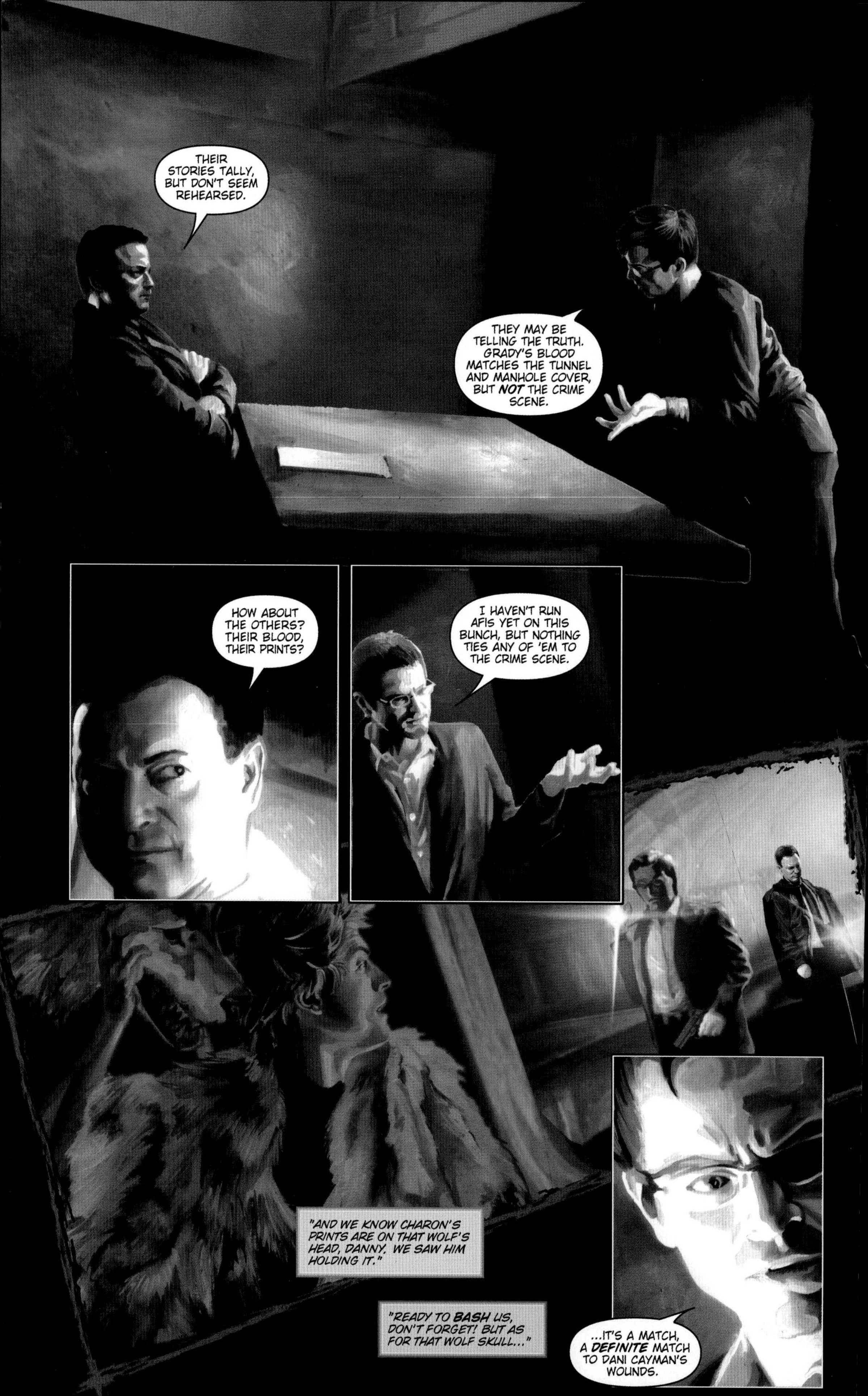
THEIR STORIES TALLY, BUT DON'T SEEM REHEARSED.
THEY MAY BE TELLING THE TRUTH. GRADY'S BLOOD MATCHES THE TUNNEL AND MANHOLE COVER, BUT NOT THE CRIME SCENE.
HOW ABOUT THE OTHERS? THEIR BLOOD, THEIR PRINTS?
I HAVEN'T RUN AFIS YET ON THIS BUNCH, BUT NOTHING TIES ANY OF 'EM TO THE CRIME SCENE.
"AND WE KNOW CHARON'S PRINTS ARE ON THAT WOLF'S HEAD, DANNY. WE SAW HIM HOLDING IT."
"READY TO BASH US, DON'T FORGET! BUT AS FOR THAT WOLF SKULL..."
...IT'S A MATCH, A DEFINITE MATCH TO DANI CAYMAN'S WOUNDS.

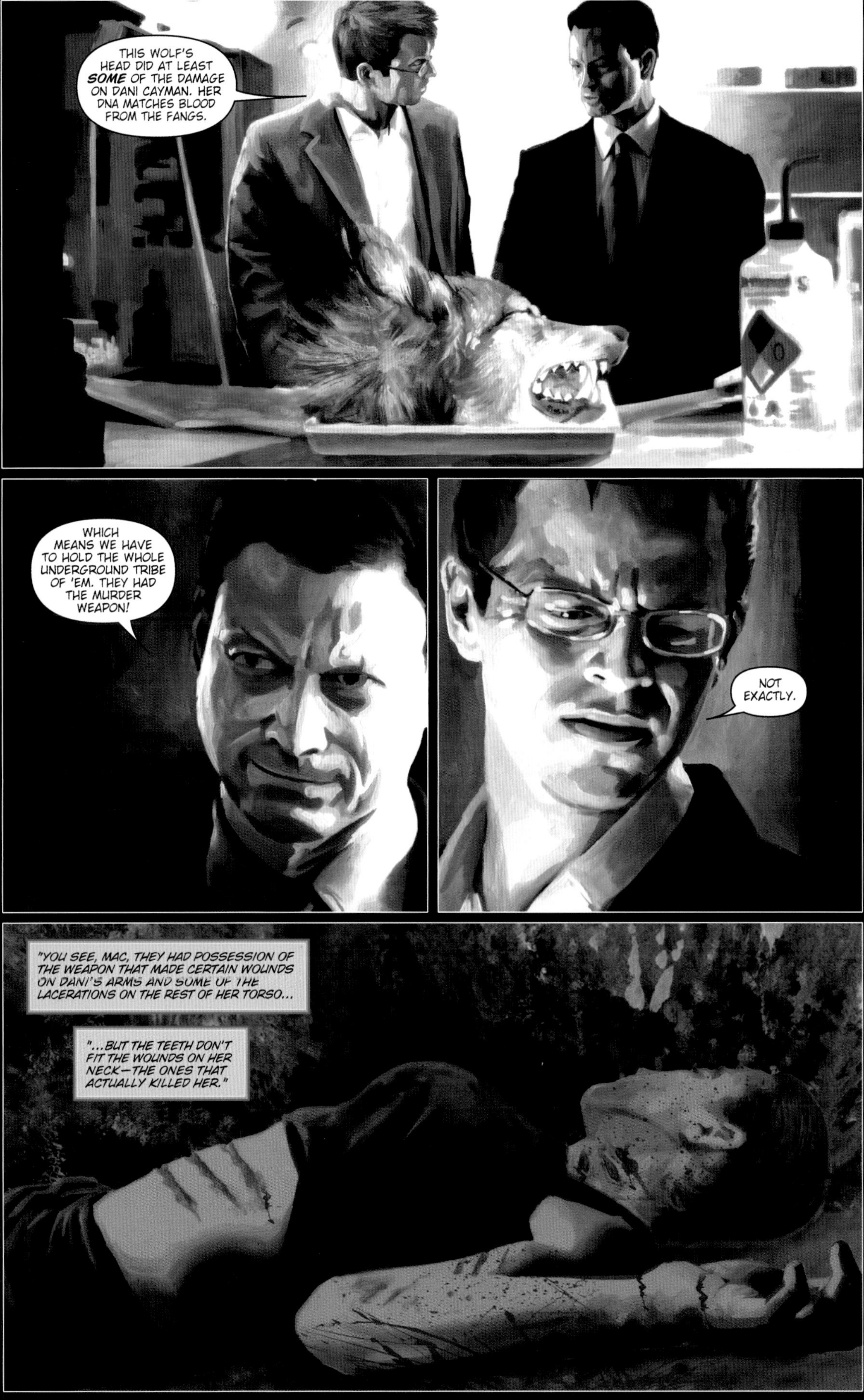
THIS WOLF'S HEAD DID AT LEAST SOME OF THE DAMAGE ON DANI CAYMAN. HER DNA MATCHES BLOOD FROM THE FANGS.
WHICH MEANS WE HAVE TO HOLD THE WHOLE UNDERGROUND TRIBE OF 'EM. THEY HAD THE MURDER WEAPON!
NOT EXACTLY.
"YOU SEE, MAC, THEY HAD POSSESSION OF THE WEAPON THAT MADE CERTAIN WOUNDS ON DANI'S ARMS AND SOME OF THE LACERATIONS ON THE REST OF HER TORSO...
"...BUT THE TEETH DON'T FIT THE WOUNDS ON HER NECK—THE ONES THAT ACTUALLY KILLED HER."

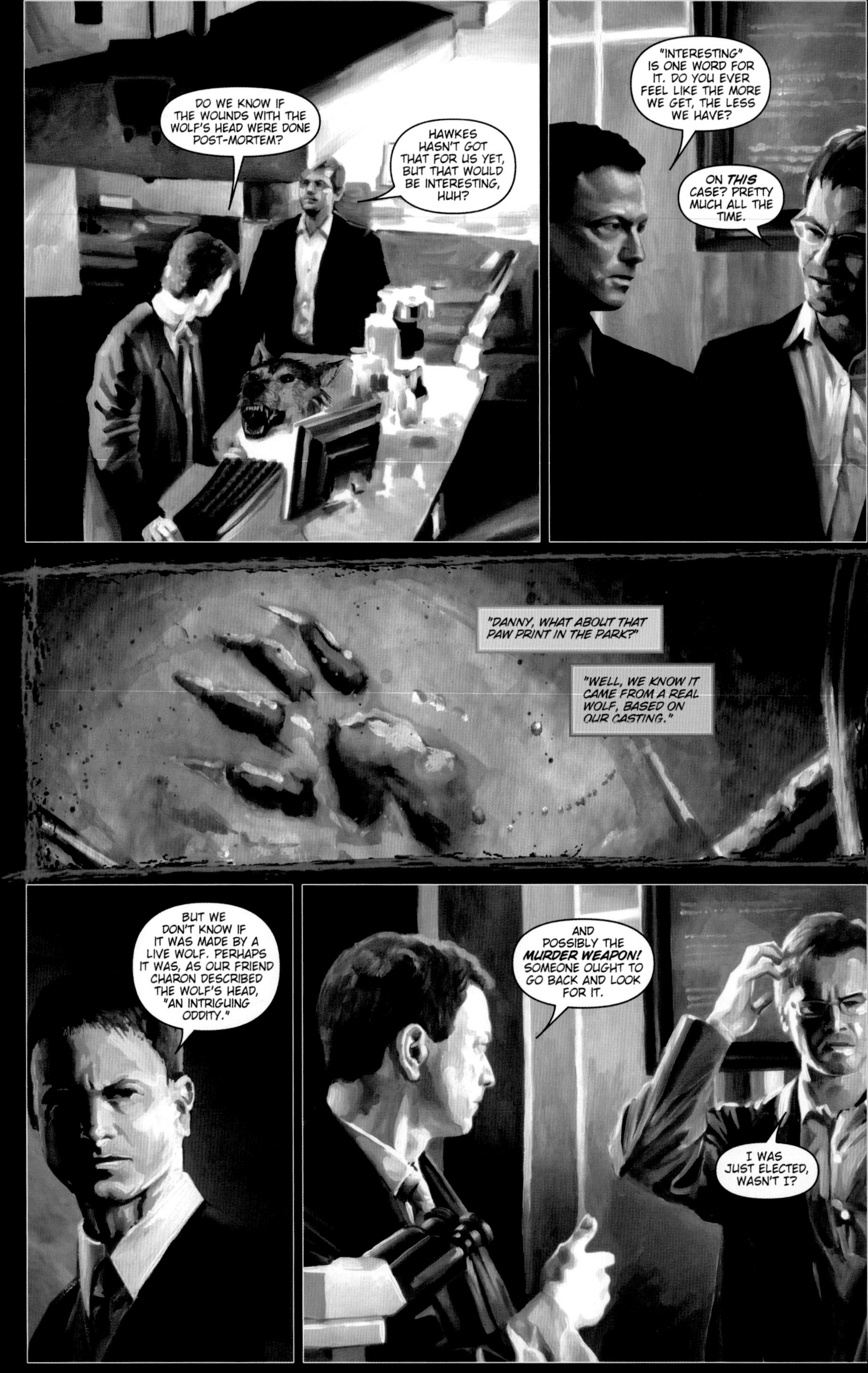
DO WE KNOW IF THE WOUNDS WITH THE WOLF'S HEAD WERE DONE POST-MORTEM?
HAWKES HASN'T GOT THAT FOR US YET, BUT THAT WOULD BE INTERESTING, HUH?
"INTERESTING" IS ONE WORD FOR IT. DO YOU EVER FEEL LIKE THE MORE WE GET, THE LESS WE HAVE?
ON *THIS* CASE? PRETTY MUCH ALL THE TIME.
"DANNY, WHAT ABOUT THAT PAW PRINT IN THE PARK?"
"WELL, WE KNOW IT CAME FROM A REAL WOLF, BASED ON OUR CASTING."
BUT WE DON'T KNOW IF IT WAS MADE BY A LIVE WOLF. PERHAPS IT WAS, AS OUR FRIEND CHARON DESCRIBED THE WOLF'S HEAD, "AN INTRIGUING ODDITY."
AND POSSIBLY THE **MURDER WEAPON!** SOMEONE OUGHT TO GO BACK AND LOOK FOR IT.
I WAS JUST ELECTED, WASN'T I?

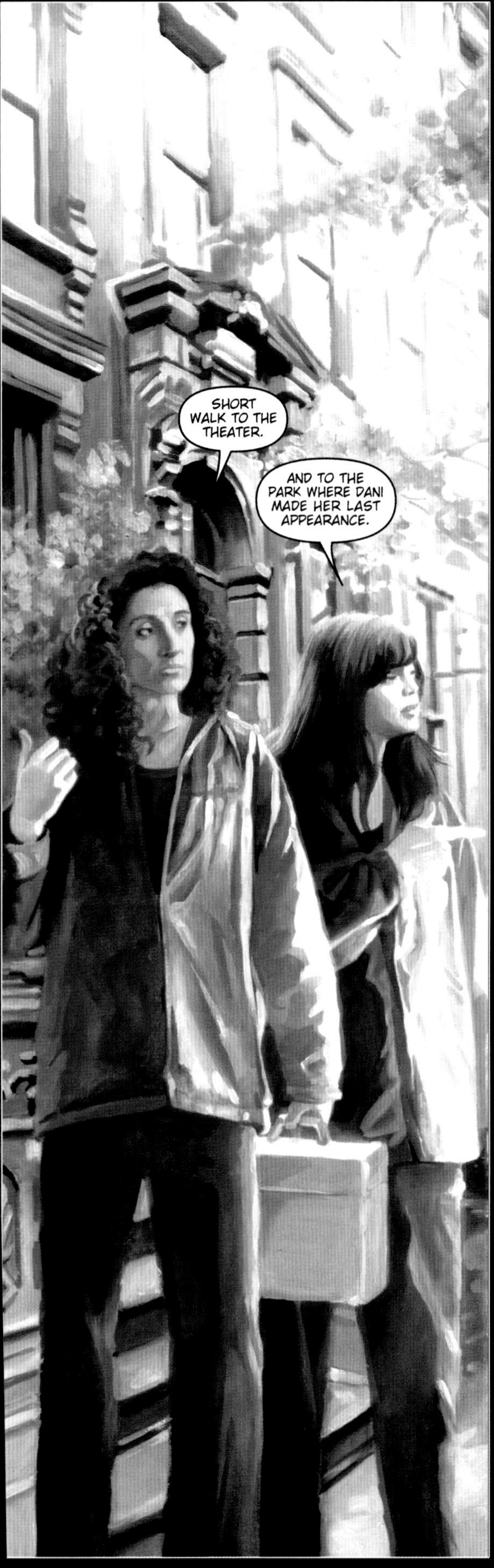
SHORT WALK TO THE THEATER.
AND TO THE PARK WHERE DANI MADE HER LAST APPEARANCE.

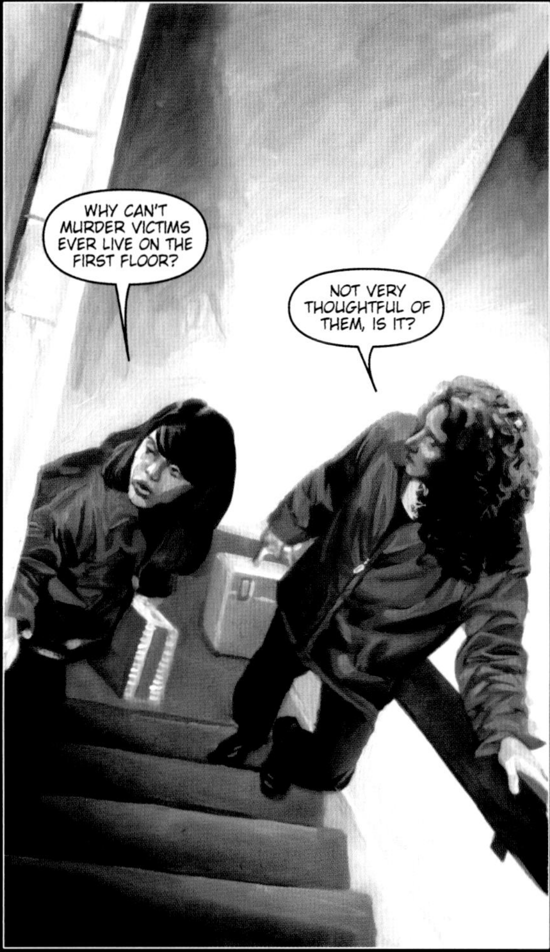
WHY CAN'T MURDER VICTIMS EVER LIVE ON THE FIRST FLOOR?
NOT VERY THOUGHTFUL OF THEM, IS IT?

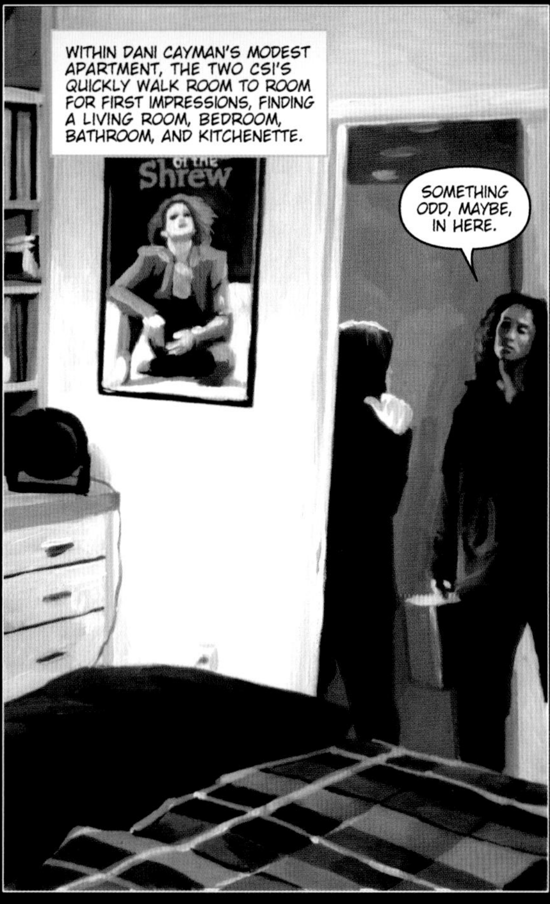
WITHIN DANI CAYMAN'S MODEST APARTMENT, THE TWO CSI'S QUICKLY WALK ROOM TO ROOM FOR FIRST IMPRESSIONS, FINDING A LIVING ROOM, BEDROOM, BATHROOM, AND KITCHENETTE.
Shrew
SOMETHING ODD, MAYBE, IN HERE.

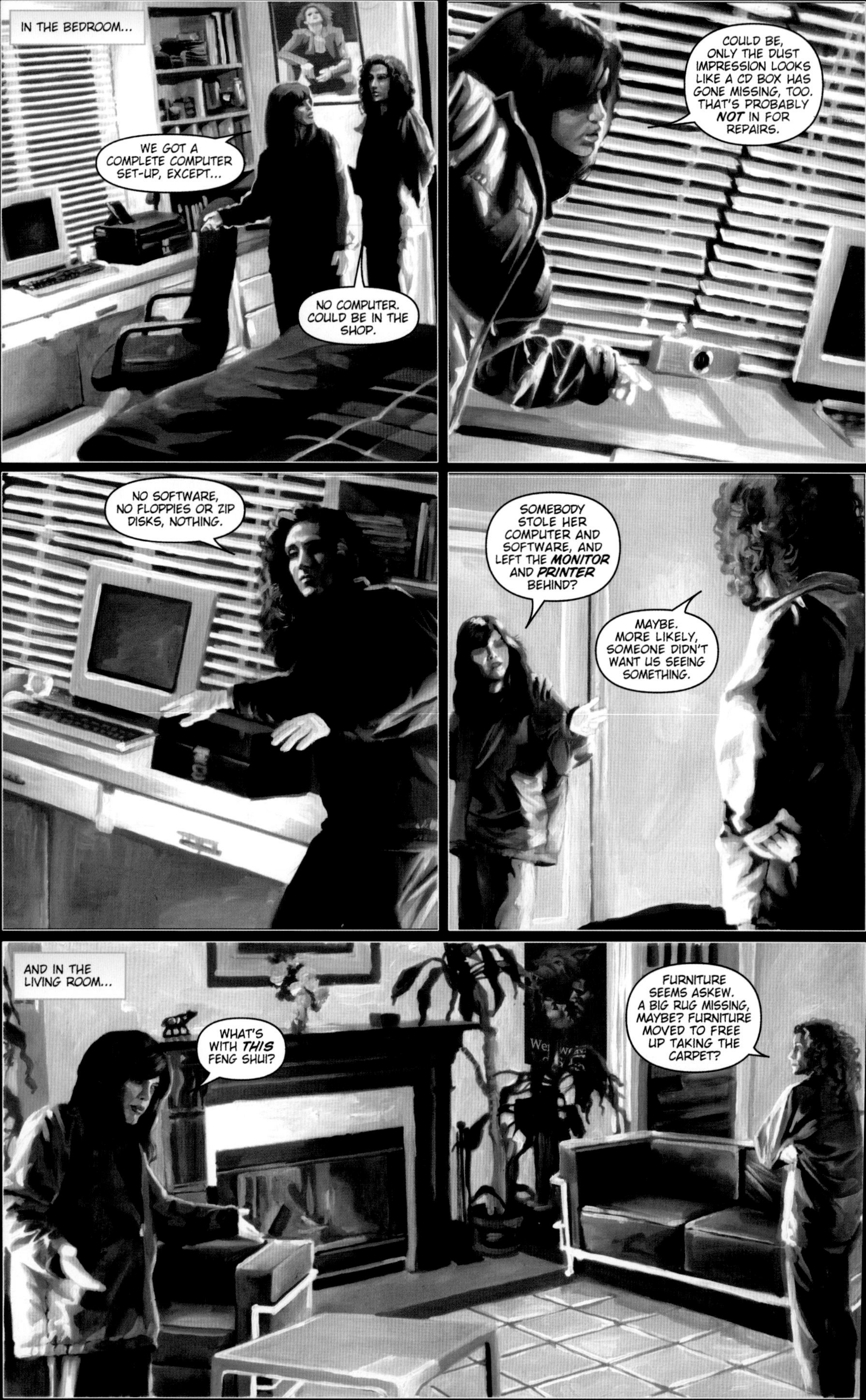
IN THE BEDROOM...
WE GOT A COMPLETE COMPUTER SET-UP, EXCEPT...
NO COMPUTER. COULD BE IN THE SHOP.
COULD BE, ONLY THE DUST IMPRESSION LOOKS LIKE A CD BOX HAS GONE MISSING, TOO. THAT'S PROBABLY NOT IN FOR REPAIRS.
NO SOFTWARE, NO FLOPPIES OR ZIP DISKS, NOTHING.
SOMEBODY STOLE HER COMPUTER AND SOFTWARE, AND LEFT THE MONITOR AND PRINTER BEHIND?
MAYBE. MORE LIKELY, SOMEONE DIDN'T WANT US SEEING SOMETHING.
AND IN THE LIVING ROOM...
WHAT'S WITH THIS FENG SHUI?
FURNITURE SEEMS ASKEW. A BIG RUG MISSING, MAYBE? FURNITURE MOVED TO FREE UP TAKING THE CARPET?

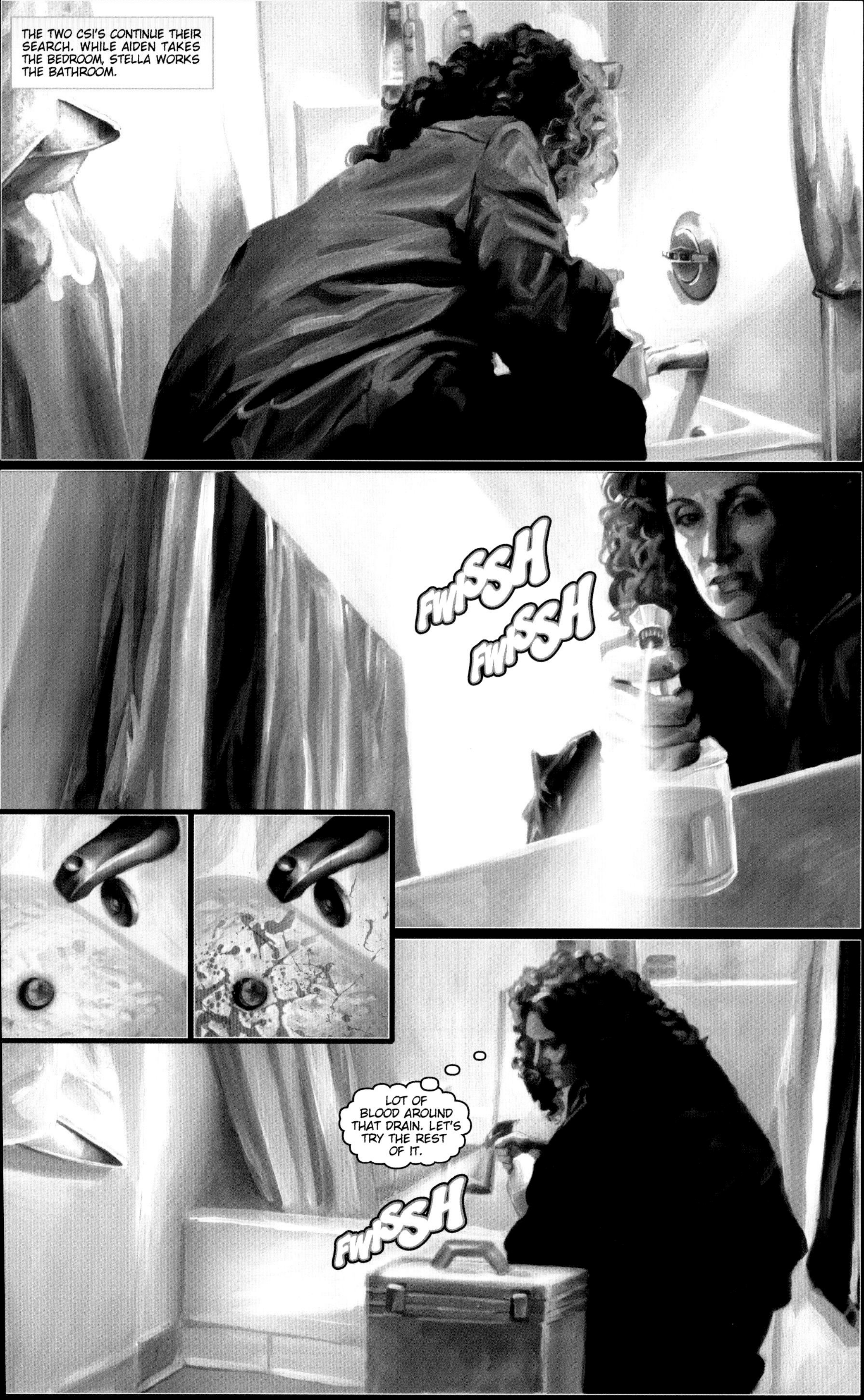
THE TWO CSI'S CONTINUE THEIR SEARCH. WHILE AIDEN TAKES THE BEDROOM, STELLA WORKS THE BATHROOM.
FWISSH
FWISSH
LOT OF BLOOD AROUND THAT DRAIN. LET'S TRY THE REST OF IT.
FWISSH

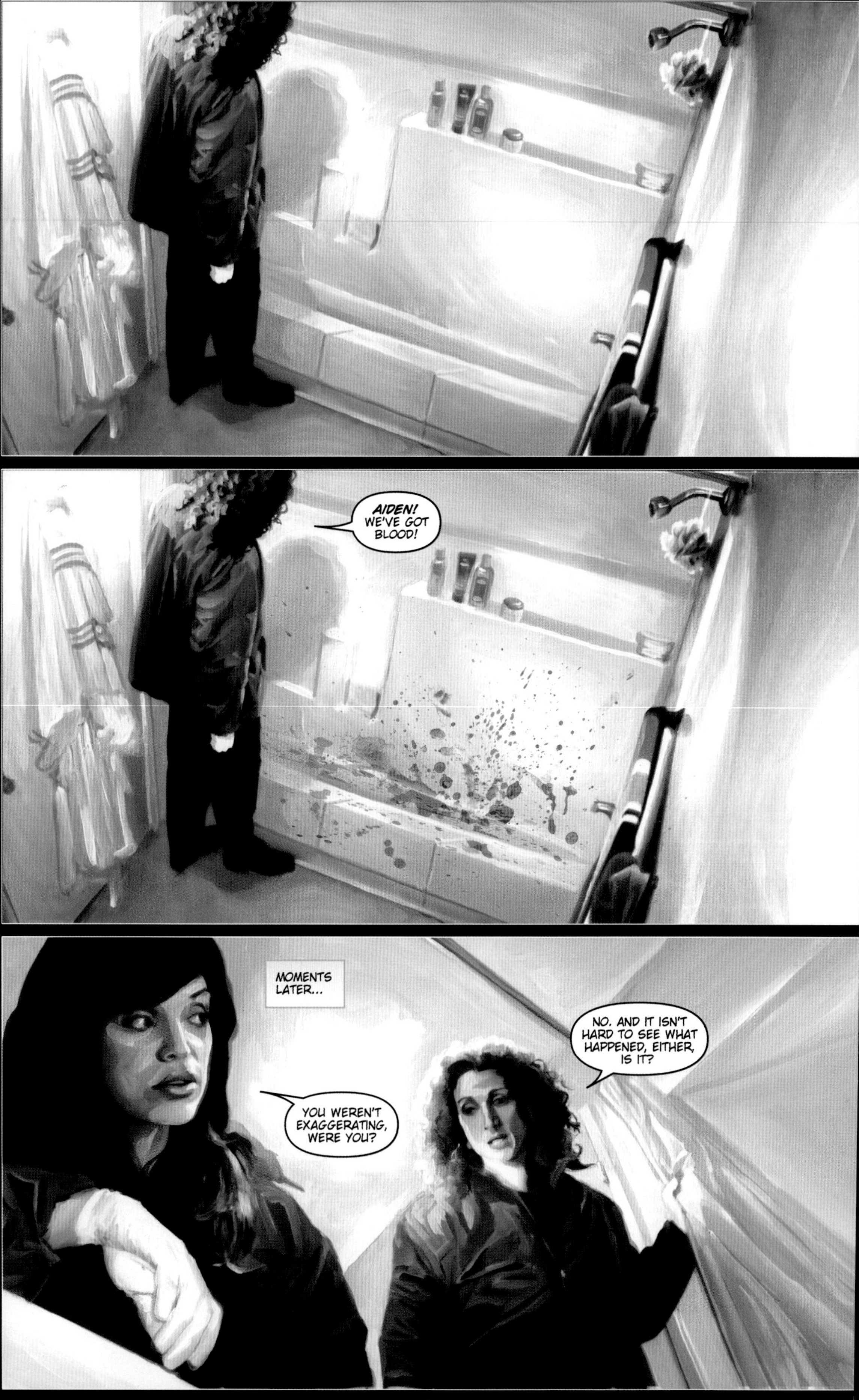
AIDEN! WE'VE GOT BLOOD!
MOMENTS LATER...
YOU WEREN'T EXAGGERATING, WERE YOU?
NO. AND IT ISN'T HARD TO SEE WHAT HAPPENED, EITHER, IS IT?

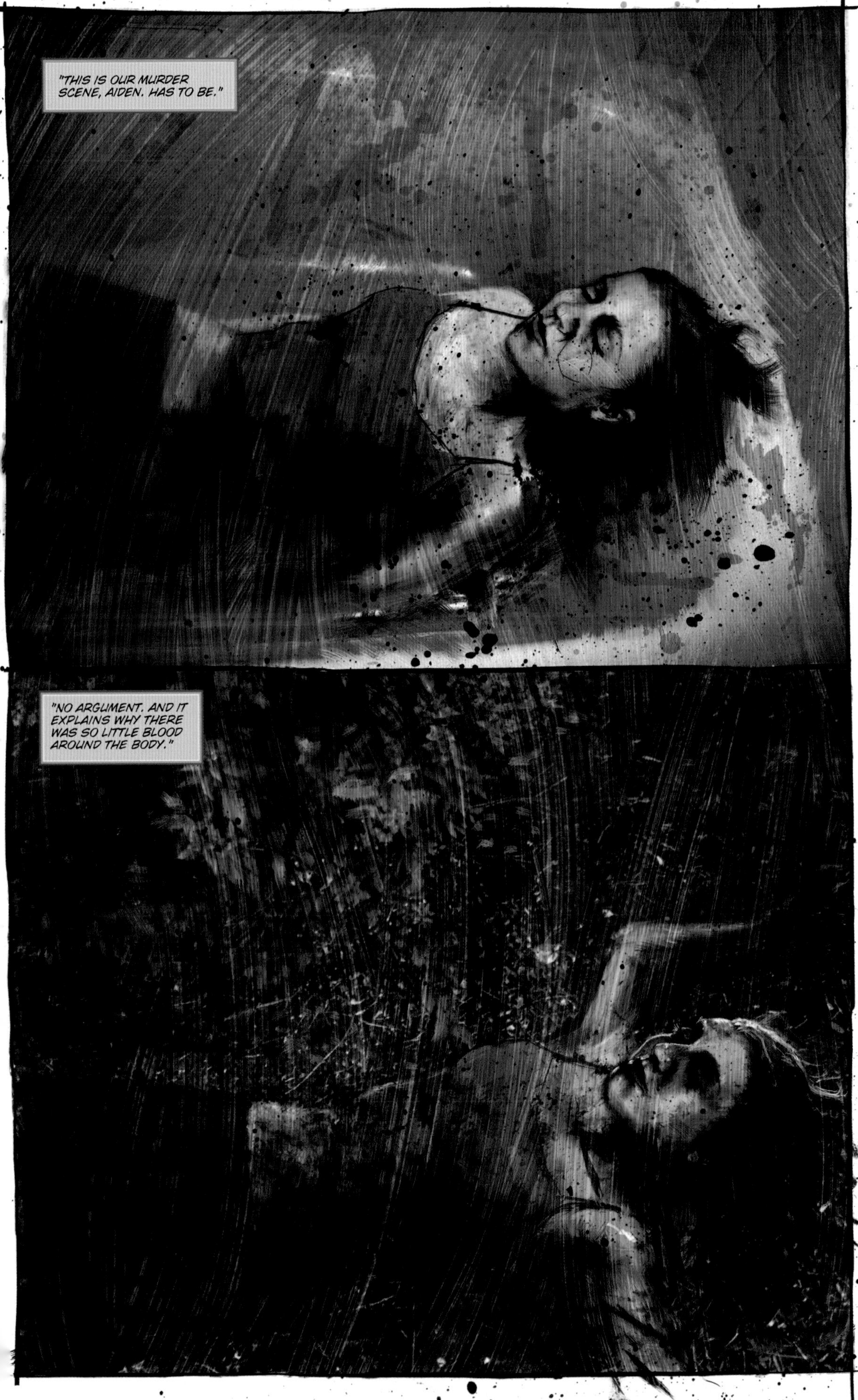
"THIS IS OUR MURDER SCENE, AIDEN. HAS TO BE."
"NO ARGUMENT. AND IT EXPLAINS WHY THERE WAS SO LITTLE BLOOD AROUND THE BODY."

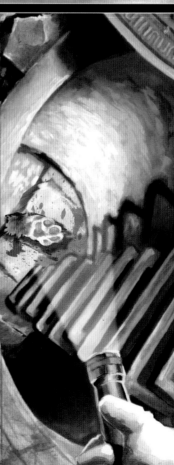

GOTCHA.

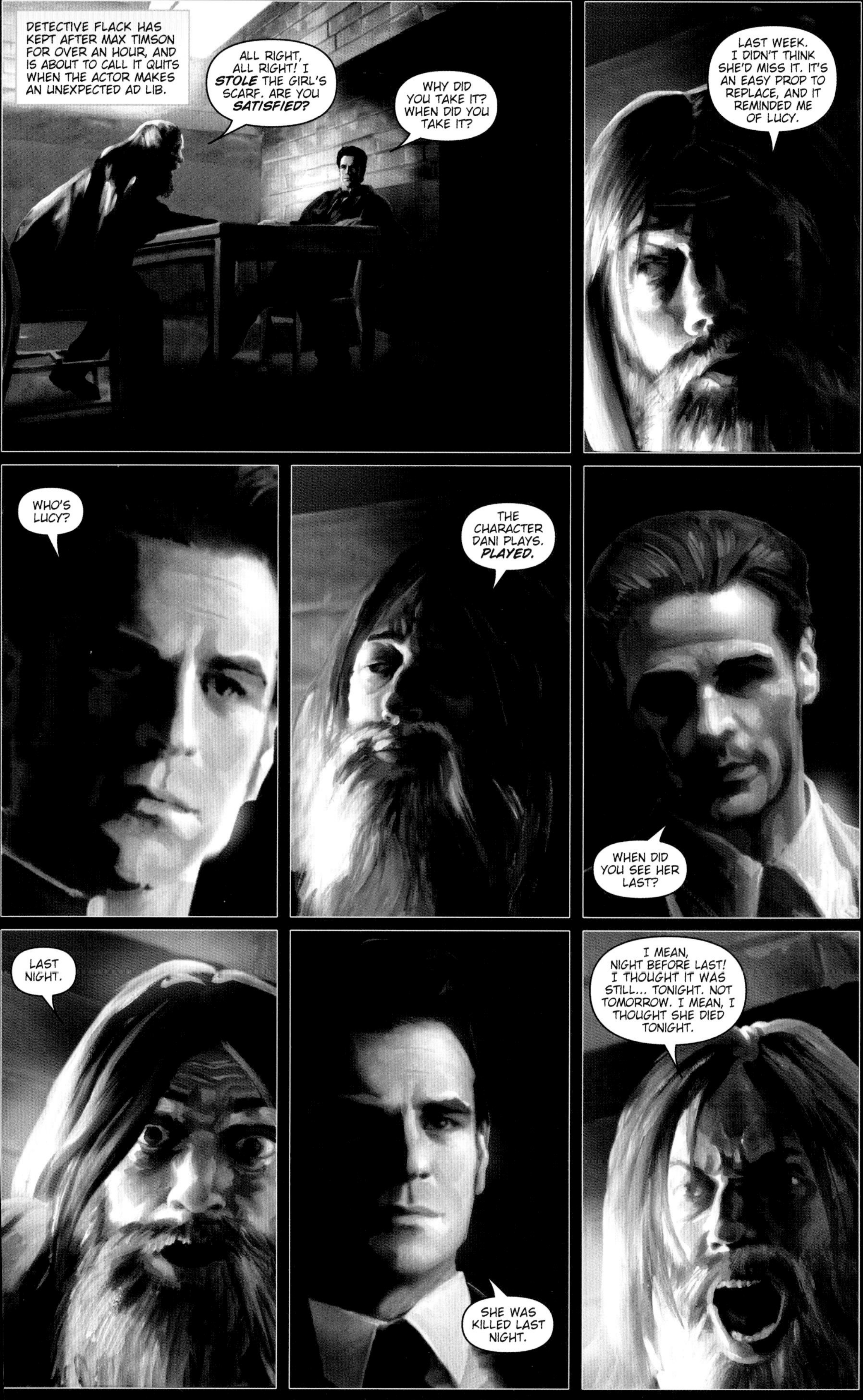
DETECTIVE FLACK HAS KEPT AFTER MAX TIMSON FOR OVER AN HOUR, AND IS ABOUT TO CALL IT QUITS WHEN THE ACTOR MAKES AN UNEXPECTED AD LIB.
ALL RIGHT, ALL RIGHT! I STOLE THE GIRL'S SCARF. ARE YOU SATISFIED?
WHY DID YOU TAKE IT? WHEN DID YOU TAKE IT?
LAST WEEK. I DIDN'T THINK SHE'D MISS IT. IT'S AN EASY PROP TO REPLACE, AND IT REMINDED ME OF LUCY.
WHO'S LUCY?
THE CHARACTER DANI PLAYS. PLAYED.
WHEN DID YOU SEE HER LAST?
LAST NIGHT.
SHE WAS KILLED LAST NIGHT.
I MEAN, NIGHT BEFORE LAST! I THOUGHT IT WAS STILL... TONIGHT. NOT TOMORROW. I MEAN, I THOUGHT SHE DIED TONIGHT.

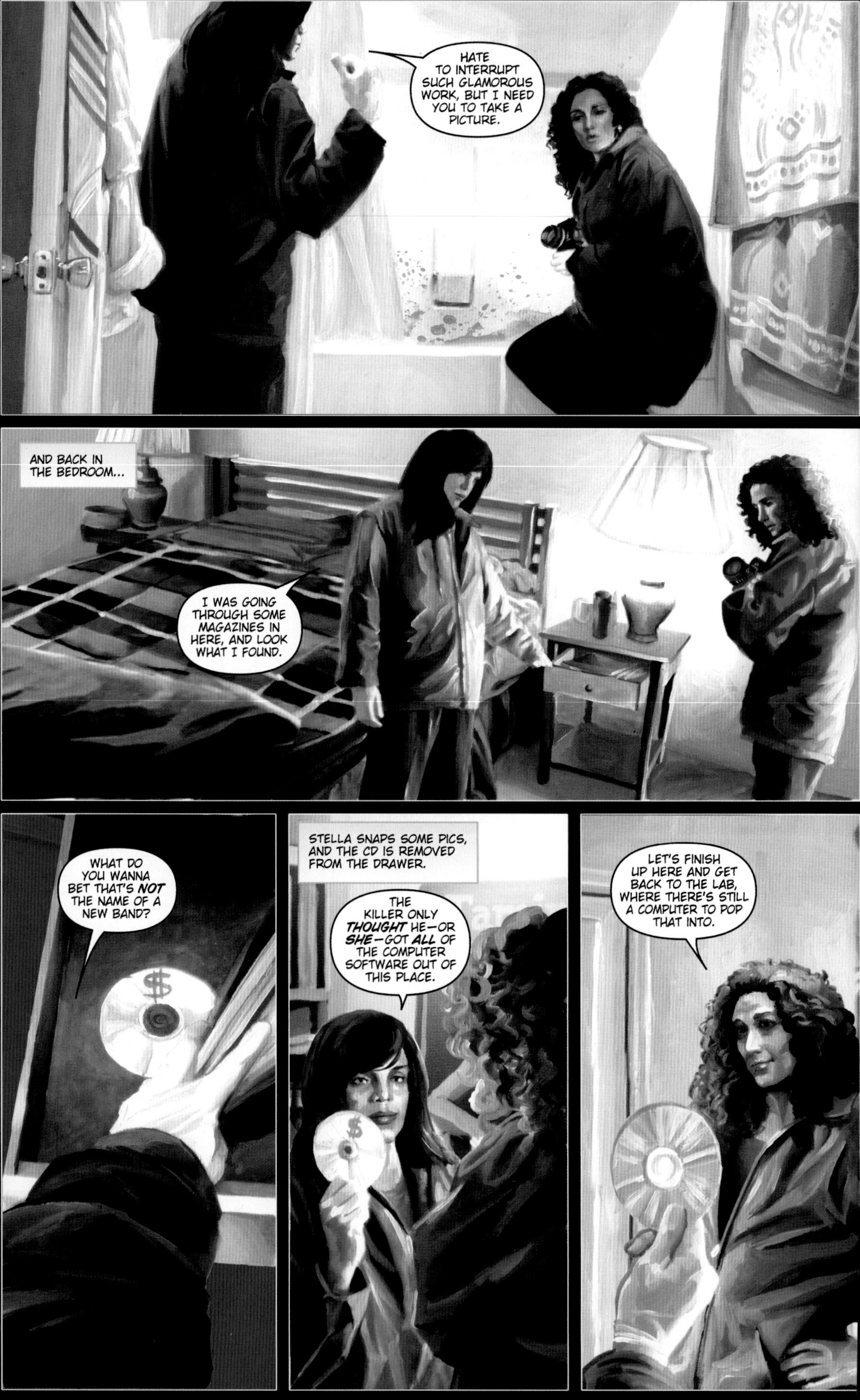
HATE TO INTERRUPT SUCH GLAMOROUS WORK, BUT I NEED YOU TO TAKE A PICTURE.
AND BACK IN THE BEDROOM...
I WAS GOING THROUGH SOME MAGAZINES IN HERE, AND LOOK WHAT I FOUND.
WHAT DO YOU WANNA BET THAT'S ***NOT*** THE NAME OF A NEW BAND?
$
STELLA SNAPS SOME PICS, AND THE CD IS REMOVED FROM THE DRAWER.
THE KILLER ONLY ***THOUGHT*** HE—OR ***SHE***—GOT ***ALL*** OF THE COMPUTER SOFTWARE OUT OF THIS PLACE.
LET'S FINISH UP HERE AND GET BACK TO THE LAB, WHERE THERE'S STILL A COMPUTER TO POP THAT INTO.

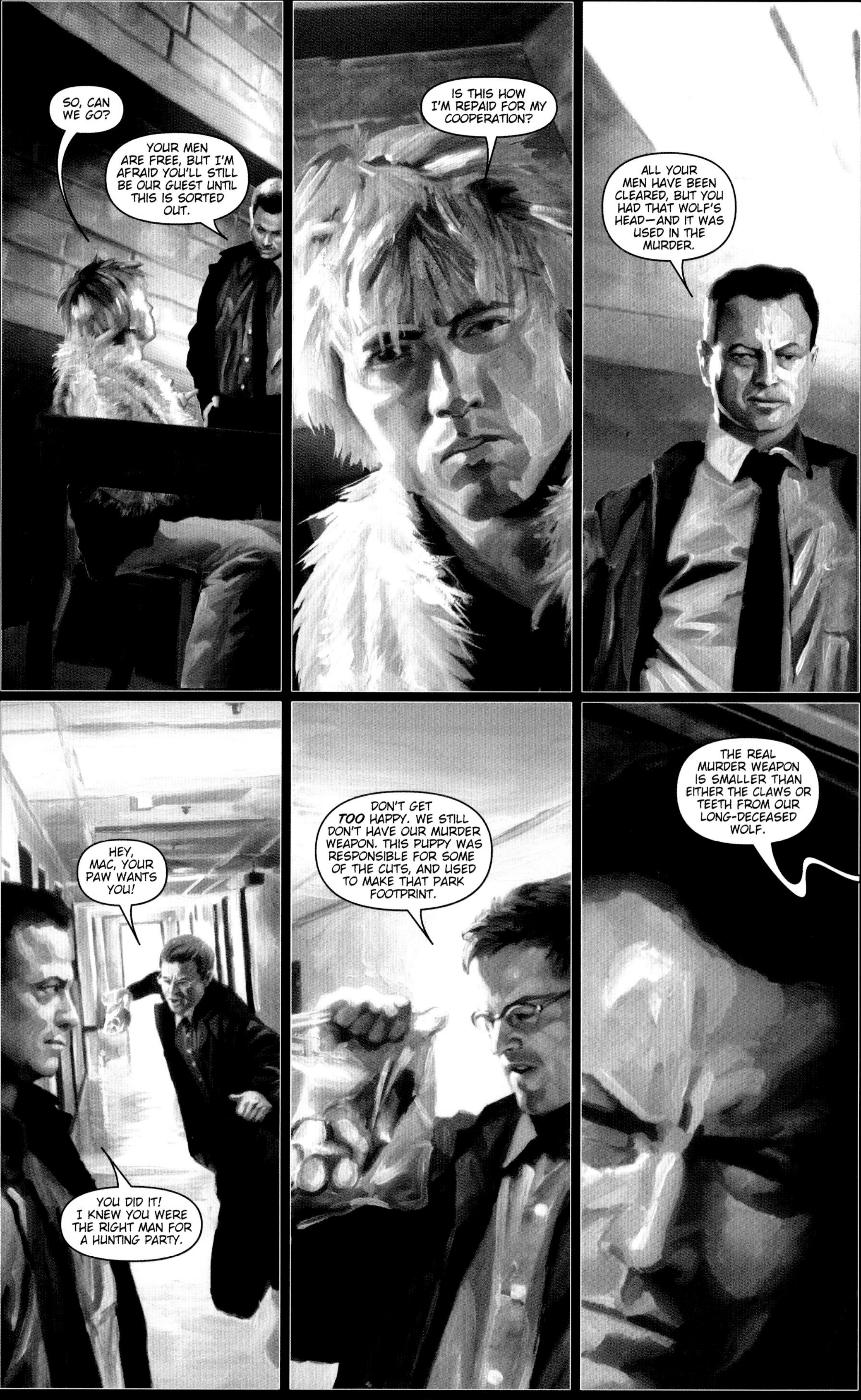
SO, CAN WE GO?
YOUR MEN ARE FREE, BUT I'M AFRAID YOU'LL STILL BE OUR GUEST UNTIL THIS IS SORTED OUT.
IS THIS HOW I'M REPAID FOR MY COOPERATION?
ALL YOUR MEN HAVE BEEN CLEARED, BUT YOU HAD THAT WOLF'S HEAD—AND IT WAS USED IN THE MURDER.
HEY, MAC, YOUR PAW WANTS YOU!
YOU DID IT! I KNEW YOU WERE THE RIGHT MAN FOR A HUNTING PARTY.
DON'T GET TOO HAPPY. WE STILL DON'T HAVE OUR MURDER WEAPON. THIS PUPPY WAS RESPONSIBLE FOR SOME OF THE CUTS, AND USED TO MAKE THAT PARK FOOTPRINT.
THE REAL MURDER WEAPON IS SMALLER THAN EITHER THE CLAWS OR TEETH FROM OUR LONG-DECEASED WOLF.

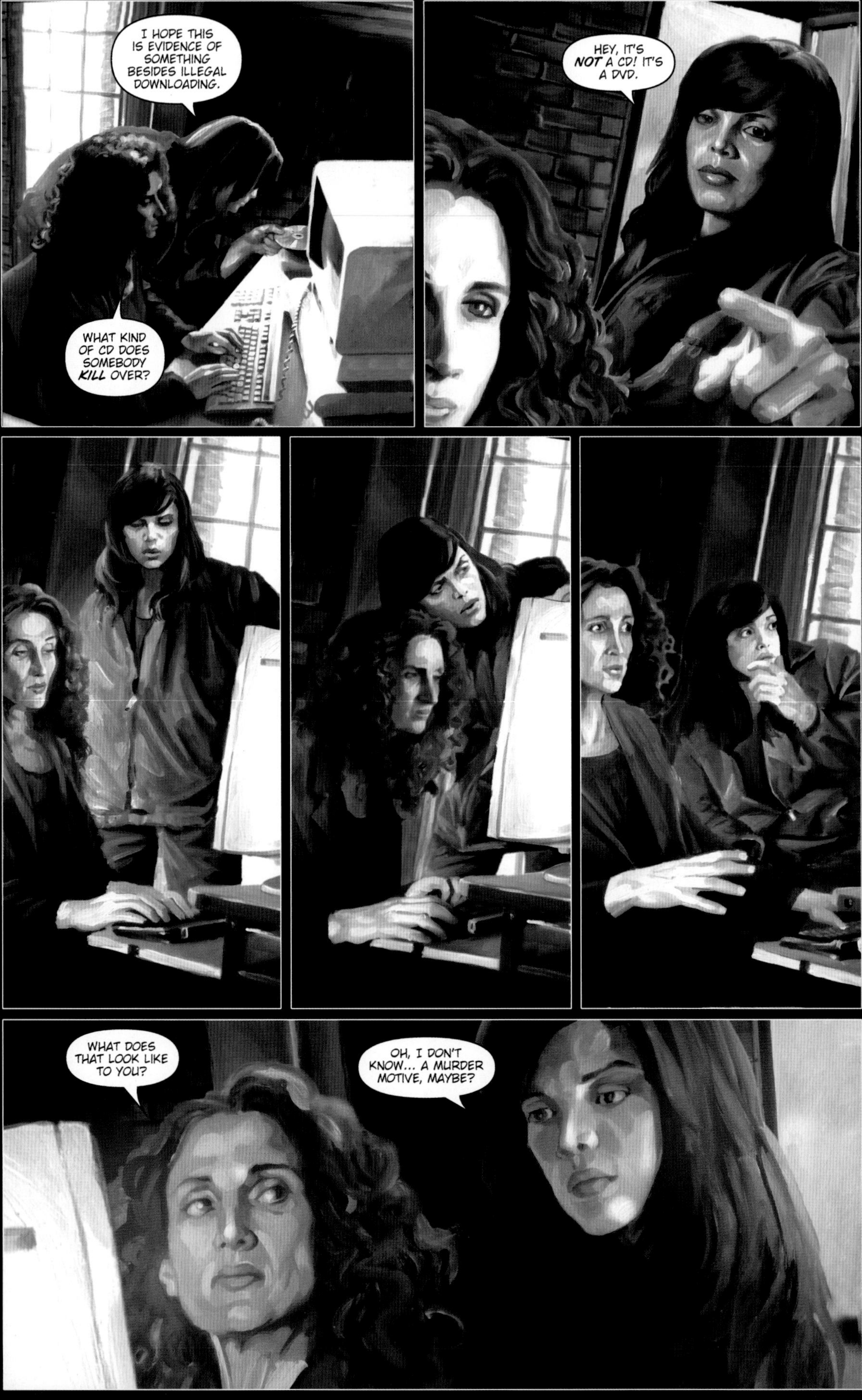
I HOPE THIS IS EVIDENCE OF SOMETHING BESIDES ILLEGAL DOWNLOADING.
WHAT KIND OF CD DOES SOMEBODY *KILL* OVER?
HEY, IT'S *NOT* A CD! IT'S A DVD.
WHAT DOES THAT LOOK LIKE TO YOU?
OH, I DON'T KNOW... A MURDER MOTIVE, MAYBE?

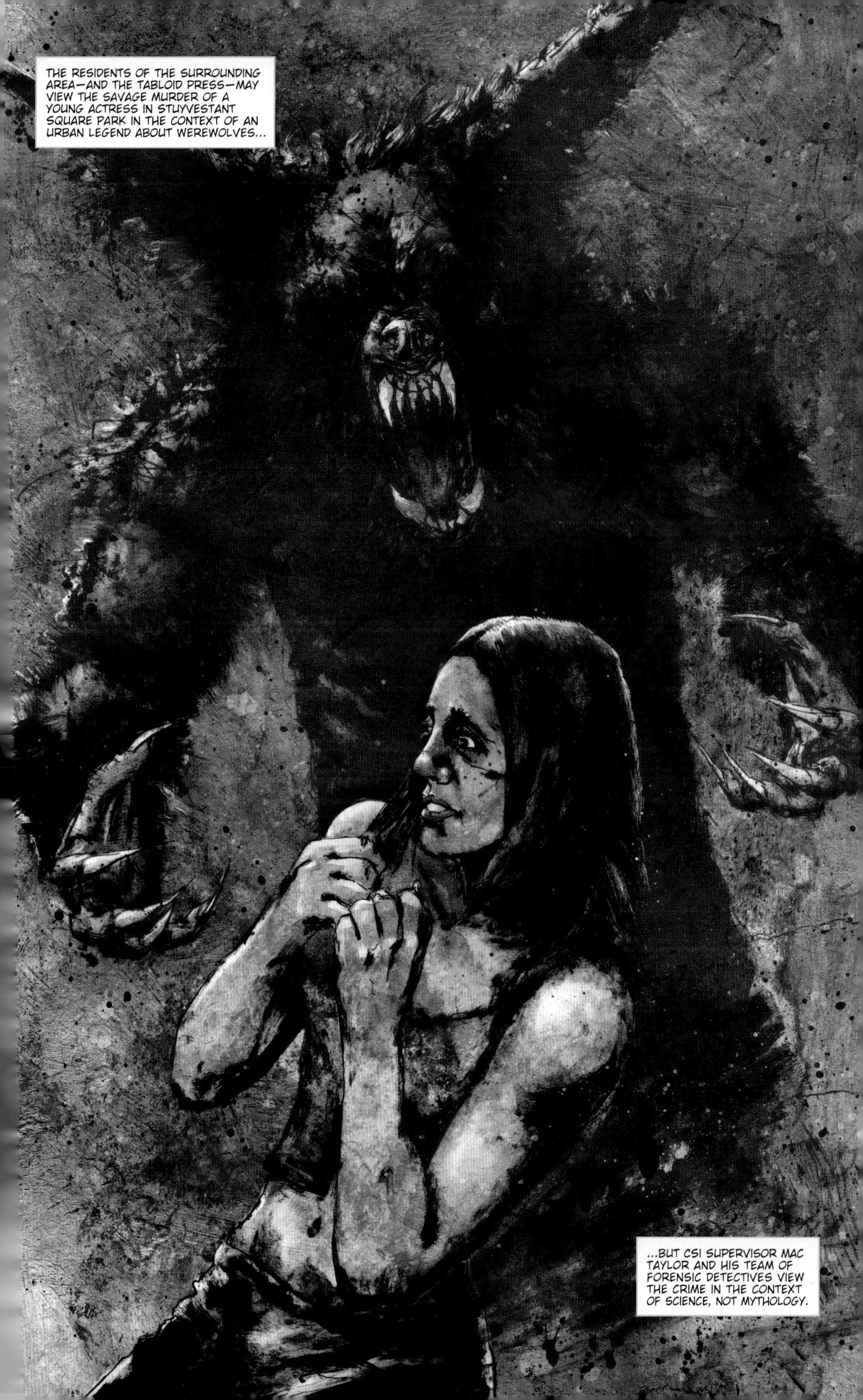
THE RESIDENTS OF THE SURROUNDING AREA—AND THE TABLOID PRESS—MAY VIEW THE SAVAGE MURDER OF A YOUNG ACTRESS IN STUYVESTANT SQUARE PARK IN THE CONTEXT OF AN URBAN LEGEND ABOUT WEREWOLVES...
...BUT CSI SUPERVISOR MAC TAYLOR AND HIS TEAM OF FORENSIC DETECTIVES VIEW THE CRIME IN THE CONTEXT OF SCIENCE, NOT MYTHOLOGY.

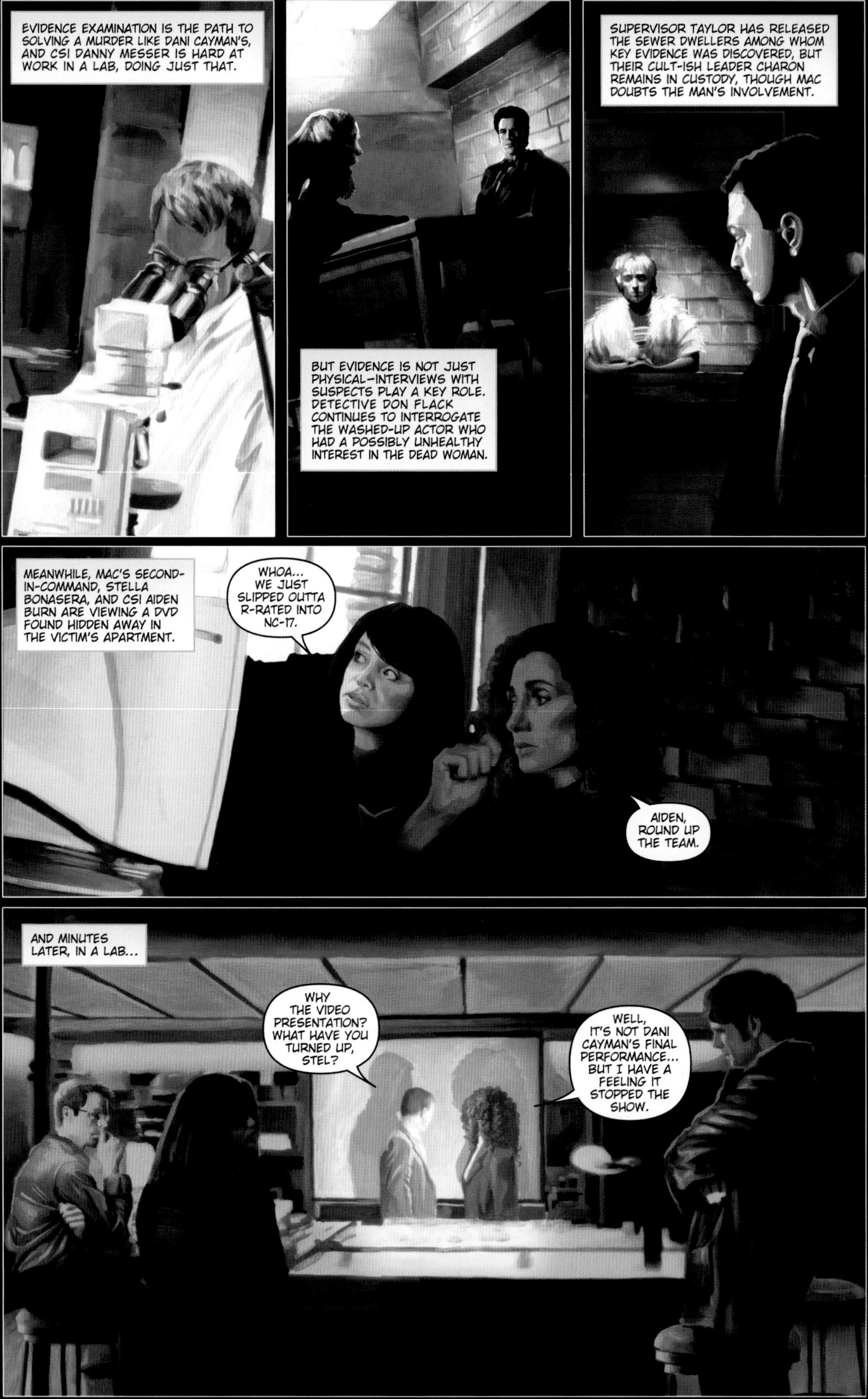

EVIDENCE EXAMINATION IS THE PATH TO SOLVING A MURDER LIKE DANI CAYMAN'S, AND CSI DANNY MESSER IS HARD AT WORK IN A LAB, DOING JUST THAT.
BUT EVIDENCE IS NOT JUST PHYSICAL—INTERVIEWS WITH SUSPECTS PLAY A KEY ROLE. DETECTIVE DON FLACK CONTINUES TO INTERROGATE THE WASHED-UP ACTOR WHO HAD A POSSIBLY UNHEALTHY INTEREST IN THE DEAD WOMAN.
SUPERVISOR TAYLOR HAS RELEASED THE SEWER DWELLERS AMONG WHOM KEY EVIDENCE WAS DISCOVERED, BUT THEIR CULT-ISH LEADER CHARON REMAINS IN CUSTODY, THOUGH MAC DOUBTS THE MAN'S INVOLVEMENT.
MEANWHILE, MAC'S SECOND-IN-COMMAND, STELLA BONASERA, AND CSI AIDEN BURN ARE VIEWING A DVD FOUND HIDDEN AWAY IN THE VICTIM'S APARTMENT.
WHOA... WE JUST SLIPPED OUTTA R-RATED INTO NC-17.
AIDEN, ROUND UP THE TEAM.
AND MINUTES LATER, IN A LAB...
WHY THE VIDEO PRESENTATION? WHAT HAVE YOU TURNED UP, STEL?
WELL, IT'S NOT DANI CAYMAN'S FINAL PERFORMANCE... BUT I HAVE A FEELING IT STOPPED THE SHOW.

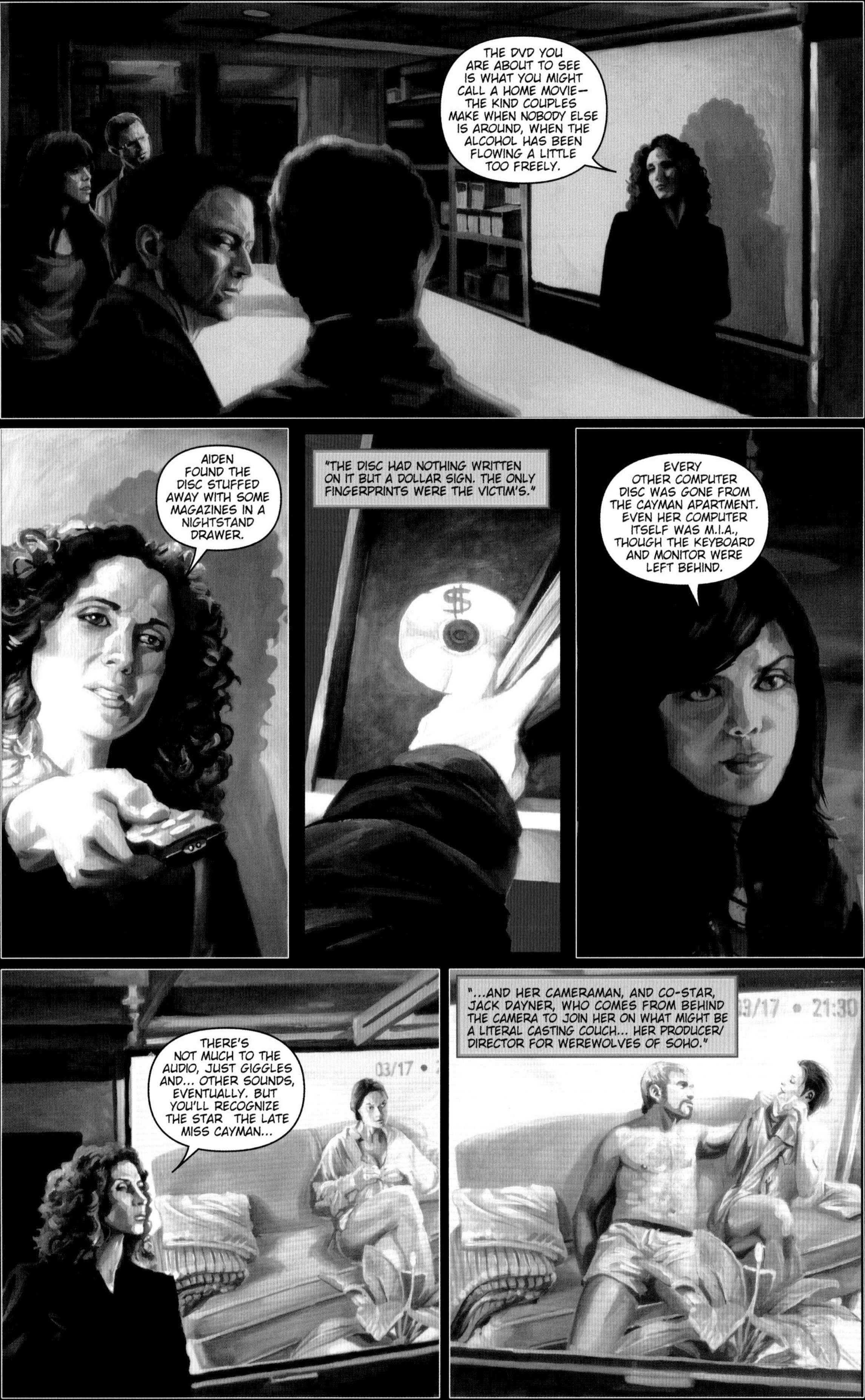
THE DVD YOU ARE ABOUT TO SEE IS WHAT YOU MIGHT CALL A HOME MOVIE— THE KIND COUPLES MAKE WHEN NOBODY ELSE IS AROUND, WHEN THE ALCOHOL HAS BEEN FLOWING A LITTLE TOO FREELY.
AIDEN FOUND THE DISC STUFFED AWAY WITH SOME MAGAZINES IN A NIGHTSTAND DRAWER.
"THE DISC HAD NOTHING WRITTEN ON IT BUT A DOLLAR SIGN. THE ONLY FINGERPRINTS WERE THE VICTIM'S."
$
EVERY OTHER COMPUTER DISC WAS GONE FROM THE CAYMAN APARTMENT. EVEN HER COMPUTER ITSELF WAS M.I.A., THOUGH THE KEYBOARD AND MONITOR WERE LEFT BEHIND.
THERE'S NOT MUCH TO THE AUDIO, JUST GIGGLES AND... OTHER SOUNDS, EVENTUALLY. BUT YOU'LL RECOGNIZE THE STAR THE LATE MISS CAYMAN...
03/17
"...AND HER CAMERAMAN, AND CO-STAR, JACK DAYNER, WHO COMES FROM BEHIND THE CAMERA TO JOIN HER ON WHAT MIGHT BE A LITERAL CASTING COUCH... HER PRODUCER/ DIRECTOR FOR WEREWOLVES OF SOHO."
03/17 • 21:30

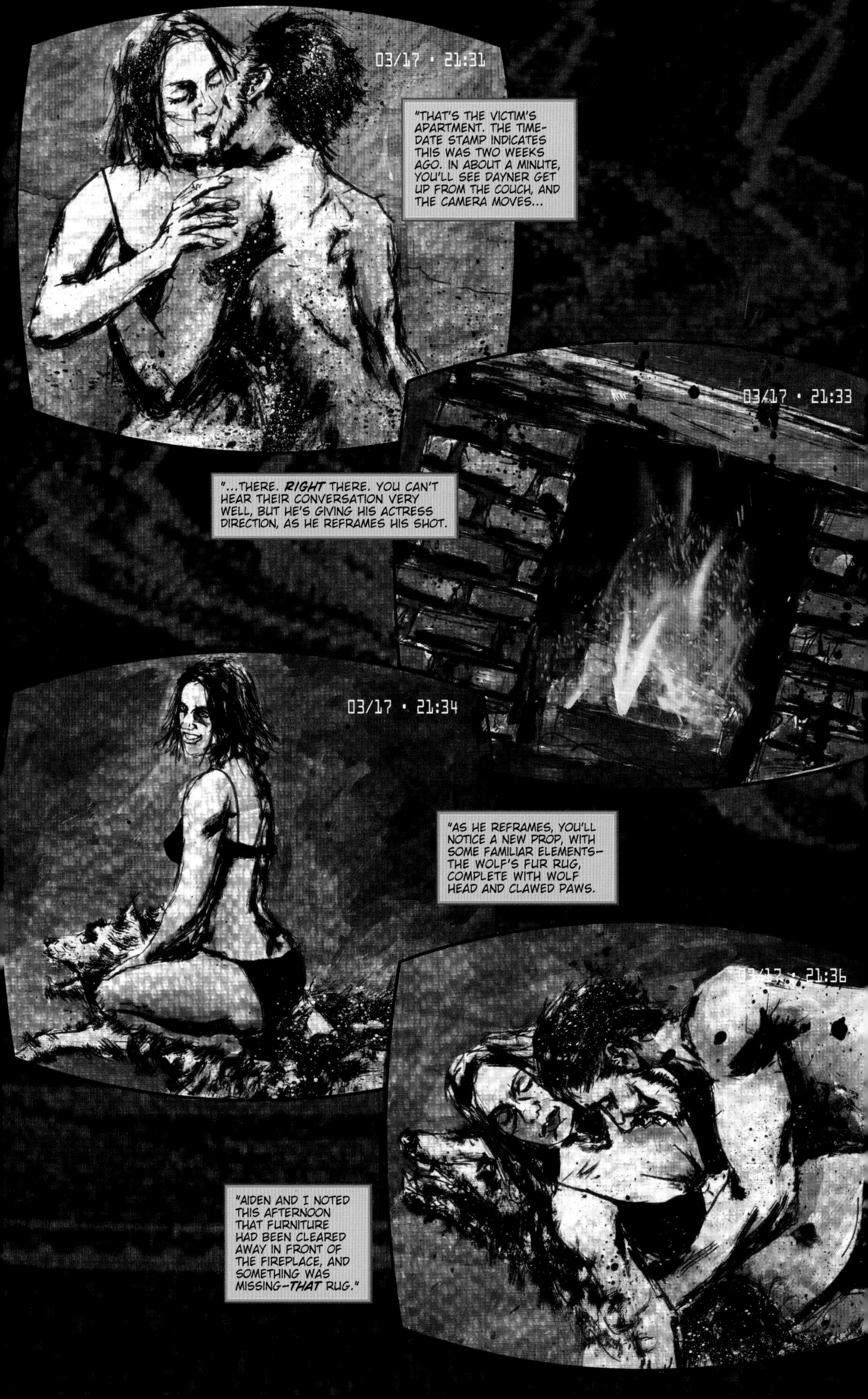
03/17 • 21:31
"THAT'S THE VICTIM'S APARTMENT. THE TIME-DATE STAMP INDICATES THIS WAS TWO WEEKS AGO. IN ABOUT A MINUTE, YOU'LL SEE DAYNER GET UP FROM THE COUCH, AND THE CAMERA MOVES...
03/17 • 21:33
"...THERE. RIGHT THERE. YOU CAN'T HEAR THEIR CONVERSATION VERY WELL, BUT HE'S GIVING HIS ACTRESS DIRECTION, AS HE REFRAMES HIS SHOT.
03/17 • 21:34
"AS HE REFRAMES, YOU'LL NOTICE A NEW PROP, WITH SOME FAMILIAR ELEMENTS—THE WOLF'S FUR RUG, COMPLETE WITH WOLF HEAD AND CLAWED PAWS.
21:36
"AIDEN AND I NOTED THIS AFTERNOON THAT FURNITURE HAD BEEN CLEARED AWAY IN FRONT OF THE FIREPLACE, AND SOMETHING WAS MISSING—THAT RUG."

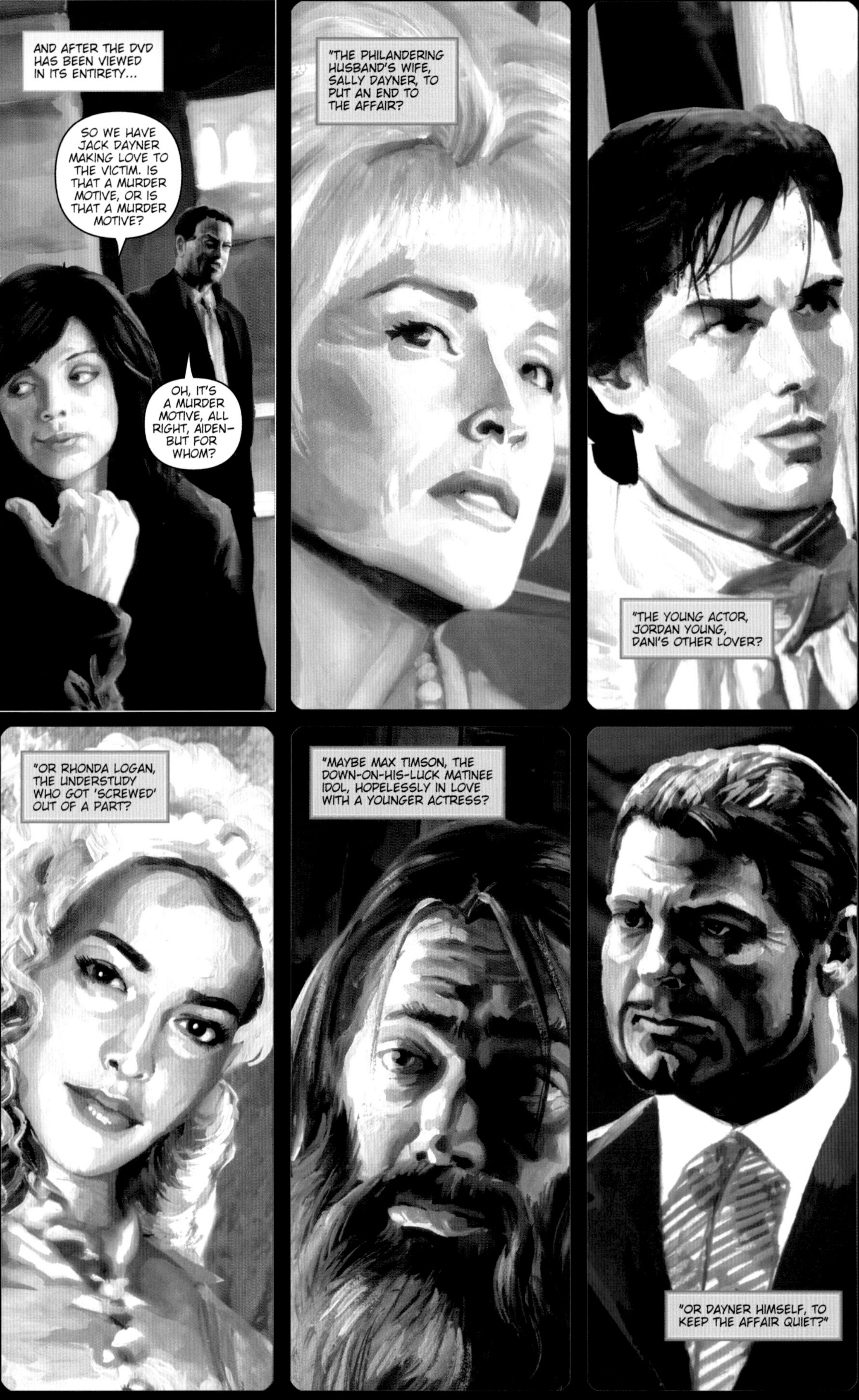
AND AFTER THE DVD HAS BEEN VIEWED IN ITS ENTIRETY...
SO WE HAVE JACK DAYNER MAKING LOVE TO THE VICTIM. IS THAT A MURDER MOTIVE, OR IS THAT A MURDER MOTIVE?
OH, IT'S A MURDER MOTIVE, ALL RIGHT, AIDEN-- BUT FOR WHOM?
"THE PHILANDERING HUSBAND'S WIFE, SALLY DAYNER, TO PUT AN END TO THE AFFAIR?
"THE YOUNG ACTOR, JORDAN YOUNG, DANI'S OTHER LOVER?
"OR RHONDA LOGAN, THE UNDERSTUDY WHO GOT 'SCREWED' OUT OF A PART?
"MAYBE MAX TIMSON, THE DOWN-ON-HIS-LUCK MATINEE IDOL, HOPELESSLY IN LOVE WITH A YOUNGER ACTRESS?
"OR DAYNER HIMSELF, TO KEEP THE AFFAIR QUIET?"

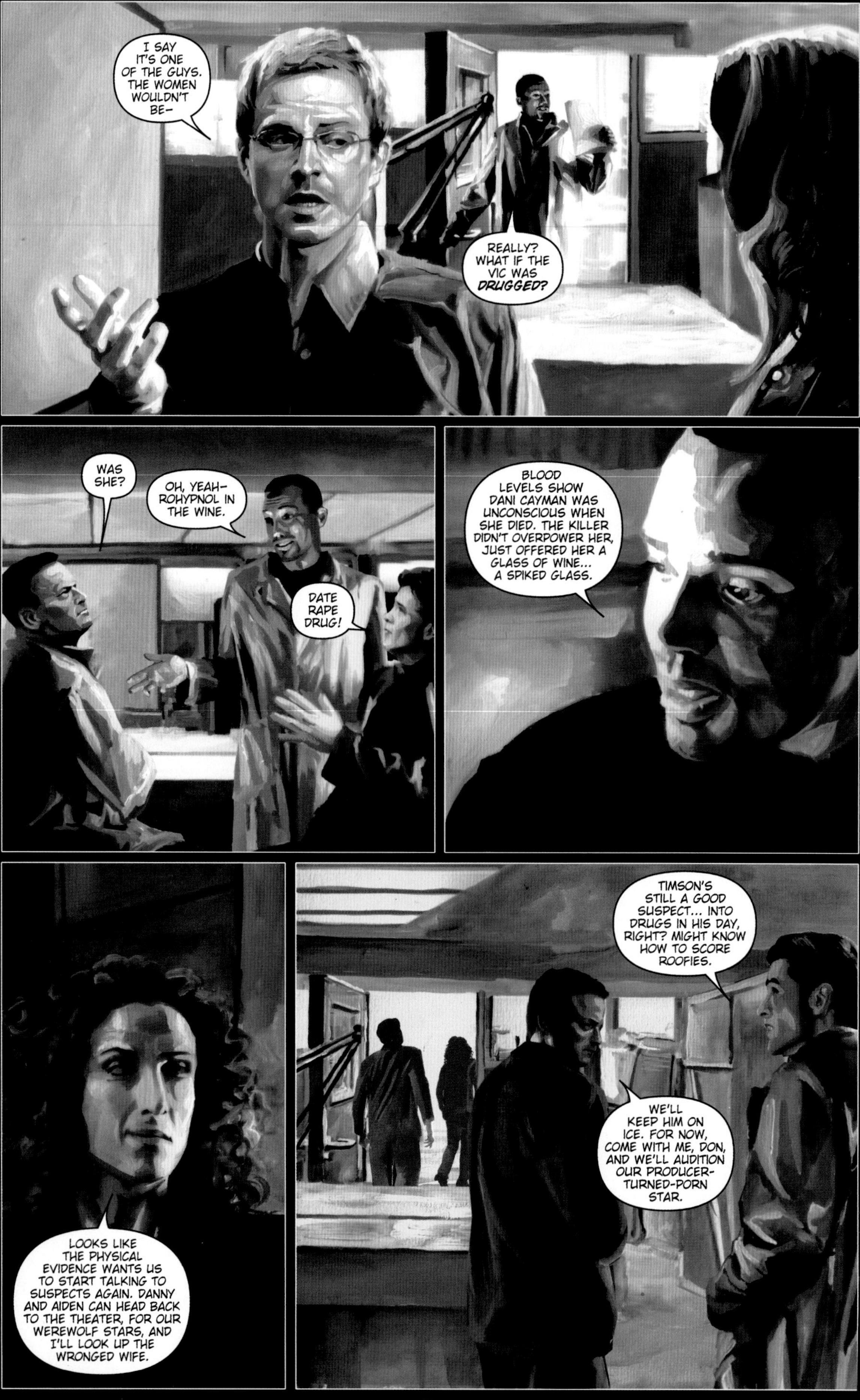
I SAY IT'S ONE OF THE GUYS. THE WOMEN WOULDN'T BE–
REALLY? WHAT IF THE VIC WAS DRUGGED?
WAS SHE?
OH, YEAH– ROHYPNOL IN THE WINE.
DATE RAPE DRUG!
BLOOD LEVELS SHOW DANI CAYMAN WAS UNCONSCIOUS WHEN SHE DIED. THE KILLER DIDN'T OVERPOWER HER, JUST OFFERED HER A GLASS OF WINE... A SPIKED GLASS.
LOOKS LIKE THE PHYSICAL EVIDENCE WANTS US TO START TALKING TO SUSPECTS AGAIN. DANNY AND AIDEN CAN HEAD BACK TO THE THEATER, FOR OUR WEREWOLF STARS, AND I'LL LOOK UP THE WRONGED WIFE.
TIMSON'S STILL A GOOD SUSPECT... INTO DRUGS IN HIS DAY, RIGHT? MIGHT KNOW HOW TO SCORE ROOFIES.
WE'LL KEEP HIM ON ICE. FOR NOW, COME WITH ME, DON, AND WE'LL AUDITION OUR PRODUCER-TURNED-PORN STAR.

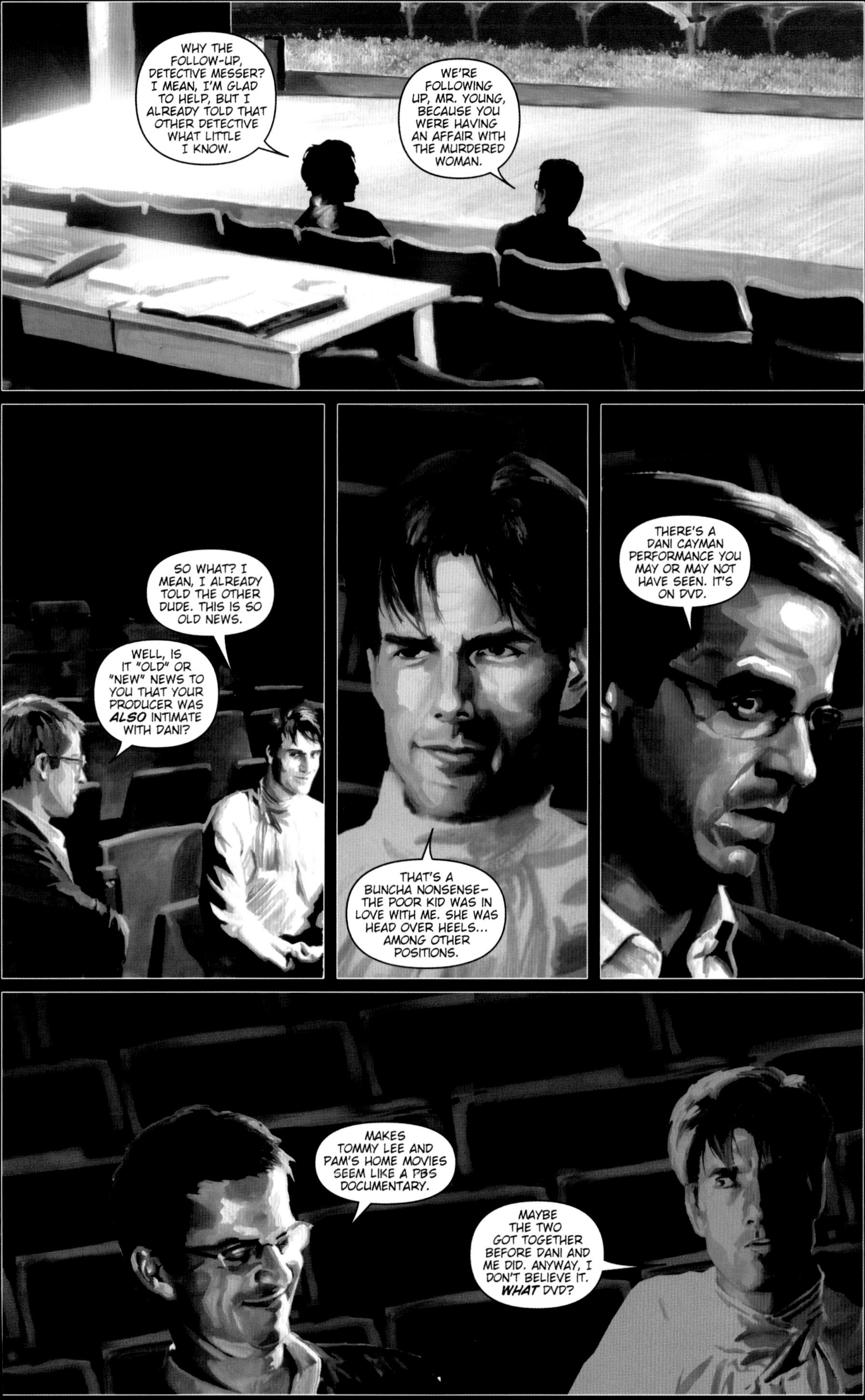
WHY THE FOLLOW-UP, DETECTIVE MESSER? I MEAN, I'M GLAD TO HELP, BUT I ALREADY TOLD THAT OTHER DETECTIVE WHAT LITTLE I KNOW.
WE'RE FOLLOWING UP, MR. YOUNG, BECAUSE YOU WERE HAVING AN AFFAIR WITH THE MURDERED WOMAN.
SO WHAT? I MEAN, I ALREADY TOLD THE OTHER DUDE. THIS IS SO OLD NEWS.
WELL, IS IT "OLD" OR "NEW" NEWS TO YOU THAT YOUR PRODUCER WAS ALSO INTIMATE WITH DANI?
THAT'S A BUNCHA NONSENSE– THE POOR KID WAS IN LOVE WITH ME. SHE WAS HEAD OVER HEELS... AMONG OTHER POSITIONS.
THERE'S A DANI CAYMAN PERFORMANCE YOU MAY OR MAY NOT HAVE SEEN. IT'S ON DVD.
MAKES TOMMY LEE AND PAM'S HOME MOVIES SEEM LIKE A PBS DOCUMENTARY.
MAYBE THE TWO GOT TOGETHER BEFORE DANI AND ME DID. ANYWAY, I DON'T BELIEVE IT. WHAT DVD?

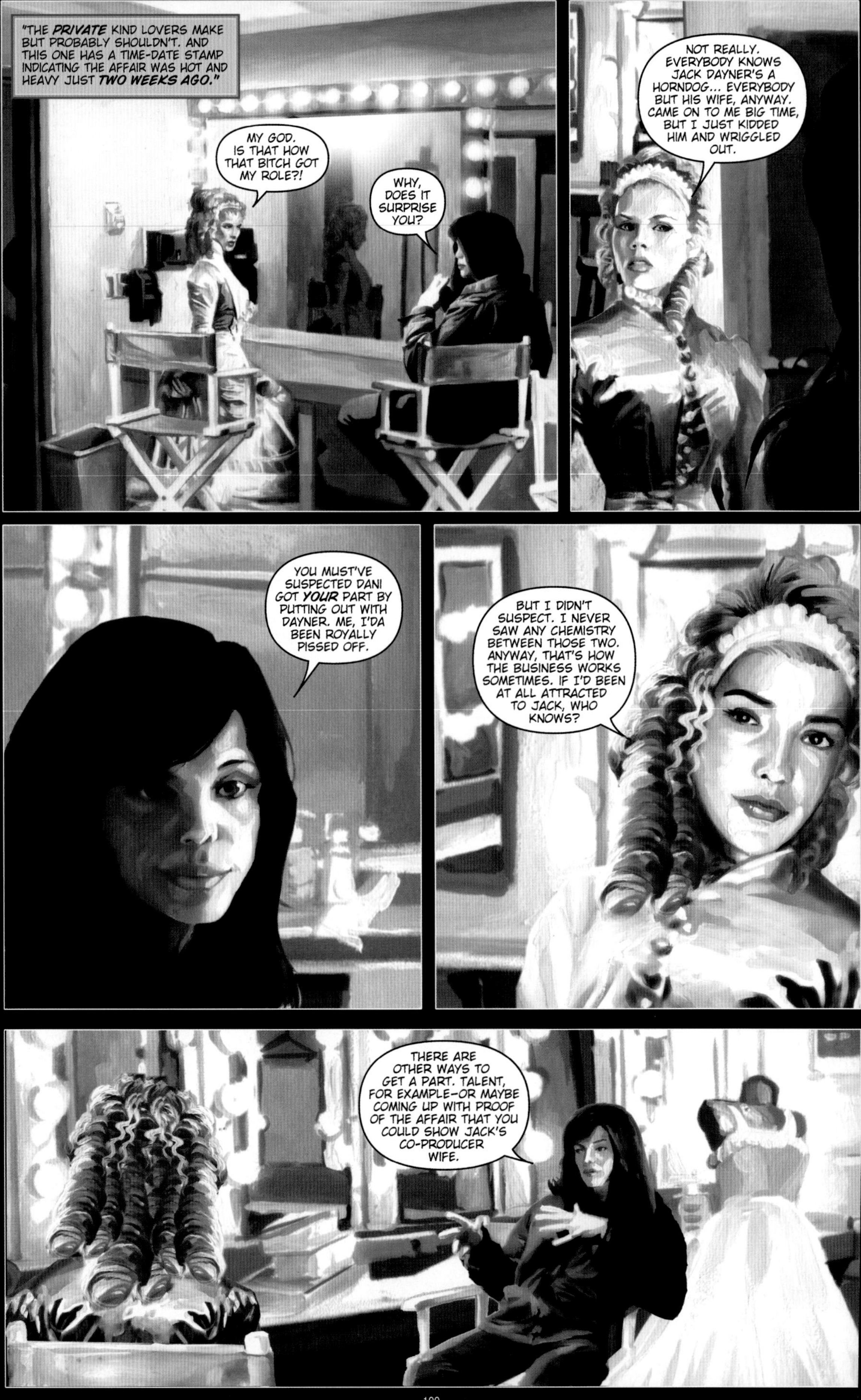
"THE PRIVATE KIND LOVERS MAKE BUT PROBABLY SHOULDN'T. AND THIS ONE HAS A TIME-DATE STAMP INDICATING THE AFFAIR WAS HOT AND HEAVY JUST TWO WEEKS AGO."
MY GOD. IS THAT HOW THAT BITCH GOT MY ROLE?!
WHY, DOES IT SURPRISE YOU?
NOT REALLY. EVERYBODY KNOWS JACK DAYNER'S A HORNDOG... EVERYBODY BUT HIS WIFE, ANYWAY. CAME ON TO ME BIG TIME, BUT I JUST KIDDED HIM AND WRIGGLED OUT.
YOU MUST'VE SUSPECTED DANI GOT YOUR PART BY PUTTING OUT WITH DAYNER. ME, I'DA BEEN ROYALLY PISSED OFF.
BUT I DIDN'T SUSPECT. I NEVER SAW ANY CHEMISTRY BETWEEN THOSE TWO. ANYWAY, THAT'S HOW THE BUSINESS WORKS SOMETIMES. IF I'D BEEN AT ALL ATTRACTED TO JACK, WHO KNOWS?
THERE ARE OTHER WAYS TO GET A PART. TALENT, FOR EXAMPLE—OR MAYBE COMING UP WITH PROOF OF THE AFFAIR THAT YOU COULD SHOW JACK'S CO-PRODUCER WIFE.

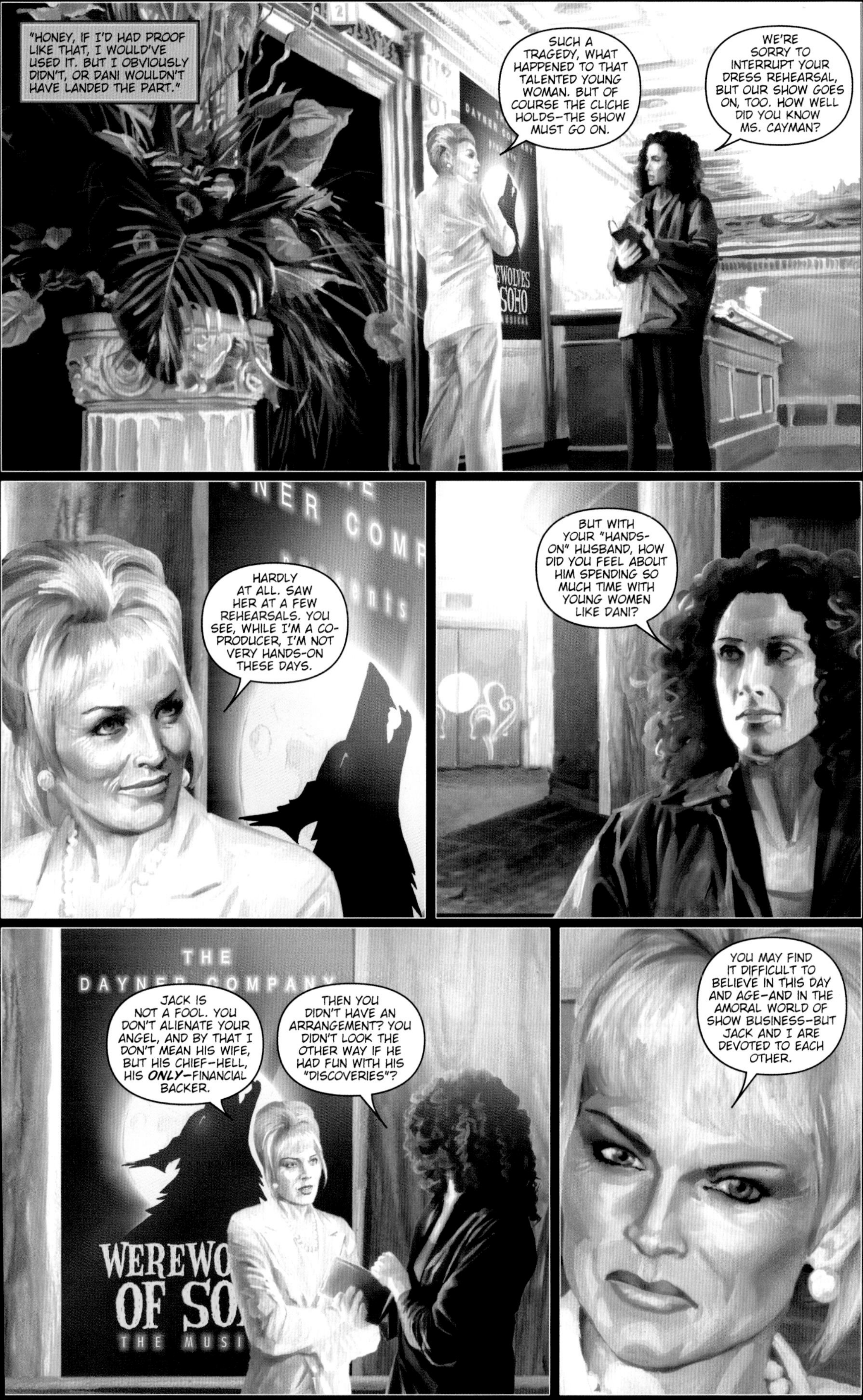
"HONEY, IF I'D HAD PROOF LIKE THAT, I WOULD'VE USED IT. BUT I OBVIOUSLY DIDN'T, OR DANI WOULDN'T HAVE LANDED THE PART."
SUCH A TRAGEDY, WHAT HAPPENED TO THAT TALENTED YOUNG WOMAN. BUT OF COURSE THE CLICHE HOLDS–THE SHOW MUST GO ON.
WE'RE SORRY TO INTERRUPT YOUR DRESS REHEARSAL, BUT OUR SHOW GOES ON, TOO. HOW WELL DID YOU KNOW MS. CAYMAN?
HARDLY AT ALL. SAW HER AT A FEW REHEARSALS. YOU SEE, WHILE I'M A CO-PRODUCER, I'M NOT VERY HANDS-ON THESE DAYS.
BUT WITH YOUR "HANDS-ON" HUSBAND, HOW DID YOU FEEL ABOUT HIM SPENDING SO MUCH TIME WITH YOUNG WOMEN LIKE DANI?
THE DAYNER COMPANY
JACK IS NOT A FOOL. YOU DON'T ALIENATE YOUR ANGEL, AND BY THAT I DON'T MEAN HIS WIFE, BUT HIS CHIEF–HELL, HIS *ONLY*–FINANCIAL BACKER.
THEN YOU DIDN'T HAVE AN ARRANGEMENT? YOU DIDN'T LOOK THE OTHER WAY IF HE HAD FUN WITH HIS "DISCOVERIES"?
YOU MAY FIND IT DIFFICULT TO BELIEVE IN THIS DAY AND AGE–AND IN THE AMORAL WORLD OF SHOW BUSINESS–BUT JACK AND I ARE DEVOTED TO EACH OTHER.

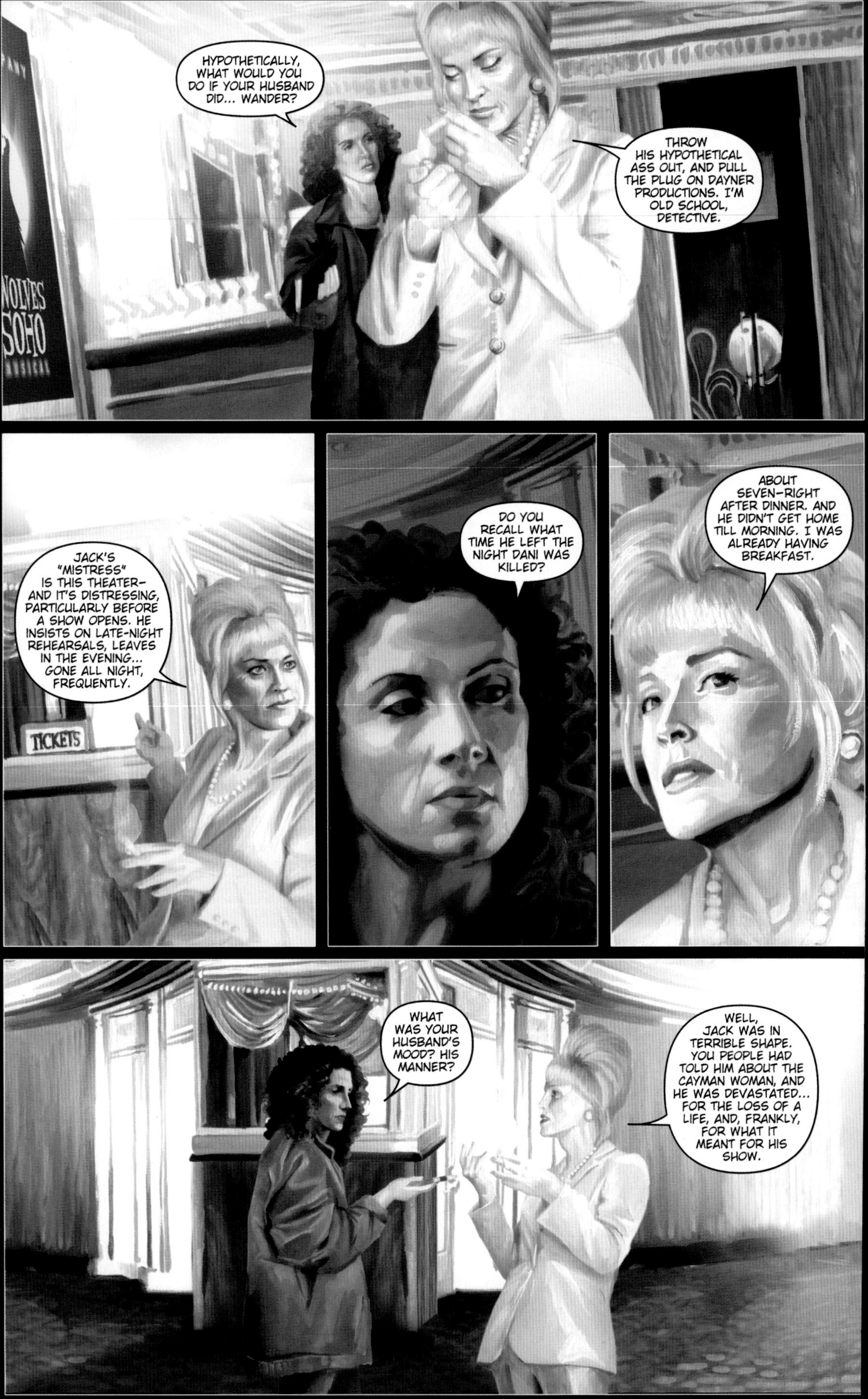
HYPOTHETICALLY, WHAT WOULD YOU DO IF YOUR HUSBAND DID... WANDER?
THROW HIS HYPOTHETICAL ASS OUT, AND PULL THE PLUG ON DAYNER PRODUCTIONS. I'M OLD SCHOOL, DETECTIVE.
WOLVES SOHO
TICKETS
"JACK'S "MISTRESS" IS THIS THEATER– AND IT'S DISTRESSING, PARTICULARLY BEFORE A SHOW OPENS. HE INSISTS ON LATE-NIGHT REHEARSALS, LEAVES IN THE EVENING... GONE ALL NIGHT, FREQUENTLY.
DO YOU RECALL WHAT TIME HE LEFT THE NIGHT DANI WAS KILLED?
ABOUT SEVEN–RIGHT AFTER DINNER. AND HE DIDN'T GET HOME TILL MORNING. I WAS ALREADY HAVING BREAKFAST.
WHAT WAS YOUR HUSBAND'S MOOD? HIS MANNER?
WELL, JACK WAS IN TERRIBLE SHAPE. YOU PEOPLE HAD TOLD HIM ABOUT THE CAYMAN WOMAN, AND HE WAS DEVASTATED... FOR THE LOSS OF A LIFE, AND, FRANKLY, FOR WHAT IT MEANT FOR HIS SHOW.

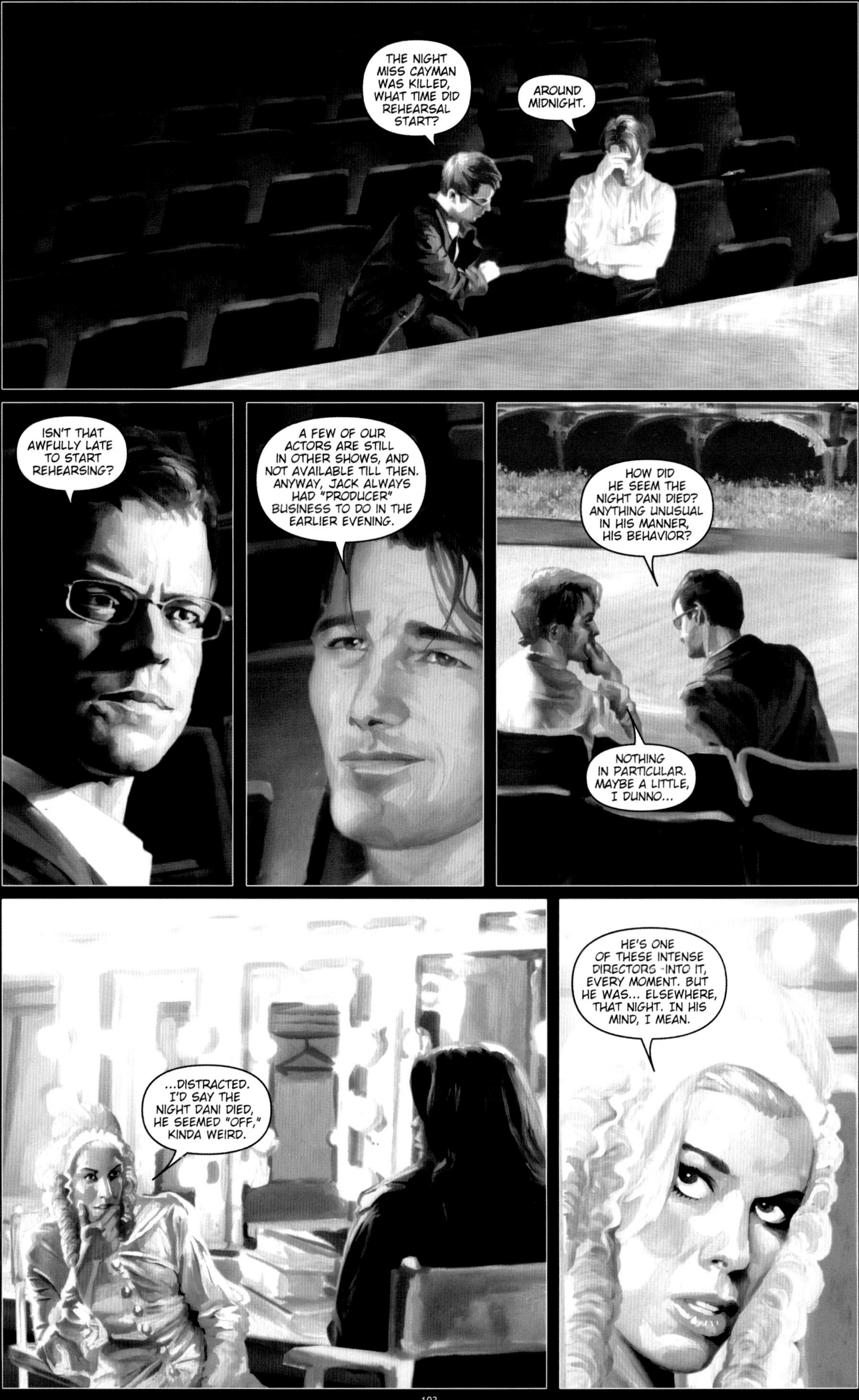
THE NIGHT MISS CAYMAN WAS KILLED, WHAT TIME DID REHEARSAL START?
AROUND MIDNIGHT.
ISN'T THAT AWFULLY LATE TO START REHEARSING?
A FEW OF OUR ACTORS ARE STILL IN OTHER SHOWS, AND NOT AVAILABLE TILL THEN. ANYWAY, JACK ALWAYS HAD "PRODUCER" BUSINESS TO DO IN THE EARLIER EVENING.
HOW DID HE SEEM THE NIGHT DANI DIED? ANYTHING UNUSUAL IN HIS MANNER, HIS BEHAVIOR?
NOTHING IN PARTICULAR. MAYBE A LITTLE, I DUNNO...
...DISTRACTED. I'D SAY THE NIGHT DANI DIED, HE SEEMED "OFF," KINDA WEIRD.
HE'S ONE OF THESE INTENSE DIRECTORS -INTO IT, EVERY MOMENT. BUT HE WAS... ELSEWHERE, THAT NIGHT. IN HIS MIND, I MEAN.

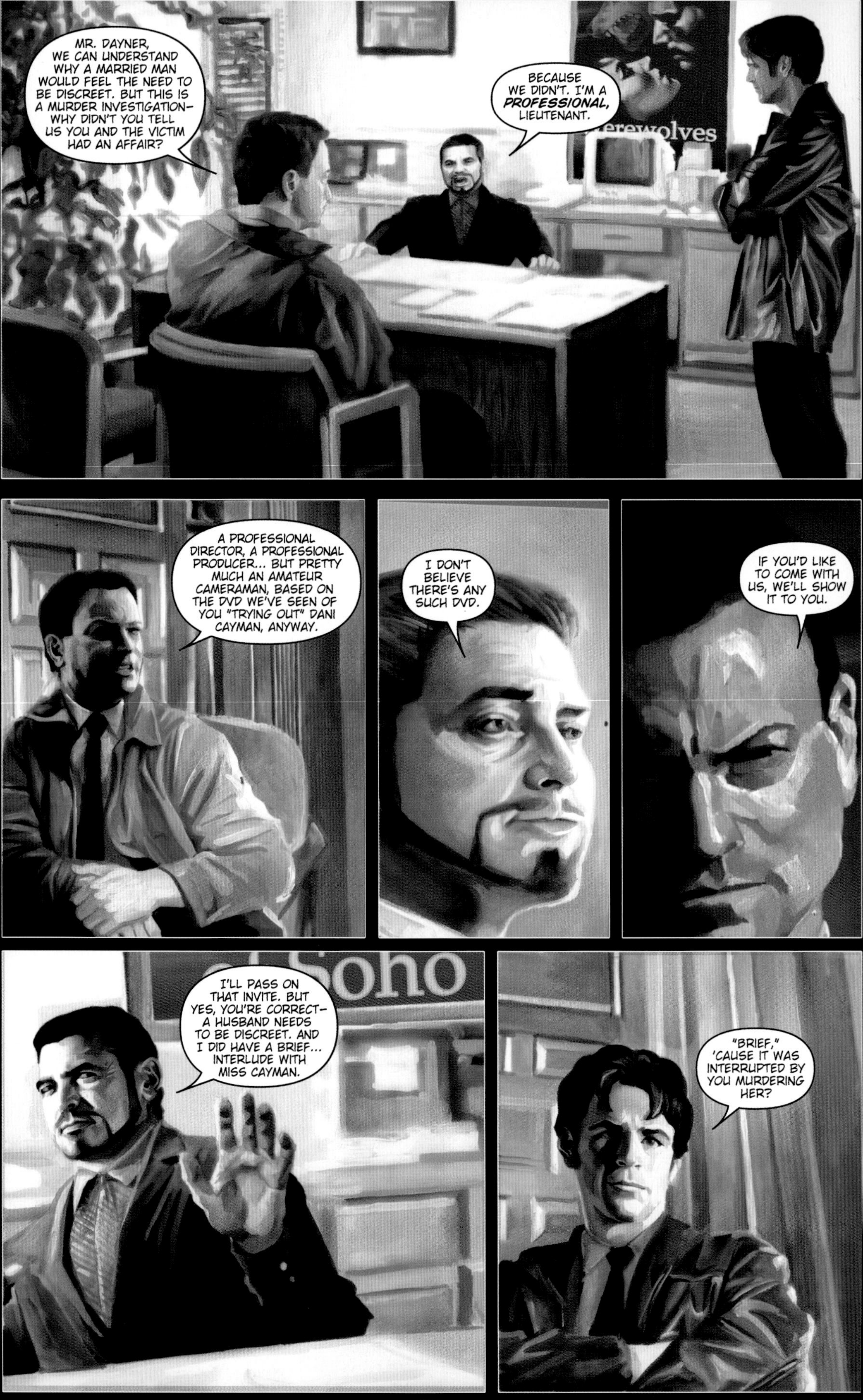
MR. DAYNER, WE CAN UNDERSTAND WHY A MARRIED MAN WOULD FEEL THE NEED TO BE DISCREET. BUT THIS IS A MURDER INVESTIGATION-WHY DIDN'T YOU TELL US YOU AND THE VICTIM HAD AN AFFAIR?
BECAUSE WE DIDN'T. I'M A *PROFESSIONAL,* LIEUTENANT.
erewolves
A PROFESSIONAL DIRECTOR, A PROFESSIONAL PRODUCER... BUT PRETTY MUCH AN AMATEUR CAMERAMAN, BASED ON THE DVD WE'VE SEEN OF YOU "TRYING OUT" DANI CAYMAN, ANYWAY.
I DON'T BELIEVE THERE'S ANY SUCH DVD.
IF YOU'D LIKE TO COME WITH US, WE'LL SHOW IT TO YOU.
Soho
I'LL PASS ON THAT INVITE. BUT YES, YOU'RE CORRECT-A HUSBAND NEEDS TO BE DISCREET. AND I DID HAVE A BRIEF... INTERLUDE WITH MISS CAYMAN.
"BRIEF," 'CAUSE IT WAS INTERRUPTED BY YOU MURDERING HER?

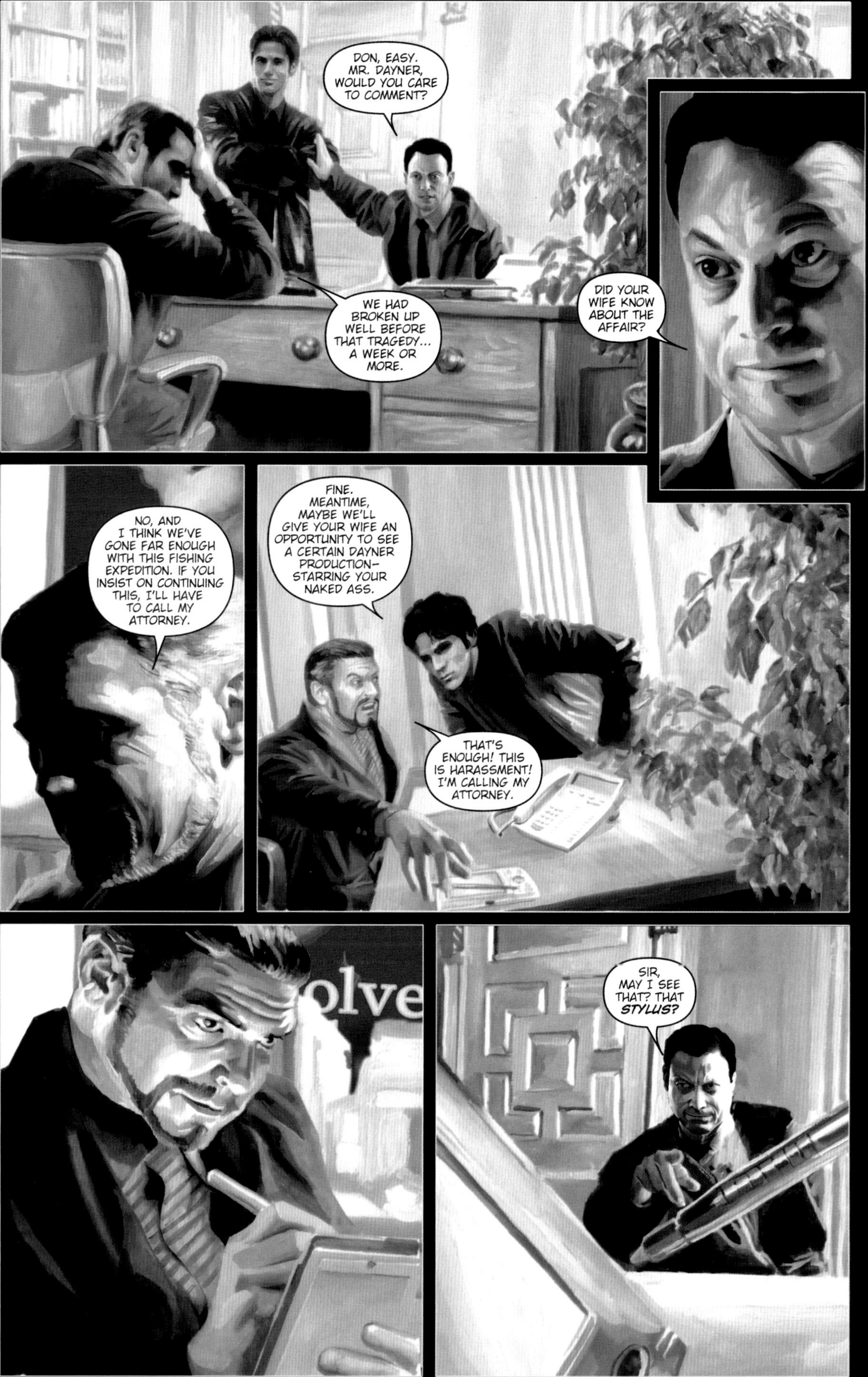
DON, EASY. MR. DAYNER, WOULD YOU CARE TO COMMENT?
WE HAD BROKEN UP WELL BEFORE THAT TRAGEDY... A WEEK OR MORE.
DID YOUR WIFE KNOW ABOUT THE AFFAIR?
NO, AND I THINK WE'VE GONE FAR ENOUGH WITH THIS FISHING EXPEDITION. IF YOU INSIST ON CONTINUING THIS, I'LL HAVE TO CALL MY ATTORNEY.
FINE. MEANTIME, MAYBE WE'LL GIVE YOUR WIFE AN OPPORTUNITY TO SEE A CERTAIN DAYNER PRODUCTION– STARRING YOUR NAKED ASS.
THAT'S ENOUGH! THIS IS HARASSMENT! I'M CALLING MY ATTORNEY.
olve
SIR, MAY I SEE THAT? THAT ***STYLUS?***

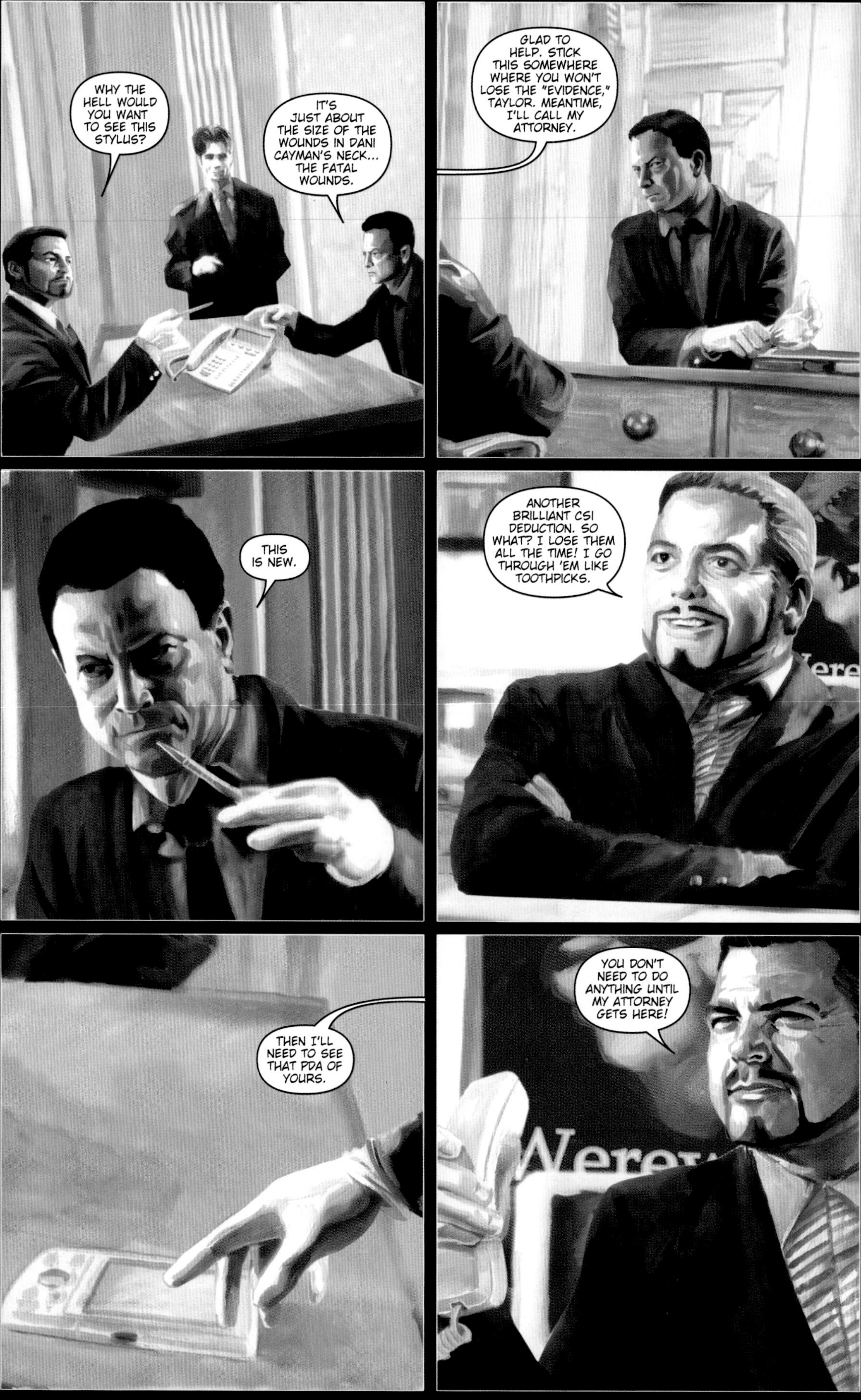
WHY THE HELL WOULD YOU WANT TO SEE THIS STYLUS?
IT'S JUST ABOUT THE SIZE OF THE WOUNDS IN DANI CAYMAN'S NECK... THE FATAL WOUNDS.
GLAD TO HELP. STICK THIS SOMEWHERE WHERE YOU WON'T LOSE THE "EVIDENCE," TAYLOR. MEANTIME, I'LL CALL MY ATTORNEY.
THIS IS NEW.
ANOTHER BRILLIANT CSI DEDUCTION. SO WHAT? I LOSE THEM ALL THE TIME! I GO THROUGH 'EM LIKE TOOTHPICKS.
THEN I'LL NEED TO SEE THAT PDA OF YOURS.
YOU DON'T NEED TO DO ANYTHING UNTIL MY ATTORNEY GETS HERE!

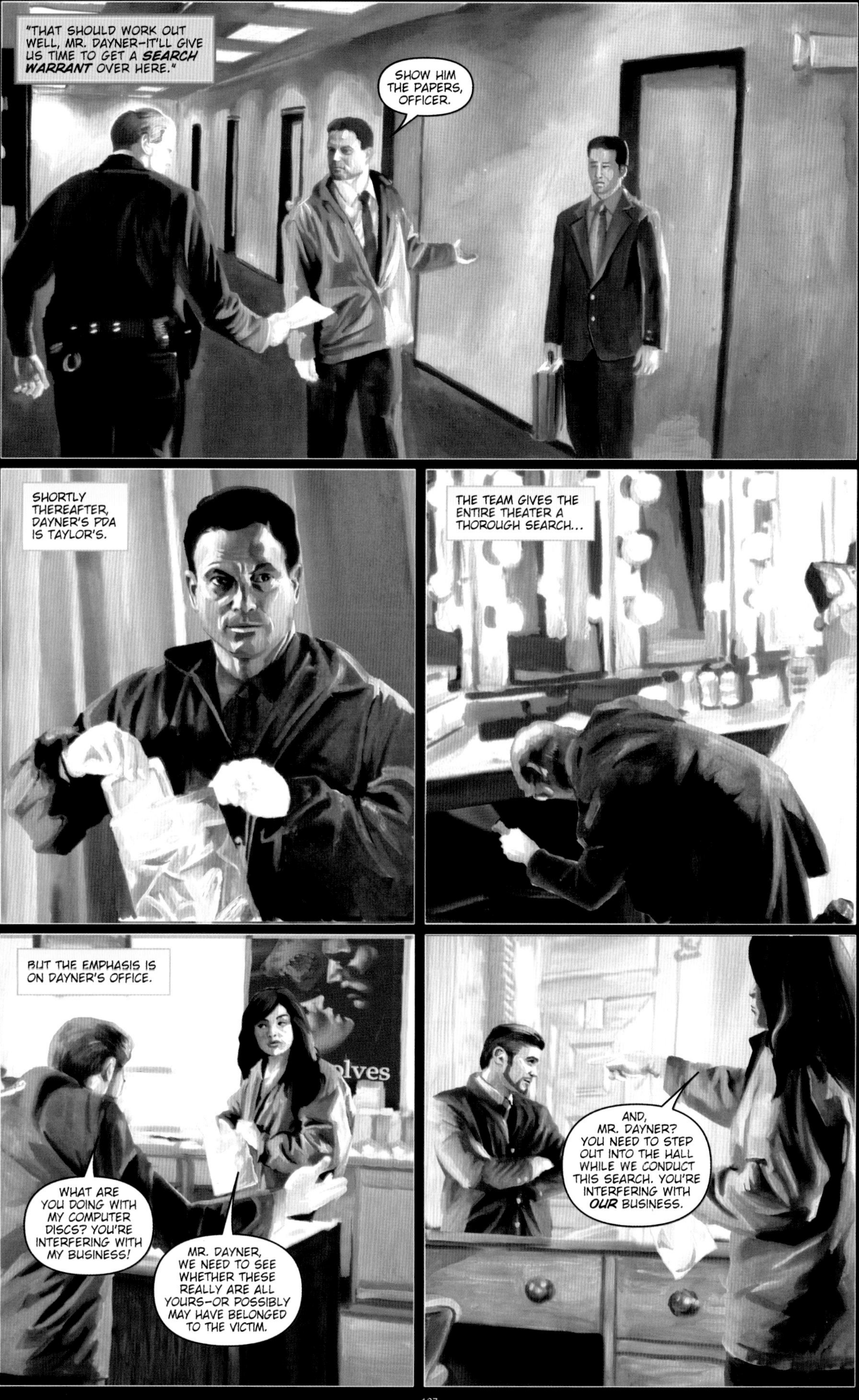

"THAT SHOULD WORK OUT WELL, MR. DAYNER–IT'LL GIVE US TIME TO GET A ***SEARCH WARRANT*** OVER HERE."
SHOW HIM THE PAPERS, OFFICER.
SHORTLY THEREAFTER, DAYNER'S PDA IS TAYLOR'S.
THE TEAM GIVES THE ENTIRE THEATER A THOROUGH SEARCH...
BUT THE EMPHASIS IS ON DAYNER'S OFFICE.
WHAT ARE YOU DOING WITH MY COMPUTER DISCS? YOU'RE INTERFERING WITH MY BUSINESS!
MR. DAYNER, WE NEED TO SEE WHETHER THESE REALLY ARE ALL YOURS–OR POSSIBLY MAY HAVE BELONGED TO THE VICTIM.
AND, MR. DAYNER? YOU NEED TO STEP OUT INTO THE HALL WHILE WE CONDUCT THIS SEARCH. YOU'RE INTERFERING WITH ***OUR*** BUSINESS.

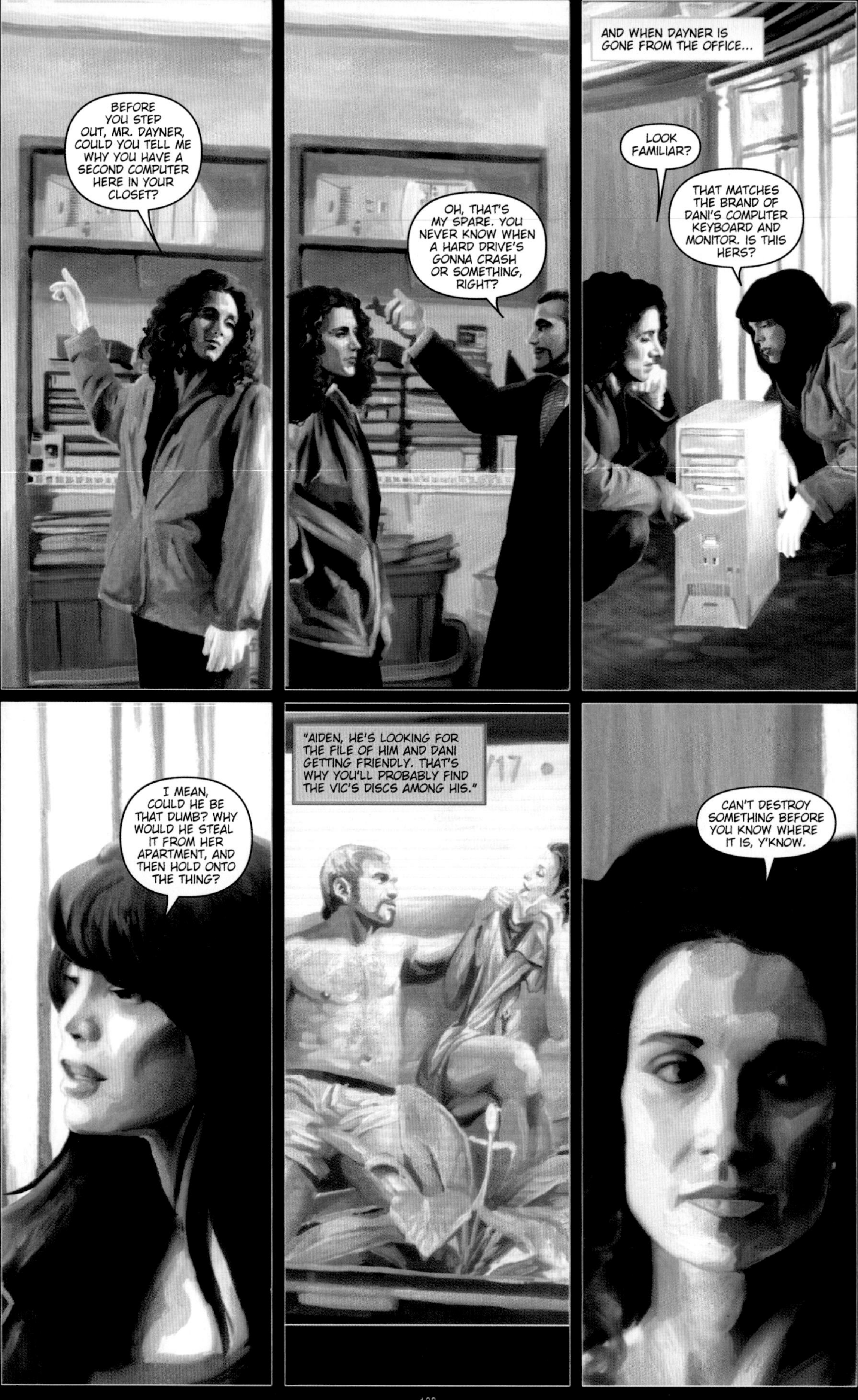
BEFORE YOU STEP OUT, MR. DAYNER, COULD YOU TELL ME WHY YOU HAVE A SECOND COMPUTER HERE IN YOUR CLOSET?
OH, THAT'S MY SPARE. YOU NEVER KNOW WHEN A HARD DRIVE'S GONNA CRASH OR SOMETHING, RIGHT?
AND WHEN DAYNER IS GONE FROM THE OFFICE...
LOOK FAMILIAR?
THAT MATCHES THE BRAND OF DANI'S COMPUTER KEYBOARD AND MONITOR. IS THIS HERS?
I MEAN, COULD HE BE THAT DUMB? WHY WOULD HE STEAL IT FROM HER APARTMENT, AND THEN HOLD ONTO THE THING?
"AIDEN, HE'S LOOKING FOR THE FILE OF HIM AND DANI GETTING FRIENDLY. THAT'S WHY YOU'LL PROBABLY FIND THE VIC'S DISCS AMONG HIS."
CAN'T DESTROY SOMETHING BEFORE YOU KNOW WHERE IT IS, Y'KNOW.

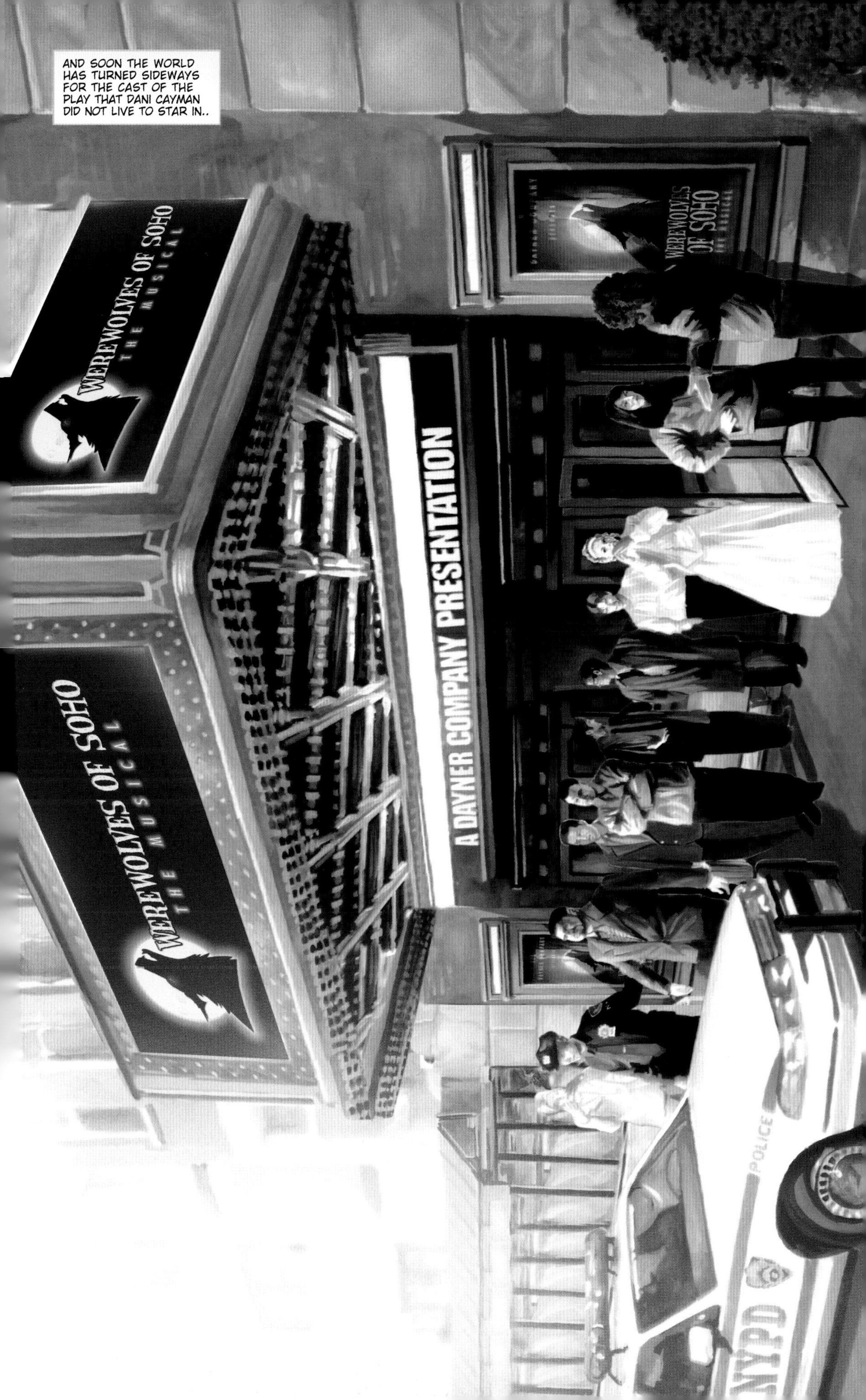
AND SOON THE WORLD HAS TURNED SIDEWAYS FOR THE CAST OF THE PLAY THAT DANI CAYMAN DID NOT LIVE TO STAR IN..
WEREWOLVES OF SOHO
THE MUSICAL
WEREWOLVES OF SOHO
THE MUSICAL
A DAYNER COMPANY PRESENTATION
WEREWOLVES OF SOHO
THE MUSICAL
POLICE
NYPD

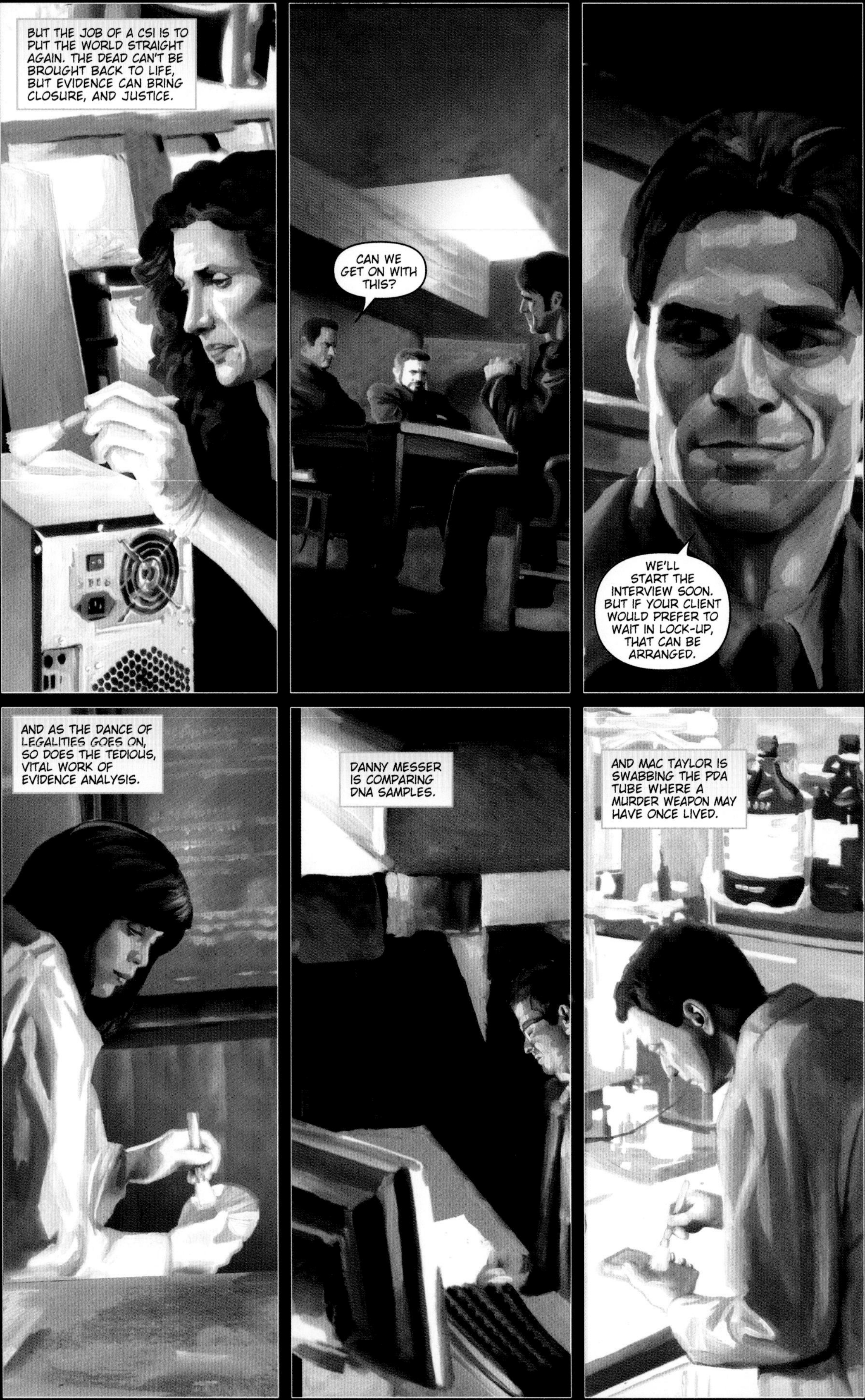
BUT THE JOB OF A CSI IS TO PUT THE WORLD STRAIGHT AGAIN. THE DEAD CAN'T BE BROUGHT BACK TO LIFE, BUT EVIDENCE CAN BRING CLOSURE, AND JUSTICE.
CAN WE GET ON WITH THIS?
WE'LL START THE INTERVIEW SOON. BUT IF YOUR CLIENT WOULD PREFER TO WAIT IN LOCK-UP, THAT CAN BE ARRANGED.
AND AS THE DANCE OF LEGALITIES GOES ON, SO DOES THE TEDIOUS, VITAL WORK OF EVIDENCE ANALYSIS.
DANNY MESSER IS COMPARING DNA SAMPLES.
AND MAC TAYLOR IS SWABBING THE PDA TUBE WHERE A MURDER WEAPON MAY HAVE ONCE LIVED.

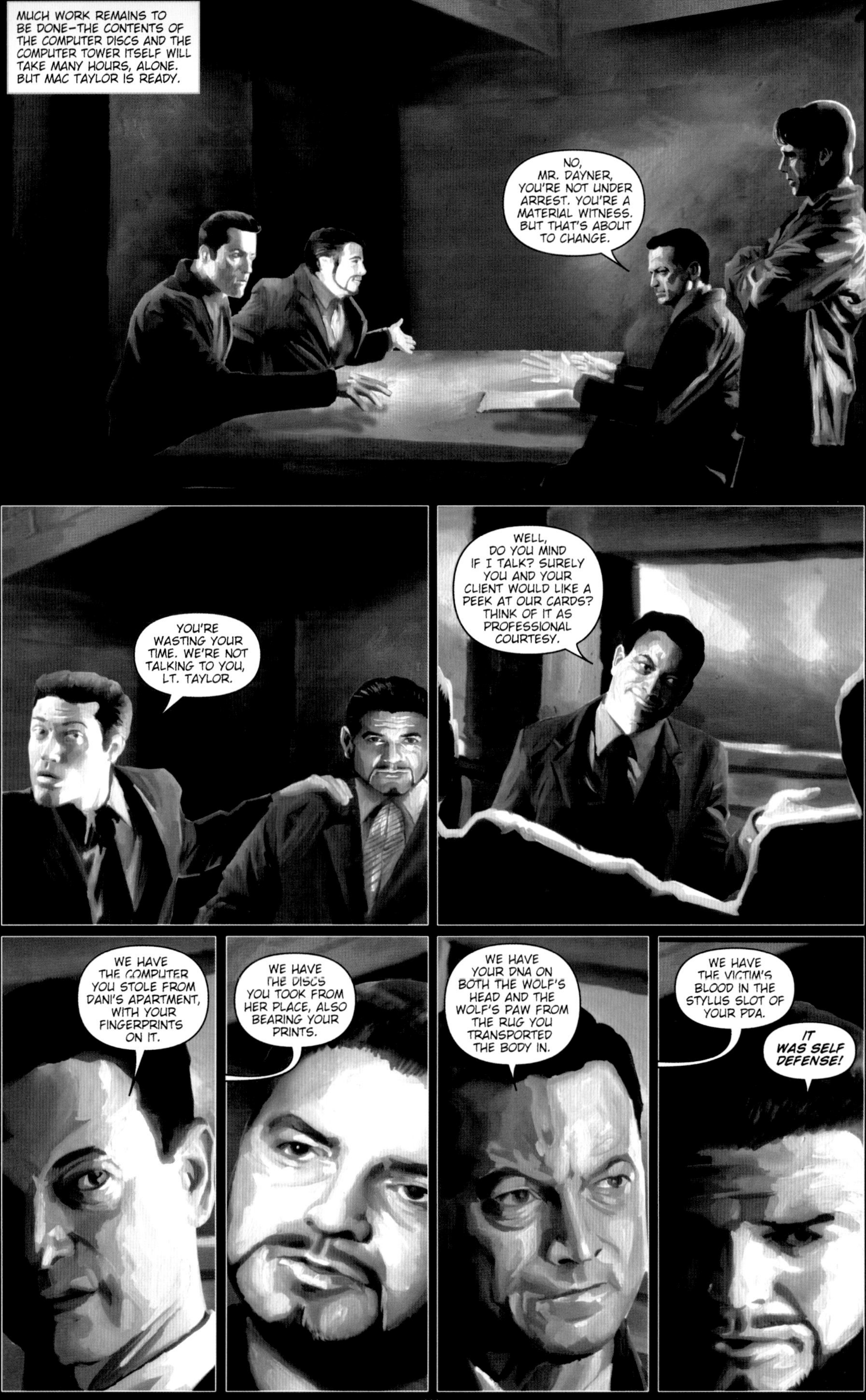

MUCH WORK REMAINS TO BE DONE—THE CONTENTS OF THE COMPUTER DISCS AND THE COMPUTER TOWER ITSELF WILL TAKE MANY HOURS, ALONE. BUT MAC TAYLOR IS READY.
NO, MR. DAYNER, YOU'RE NOT UNDER ARREST. YOU'RE A MATERIAL WITNESS. BUT THAT'S ABOUT TO CHANGE.
YOU'RE WASTING YOUR TIME. WE'RE NOT TALKING TO YOU, LT. TAYLOR.
WELL, DO YOU MIND IF I TALK? SURELY YOU AND YOUR CLIENT WOULD LIKE A PEEK AT OUR CARDS? THINK OF IT AS PROFESSIONAL COURTESY.
WE HAVE THE COMPUTER YOU STOLE FROM DANI'S APARTMENT, WITH YOUR FINGERPRINTS ON IT.
WE HAVE THE DISCS YOU TOOK FROM HER PLACE, ALSO BEARING YOUR PRINTS.
WE HAVE YOUR DNA ON BOTH THE WOLF'S HEAD AND THE WOLF'S PAW FROM THE RUG YOU TRANSPORTED THE BODY IN.
WE HAVE THE VICTIM'S BLOOD IN THE STYLUS SLOT OF YOUR PDA.
IT WAS SELF DEFENSE!

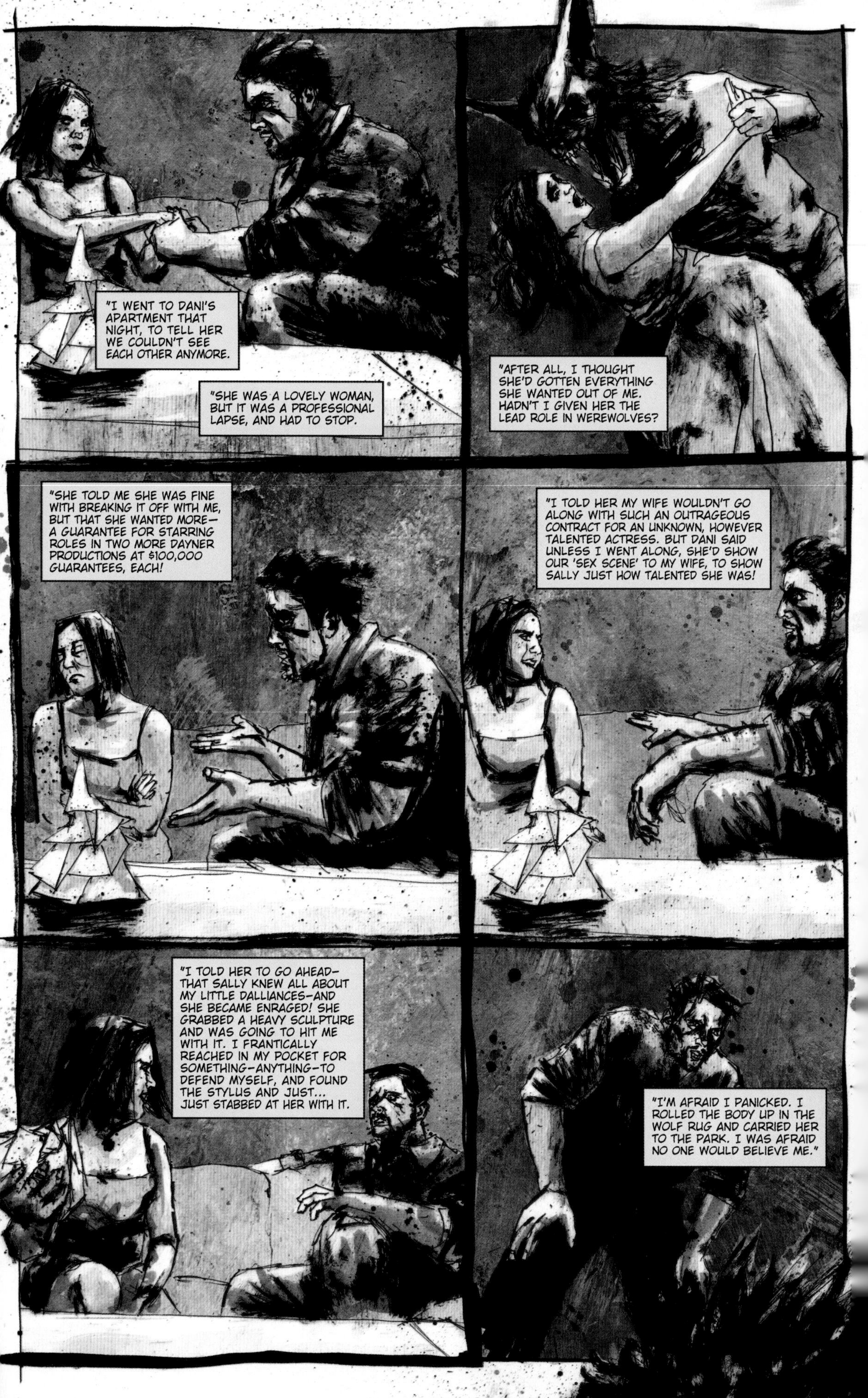
"I WENT TO DANI'S APARTMENT THAT NIGHT, TO TELL HER WE COULDN'T SEE EACH OTHER ANYMORE.
"SHE WAS A LOVELY WOMAN, BUT IT WAS A PROFESSIONAL LAPSE, AND HAD TO STOP.
"AFTER ALL, I THOUGHT SHE'D GOTTEN EVERYTHING SHE WANTED OUT OF ME. HADN'T I GIVEN HER THE LEAD ROLE IN WEREWOLVES?
"SHE TOLD ME SHE WAS FINE WITH BREAKING IT OFF WITH ME, BUT THAT SHE WANTED MORE— A GUARANTEE FOR STARRING ROLES IN TWO MORE DAYNER PRODUCTIONS AT $100,000 GUARANTEES, EACH!
"I TOLD HER MY WIFE WOULDN'T GO ALONG WITH SUCH AN OUTRAGEOUS CONTRACT FOR AN UNKNOWN, HOWEVER TALENTED ACTRESS. BUT DANI SAID UNLESS I WENT ALONG, SHE'D SHOW OUR 'SEX SCENE' TO MY WIFE, TO SHOW SALLY JUST HOW TALENTED SHE WAS!
"I TOLD HER TO GO AHEAD— THAT SALLY KNEW ALL ABOUT MY LITTLE DALLIANCES—AND SHE BECAME ENRAGED! SHE GRABBED A HEAVY SCULPTURE AND WAS GOING TO HIT ME WITH IT. I FRANTICALLY REACHED IN MY POCKET FOR SOMETHING—ANYTHING—TO DEFEND MYSELF, AND FOUND THE STYLUS AND JUST... JUST STABBED AT HER WITH IT.
"I'M AFRAID I PANICKED. I ROLLED THE BODY UP IN THE WOLF RUG AND CARRIED HER TO THE PARK. I WAS AFRAID NO ONE WOULD BELIEVE ME."

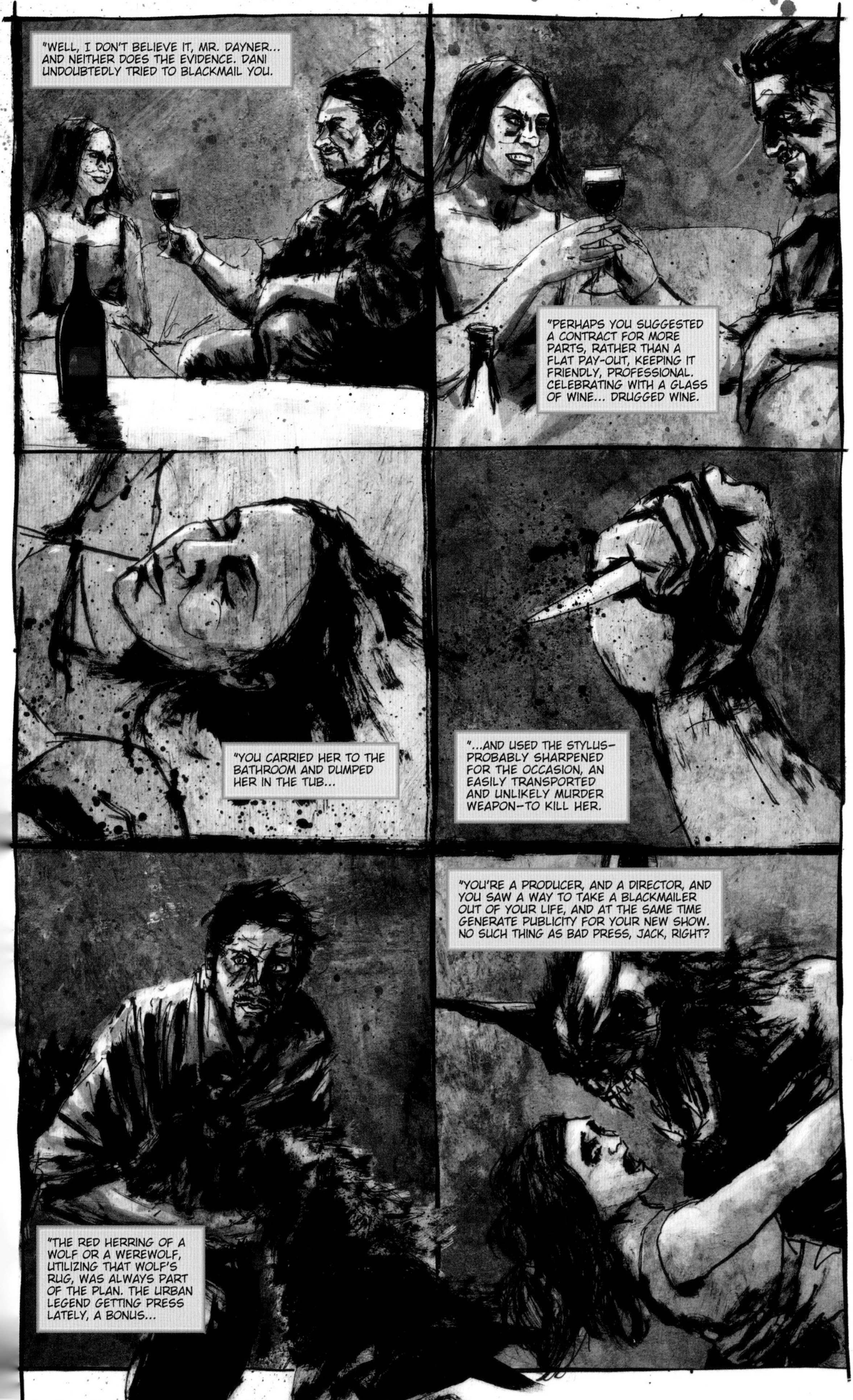
"WELL, I DON'T BELIEVE IT, MR. DAYNER... AND NEITHER DOES THE EVIDENCE. DANI UNDOUBTEDLY TRIED TO BLACKMAIL YOU.
"PERHAPS YOU SUGGESTED A CONTRACT FOR MORE PARTS, RATHER THAN A FLAT PAY-OUT, KEEPING IT FRIENDLY, PROFESSIONAL. CELEBRATING WITH A GLASS OF WINE... DRUGGED WINE.
"YOU CARRIED HER TO THE BATHROOM AND DUMPED HER IN THE TUB...
"...AND USED THE STYLUS–PROBABLY SHARPENED FOR THE OCCASION, AN EASILY TRANSPORTED AND UNLIKELY MURDER WEAPON–TO KILL HER.
"THE RED HERRING OF A WOLF OR A WEREWOLF, UTILIZING THAT WOLF'S RUG, WAS ALWAYS PART OF THE PLAN. THE URBAN LEGEND GETTING PRESS LATELY, A BONUS...
"YOU'RE A PRODUCER, AND A DIRECTOR, AND YOU SAW A WAY TO TAKE A BLACKMAILER OUT OF YOUR LIFE, AND AT THE SAME TIME GENERATE PUBLICITY FOR YOUR NEW SHOW. NO SUCH THING AS BAD PRESS, JACK, RIGHT?

"MAKING THE ATTACK SUGGEST A WOLF OR A WEREWOLF, USING THE WOLF'S HEAD AND CLAWED PAW, WAS A NICE DISTRACTION, RIGHT? SEND THE POLICE DOWN THE WRONG ROAD WHILE GAINING PRESS FOR THE NEW PRODUCTION."

WITH DANI GONE, SALLY— YOUR ANGEL—COULD CONTINUE FUNDING THE ART OF A REAL-LIFE MONSTER.

"WHEN YOU STOLE THE DISCS AND THE COMPUTER FROM DANI'S PLACE, YOU MISSED THE ONLY DISC THAT REALLY COUNTED— THAT HOMEMADE EROTICA, A DVD THAT'LL BE THE HIT OF YOUR TRIAL.

03/17

"YOU EVEN HAD A BUILT-IN FALL GUY IN POOR MAX TIMSON. I WONDER IF YOU REALLY FELT SORRY FOR YOUR FORMER STAR, OR HAD THIS ROLE IN MIND FOR HIM ALL ALONG."

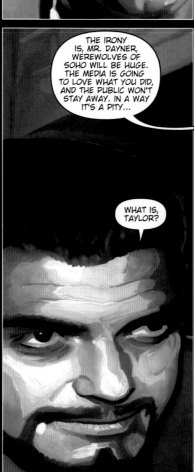

THE IRONY IS, MR. DAYNER, WEREWOLVES OF SOHO WILL BE HUGE. THE MEDIA IS GOING TO LOVE WHAT YOU DID, AND THE PUBLIC WON'T STAY AWAY. IN A WAY IT'S A PITY...

WHAT IS, TAYLOR?

THAT AT YOUR MURDER TRIAL, THE SEATING WILL BE SO LIMITED.

THE END

CSI: NY™

BLOODY MURDER

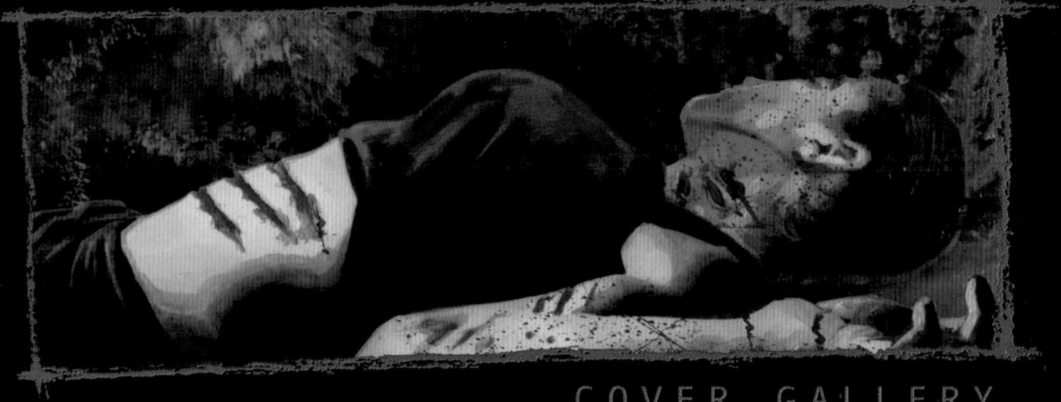

COVER GALLERY

Photos: Timothy White

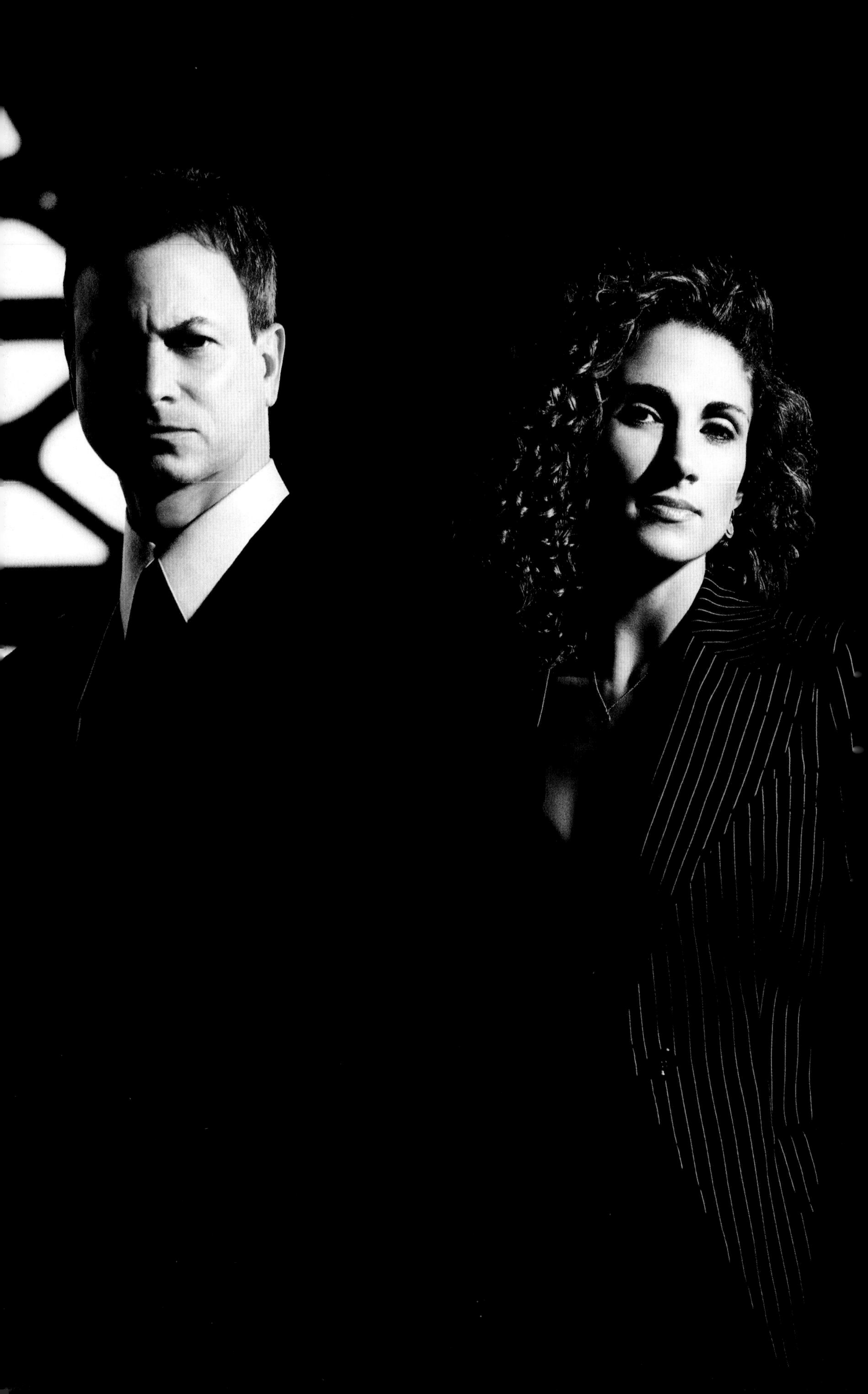

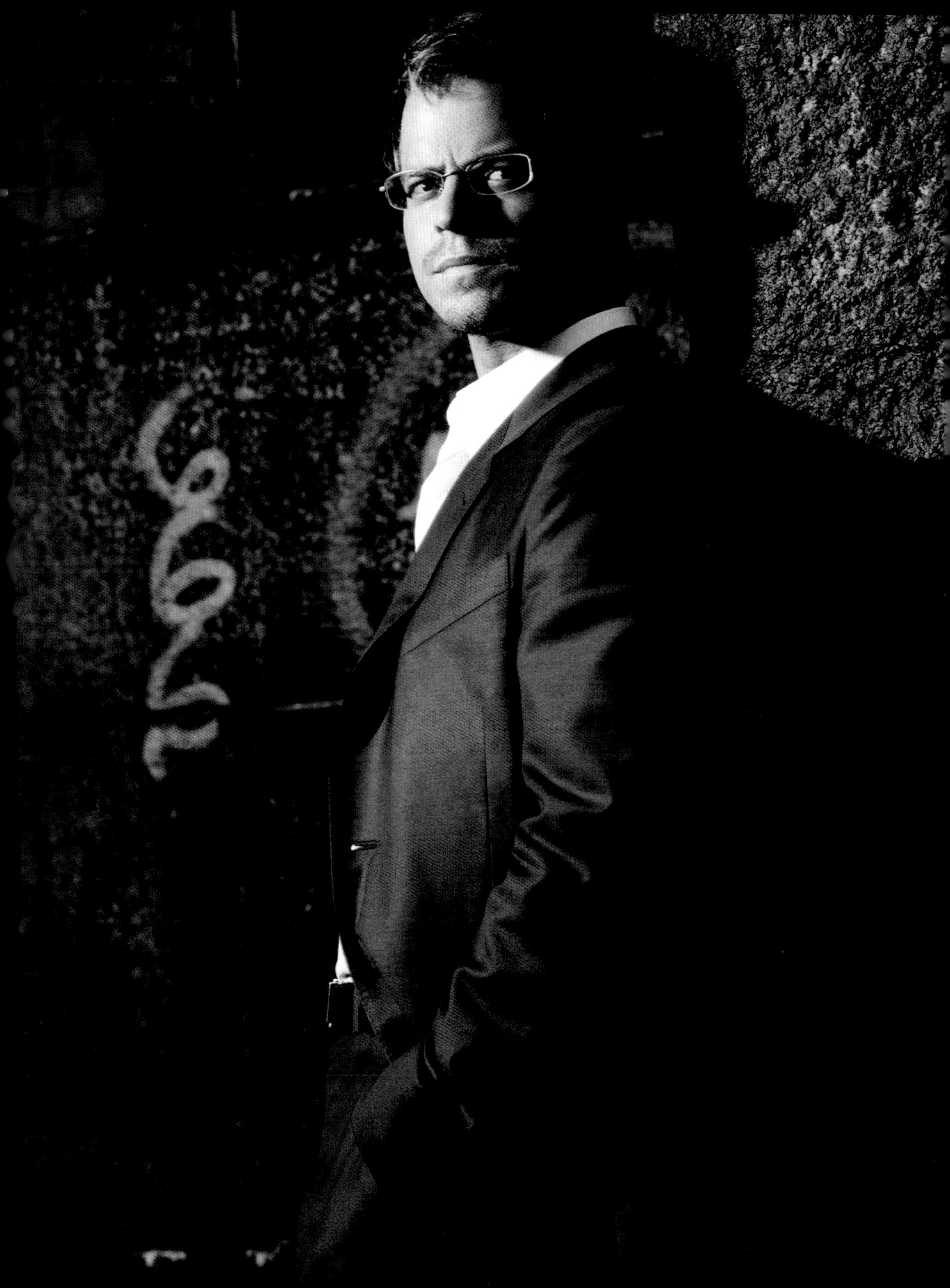

<illegible graffiti not transcribed>

Cover Issue #1 : Opposite Page
Cover Issue #2 : This Page

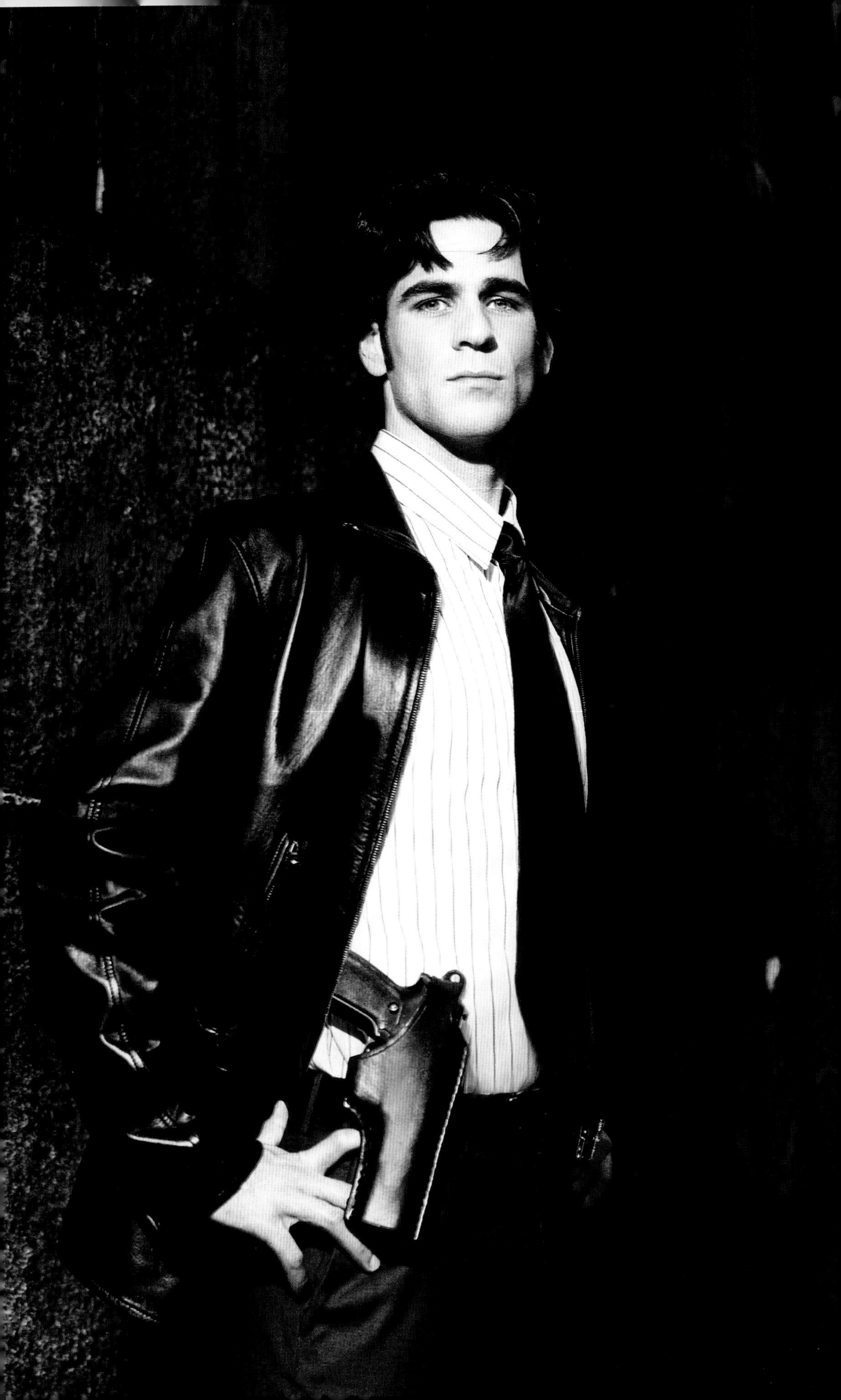

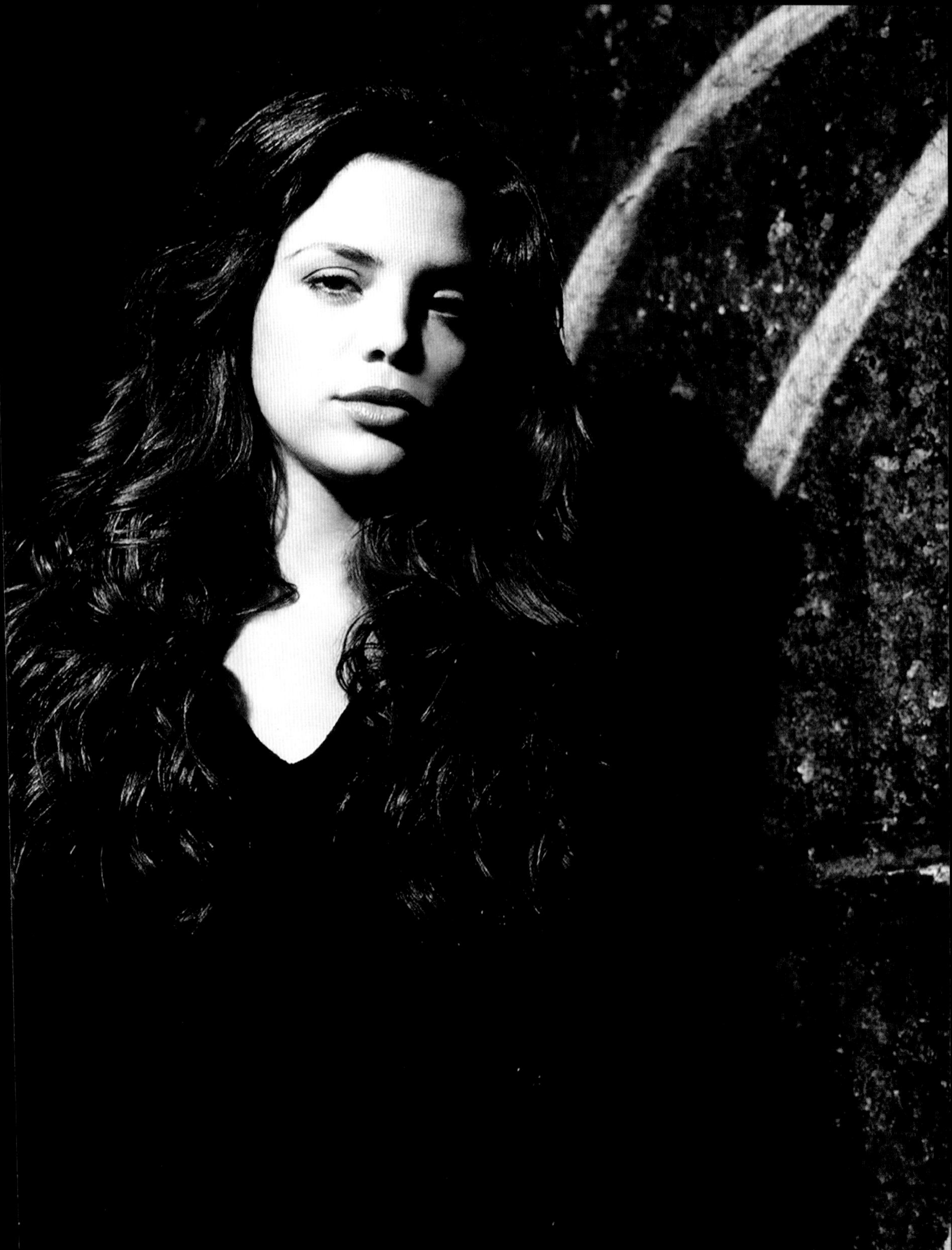

Cover Issue #3 : Opposite Page
Cover Issue #4 : This Page
Cover Issue #5 : Next Page

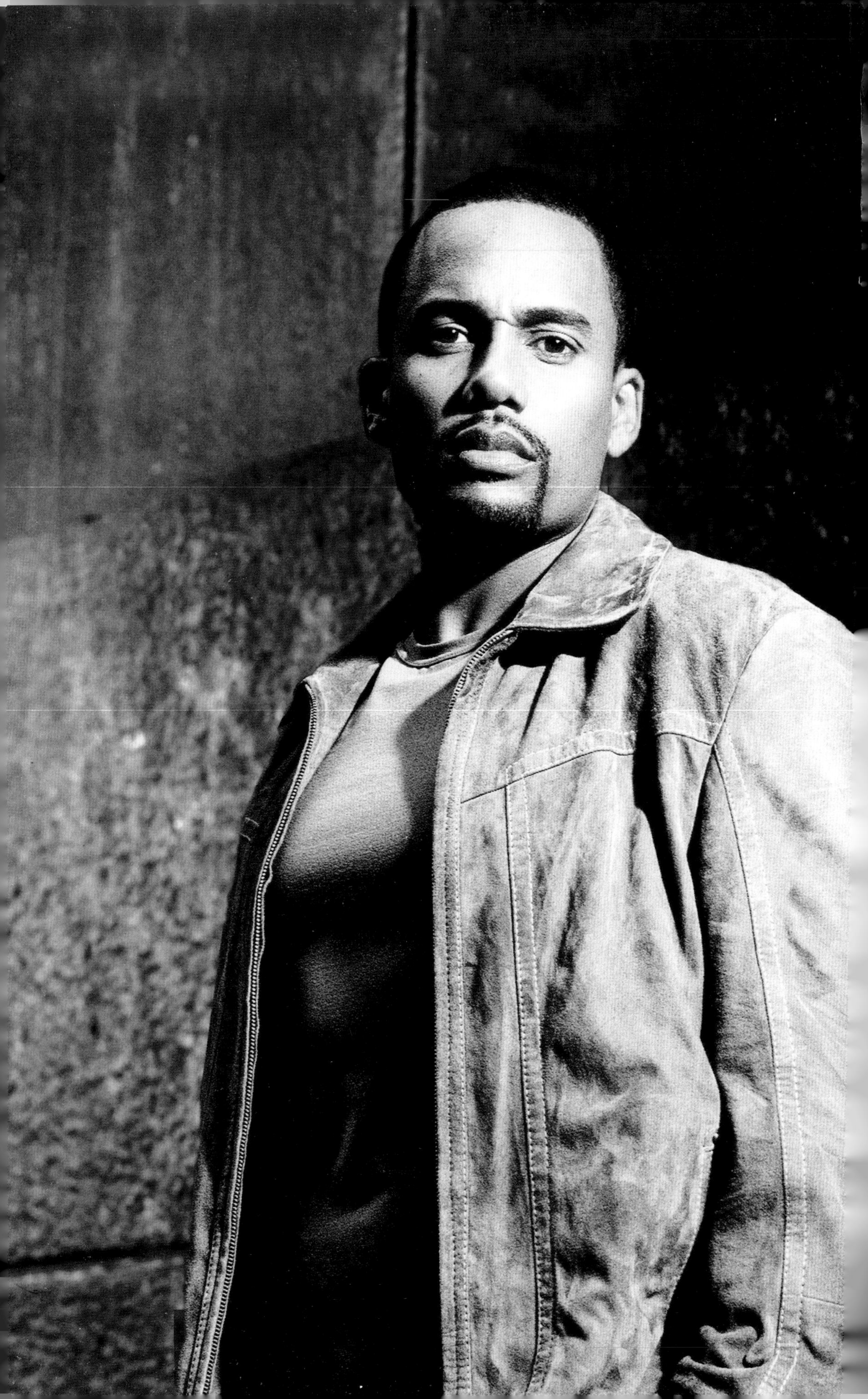